# Exit Zero

# Exit Zero

Family and Class in Postindustrial Chicago

CHRISTINE J. WALLEY

The University of Chicago Press
Chicago and London

Christine J. Walley is associate professor of anthropology at MIT and the author of *Rough Waters: Nature and Development in an East African Marine Park*.

The University of Chicago Press, Chicago 60637
The University of Chicago Press, Ltd., London
© 2013 by The University of Chicago
All rights reserved. Published 2013.
Printed in the United States of America

22 21 20 19 18 17 16 15 14 13      1 2 3 4 5

ISBN-13: 978-0-226-87179-0 (cloth)
ISBN-13: 978-0-226-87180-6 (paper)
ISBN-13: 978-0-226-87181-3 (e-book)
ISBN-10: 0-226-87179-7 (cloth)
ISBN-10: 0-226-87180-0 (paper)
ISBN-10: 0-226-87181-9 (e-book)

Library of Congress Cataloging-in-Publication Data

Walley, Christine J., 1965–
   Exit Zero : family and class in postindustrial Chicago / Christine J. Walley.
      pages ; cm
   Includes bibliographical references and index.
   ISBN 978-0-226-87179-0 (cloth : alkaline paper)—ISBN 978-0-226-87180-6 (paperback : alkaline paper)—ISBN 0-226-87179-7 (cloth : alkaline paper)—ISBN 0-226-87180-0 (paperback : alkaline paper) 1. Steel industry and trade—Illinois—Chicago—History—20th century. 2. Working class—Illinois—Chicago—Social conditions—20th century. 3. Deindustrialization—Social aspects. 4. Walley, Christine J., 1965— Family. I. Title.
   HD9518.C4W355 2013
   338.4'76691420977311—dc23
                              2012007587

♾ This paper meets the requirements of ANSI/NISO Z39.48-1992 (Permanence of Paper).

*For my family*

# CONTENTS

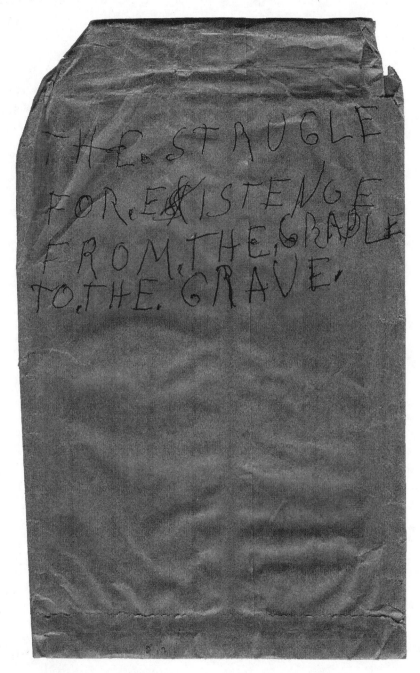

Plate 1. The sack in which my great-grandfather, John Mattson, stuffed his memoir

In October 2011, a motley group of protesters pitched their tents near Wall Street in New York City, spurring various "occupy" movements around the country and bringing the realities of expanding economic inequality to the forefront of public discussion in the United States. I followed these events from the somewhat removed vantage point of a university classroom. That fall, I was teaching a small seminar on personal stories about social class in America as found in memoirs, novels, and oral histories. As background reading, I assigned newspaper and academic articles on growing economic inequality in the United States over recent decades—a topic that my students knew little about and often found surprising. A few short weeks later, this seemingly obscure topic had captured the national limelight.

The trends leading to this growing inequality had, of course, started decades before, as many Americans, including my own family, were painfully aware. While the initial focus for New York's "occupy" movement was on Wall Street's role, at the other end of the social spectrum, this exploding inequality was also tied to a decades-long process of "deindustrialization," or the systematic collapse of manufacturing in regions throughout the country. It was the loss of stable, well-paid industrial jobs—a development linked not only to international competition but also to Wall Street's emphasis on downsizing to raise share prices—that helped knock out a rung on the ladder of upward mobility in the United States. The result has been the loss of the American dream for many.

When I began writing this book in 2006, deindustrialization was not considered a timely topic. If anything, it seemed like a tired, dated issue better suited to the 1980s. Nevertheless, I felt compelled to write about it. Growing up in Southeast Chicago as the daughter of a former steelworker, I knew that my own community, as well as large parts of the Midwest, had never recovered from the loss of industrial work. I had also come to understand the central role that deindustrialization played in generating the economic and social divides increasingly found across the United States.

This book is based on the assumption that, in order to understand this kind of contemporary inequality, we have to go back and rethink deindustrialization. Only by beginning at the historic moment when deindustrialization still seemed unfathomable does it become possible to track how things moved in this direction, the paths overlooked, and the long-term implications for the United States. This book considers such questions not in the abstract, but through events in the former steel mill region of Southeast Chicago and through family stories told across multiple generations. It is through the particulars of everyday life that it becomes possible to understand what it has meant to live these transformations, what it signifies for affected regions, and, by implication, what it might mean for US society as a whole.

Although it's impossible to know whether the current attention to inequality in the United States will continue, it is clear that understanding and addressing this issue requires reconsidering how we think about social class. Although class has been at the center of the story of deindustrialization, it has often been talked about in roundabout ways. Certainly, there has been a historically widespread tendency for Americans to downplay issues of class, and for nearly all—industrial workers included—to consider themselves to be part of a vast, amorphous "middle class." When I was growing up, this downplaying of class made it difficult to say many things—as the stories in this book attest. Nevertheless, this difficulty in speaking about class was also, in part, a holdover from something highly positive: the economic prosperity of a post–World War II United States in which large numbers of people could plausibly consider themselves to be middle class. In the wake of the "Great Recession," and at a time when upward mobility is reserved for isolated individuals even as others experience increasing economic constraints, it has become more and more difficult to maintain a belief in a broad and expansive American middle class. If our current economic difficulties are encouraging a new willingness to talk about class, it comes at an enormous cost. Nonetheless, I believe we need this language of class, not only to understand how the United States has become so divided, but to think about where we want to go in the future. Although Southeast Chicago may seem like an obscure place to some, it is the vantage point offered by such marginalized places that may offer the most revealing angle from which to view and understand what has been happening at the American center.

# ACKNOWLEDGMENTS

Although many authors observe that their intellectual and personal debts span a lifetime, it is true of this work in a more literal sense than most. First and foremost, this book is not only about my family; it is also for them, as well as for others who have shared similar experiences of deindustrialization. My deepest debt of gratitude is to my mother, Arlene Walley, and my sisters, Joelyn and Susan Walley, for allowing me to share stories of events that we lived through together. Although in an effort to protect their privacy, I have kept them at the edges, rather than at the center, of this book, their support has been fundamental to its writing. They have been incredibly generous over the years, humoring me with endless conversations about the past, submitting to formal and informal interviews, setting up interviews with other friends and acquaintances, passing along information and newspaper articles, and helping in whatever ways they could. Although I know that this account is my own and may not always accord with their version of our family history, my hope is that they will, nevertheless, find something of value in it. Although there is inevitably a sense of vulnerability that comes with publicly recounting difficult memories, the desire to write this book stems from the belief that these stories are important to tell—to others as well as to ourselves. At a time when the American dream has become increasingly elusive for many, how we understand the role of working people and think about questions of social class is crucial to determining the future in which my niece Linnea and my son Nhan will grow up. I thank you—Mom, Susie, Jo, and, now, Rocky as well—for your love and extend my own in return.

Thanks also to members of the extended Hansen and Walley clans for making my childhood in Southeast Chicago so rich in family. In particular, the Hansens—my aunt Pat and uncle Bob and my cousins Cheryl, Bobby,

David, and Marcie and their families—have always been there, ready to lend a helping hand and to share difficult times as well as happier ones. I am also indebted to Kris Sowa, and her parents' Albert and Grace, for their support and friendship from the time I was an awkward preteen through the writing of this book. Jack Bebinger, Bill Thompson, and, now, Annie are equally part of this much-valued circle. Thanks to childhood friends on the East Side who shared the awkward years of adolescence and, on occasion, even made them fun: Lisa Sabaitis, Dawn Kazmierczak, John DeCero, Dave DeCero, Rita Zicca, Diane Czasewiscz, Mary Jurkash, and Patty Flisiak. My mother's network of lifelong friends forged in Southeast Chicago were at the center of the world in which my sisters and I grew up. I thank them for demonstrating the value of lives built around a thick web of social bonds and the kinds of support this can offer, especially in difficult times. In particular, thanks to our close family friends Jack and Lesley Peterka, who were always ready with their humorous wit and perceptive insight into life in the Calumet region. During the period when my father was ill, they also became our "favorite landlords," as my husband and I jokingly referred to them. Jack, who recently passed away, is sorely missed.

The earliest seeds of this project emerged in a different form. It began in 1993 as an anthropology master's thesis at New York University under the guidance of NYU professors Faye Ginsburg and Owen Lynch. (My mother was happily surprised to learn that Faye, as a former Southeast Sider, grew up in a neighborhood adjacent to the old steel mill neighborhoods and attended the same high school as my parents). At NYU, Faye was a wonderful, formative influence. She introduced me to the study of the anthropology of the United States when it was still considered a somewhat novel choice and suggested through her own research just how rich such work could be. Owen, in turn, offered a strong grounding in studies of urban anthropology, for which I remain grateful. As mentioned later in this volume, Faye's inspiring class on feminism and the politics of the body may have quite literally saved my life, as melodramatic as that may sound, by offering me the confidence to demand a level of medical attention I never would have otherwise.

After conducting PhD research in East Africa, I returned to this project years later. Through all its stages—from the master's thesis to the subsequent research and reflection that eventually morphed into this book—the Southeast Chicago Historical Museum was an incredible resource. I owe an enormous debt to its current director, Rod Sellers. Rod, whose father was a one-time mill worker turned truck driver–salesman, is an author of various photographic books about Southeast Chicago's past as well as a renowned former East Side high school history teacher. He knows more about the area's history than anyone else, past or present. The sharp mind and meticulous care with which he has imposed order on the jumble of memorabilia, artifacts, and documents that residents have lovingly brought to this crammed one-room museum are unparalleled. His slide show talks about Southeast Chicago's history, held in church basements and local libraries, are well-attended events that quickly turn into collective acts of historical remembering. Although the museum provides a haven for an occasional researcher, it is an all-volunteer affair run by current and former residents and directed toward the community out of which it grew. I used to enjoy visiting the museum with my father, who, along with other former steelworkers and their family members, would periodically go there to "bullshit" about the "old days" in Southeast Chicago and to be among other people who knew and cared. During the time I wrote this book, Rod not only shared his remarkable knowledge of the area and its mills but also read and commented on a draft with a careful eye for detail.

My colleagues in anthropology at the Massachusetts Institute of Technology have been extraordinarily generous and supportive of this project. Although Hugh Gusterson has since left MIT, he was an early and strong influence. Hugh and Catherine Besteman organized a workshop at MIT, at which I presented the article, "Deindustrializing Chicago," from which this book would grow and which would later be published in their edited volume *The Insecure American*. Thanks to both Hugh and Catherine for their advice and encouragement as well as for the inspiration of their own work. The Anthropology Program at MIT has been a haven throughout, with a remarkably collegial group of colleagues whom I also call friends. The current anthropology chair, Susan Silbey, recently instituted a tradition of book manuscript workshops, and my MIT colleagues generously read the entire draft of this book and provided astute critiques and perceptive insights. My heartfelt thanks to Susan Silbey, Jean Jackson, Jim Howe, Mike Fischer, Stefan Helmreich, Heather Paxson, Erica James, Manduhai Buyandelger, and Graham Jones, as well as to Kate Dudley and Emily Zeamer, who also participated in the workshop. Heather and Stefan deserve special thanks both for their friendship and for their supportive input on the numerous informal occasions when our children played together.

MIT generously supported this project financially through various faculty research awards over the years. In addition to a Marion and Jaspar Whiting Foundation research grant, this university support made much of the supplemental research for this book possible. At the last moment, MIT graduate students Marie Burks and Caterina Scaramelli came in as research assistants and helpfully gathered economic statistics and collected far-flung information on the biological properties of various pollutants found in Southeast Chicago. My thanks as well to the MIT students in my American Dream classes and the DV Lab classes cotaught with Chris Boebel who offered their insights on the *Exit Zero* project in both its written and visual forms. Portions of this work also benefited from the feedback of audiences at seminars at MIT as well as at Michigan State University, College of the Holy Cross, Harvard University, and Hampshire College.

In the university town near Boston where I now live, I have been privileged to belong to a group that Jennifer Cole jokingly dubbed the "Cambridge Writing Circle." It began as a group of very junior female anthropologists in 2000, and, although some of our members have moved away, it has provided an incredible source of intellectual and personal support over the years as many of us journeyed collectively past career, individual, and family milestones. My heartfelt thanks to Ann Marie Leshkowich, Ajantha Subramanian, Heather Paxson, Smita Lahiri, Janet McIntosh, Elizabeth Ferry, Jennifer Cole, Karen Strassler, Lori Allen, Sara Freidman, Sandra Hyde, and Manduhai Buyandelger. It was members of the writing group that read the first tentative drafts of this book and provided keen insights, perceptive critiques, and enthusiastic support for a project that kept it moving at a time when I feared it might end up in the attic like my great-grandfather's memoir. Two graduate school friends and now colleagues, Ayala Fader and Beth Epstein, read an entire early draft of *Exit Zero* and offered wonderfully helpful comments that transformed the book. The work of my former NYU adviser and longtime mentor, Lila Abu-Lughod, provided an inspiring example of experimental ethnographic writing, now its own established genre. She also meticulously commented on the early article about my father— sharing the one she was writing about her deceased father as well. I can't thank them all enough for their time, insights, and generosity.

Partway through this project, my discovery of working-class studies provided a new lens through which to view this project and another intellectual home of sorts for this idiosyncratic work. Thanks to Jack Metzgar, another child of a steelworker, for his support and enthusiasm. A particularly deep debt of gratitude is owed to David Bensman and Roberta Lynch. As the authors of *Rusted Dreams*, a classic account of deindustrialization written about Wisconsin Steel, where my father had worked, they provided the base for so much that is written here. Reading *Rusted Dreams* as a young adult was a defining moment for me and was instrumental in making sense of what had happened to my family and to Southeast Chicago.

It has been a wonderful experience working with David Brent and Priya Nelson at the University of Chicago Press. Their enthusiasm and faith in an odd book that was neither fish nor fowl, not quite an academic book and not quite a memoir, are what allowed it to find a place in the world. Thanks also for their astute and helpful editorial and production advice and for being so accommodating and good natured as this work was taking on its final form. Thanks also to an enthusiastic anonymous reader and, once again, to Kate Dudley for a detailed, perceptive, and thought-provoking review that encouraged me to think much deeper. In addition, thanks to the press's Erik Carlson and Ryo Yamaguchi for their good humor and excellent work as this book came to press—particularly to Erik for his patience and careful editorial eye. Conveying a sense of Southeast Chicago's history and dramatic landscape in a book format has entailed attention to visuals as well as the written word. I am deeply grateful to Leland Belew for creating the hand-drawn map of Southeast Chicago and to my mother, Arlene Walley, for sharing boxes of family photographs. Nearly all the other images in the book come from the collection of the Southeast Chicago Historical Society, providing yet another reason to thank Rod Sellers.

In addition to those already listed, I'd like to express my gratitude to other friends and colleagues in New York, Boston, and elsewhere who listened to endless stories over the years, provided support along the way, and encouraged the visual aspects of this project in its later incarnation: Marty Baker, Laura Fair, Heather Kirkpatrick, Adam Idelson, Mike Putnam, Alice Apley, David Tames, Lisa Cliggett, Peter Twyman, Rob Shaughnessy, Ellen Remstein, Bill Bissell, Teja Ganti, Verena Paravel, Vincent Lepinay, Vince Brown, Lucien Taylor, and Lisa Barbash. Thanks also to Becca Binder for braving an Exeter reunion with me.

Over the years, this project has become firmly intertwined with a documentary film also entitled *Exit Zero*, directed by my filmmaker husband, Chris Boebel, and produced by myself. After we began shooting the documentary, Chris (and to a lesser extent myself) also became involved in making a short video about environmental issues in Southeast Chicago for the Calumet Ecological Park Association, and footage was shared between the two projects. This documentary work was in constant conversation with the book and led us to explore places I, as an anthropologist, never would have otherwise yet which are central to this account: the top of a landfill, the wetland marshes interspersed among industrial brownfields, and the fiery innards of US Steel–Gary Works. Again, we incurred many debts, particularly to those involved with CEPA: Grace and Rod yet again, as well as Judy Lihota, Aaron Rosinski, and the now-deceased Marian Byrnes. A highlight for my husband, Chris, was sharing a helicopter ride with Rod over the area's brownfields and remaining mills with a camera poised on the nose of the aircraft.

Since we met in 1994, Chris Boebel has been forced to live an obsession with Southeast Chicago and questions of social class along with me. He has profoundly shaped who I am through the emotional support and perspective he has offered over the years. Although I have kept him at the margins of this book in an effort to maintain his privacy, his influence—both personal and intellectual—is apparent on every page. Much of my ability to stand back and analyze my own and my family's past in this book is indebted in equal measures to his loving support and his remarkably clear-eyed honesty, which would never let me shy away from the more difficult moments or vulnerable places. At times when I was unable to see myself, he would become a mirror, offering a reflective surface that would never push an interpretation but would force me to come to grips with what I myself could see reflected through him. His ideas and insights also permeate the discussions throughout this book. It was Chris, for example, who suggested the problem of "speaking" as a central issue in my family life and encouraged its use as a motif for both the book and the film. For all this and much more, I can never thank him enough. Over our years of unmarried and married life together (including seven years of commuting between New York and Boston), we have gradually let our passionate commitments to various time-consuming creative and intellectual projects merge. In the process, we have become colleagues and collaborators as well as spouses, coteaching documentary film classes and making *Exit Zero* in such a way that it is no longer possible to disentangle our voices.

And, finally, to Nhan, the exuberant bundle of energy in our midst who so forcibly demonstrates the joy of the everyday. As this book goes to press, you are now four years old. You like to nestle in my lap and ask to see video clips of the grandpa you never met, questioning why it made everyone sad "when the mills went down." Thank you for this, for making clear why the future needs to be rethought, and, just as much, for holding my hand and pulling me outside to play baseball in the fleeting New England summer sun.

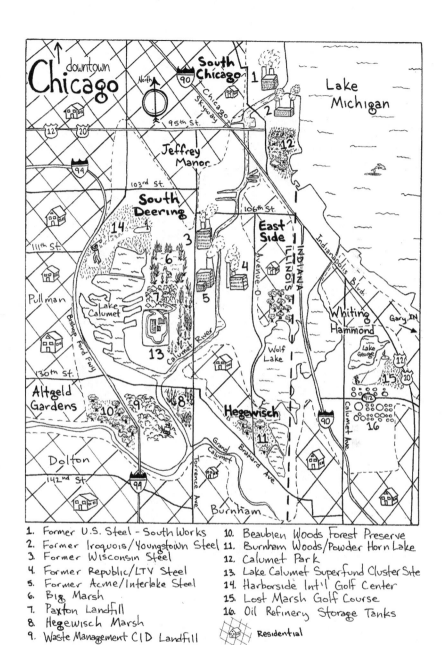

1. Former U.S. Steel - South Works
2. Former Iroquois/Youngstown Steel
3. Former Wisconsin Steel
4. Former Republic/LTV Steel
5. Former Acme/Interlake Steel
6. Big Marsh
7. Paxton Landfill
8. Hegewisch Marsh
9. Waste Management CID Landfill
10. Beaubien Woods Forest Preserve
11. Burnham Woods/Powder Horn Lake
12. Calumet Park
13. Lake Calumet Superfund Cluster Site
14. Harborside Int'l Golf Center
15. Lost Marsh Golf Course
16. Oil Refinery Storage Tanks

Residential

Map. 1. Map of Southeast Chicago. Created by Leland Belew.

Early one morning when I was fourteen years old, my mom entered my bedroom and shook me awake. "Don't worry," she said quietly, "it'll be OK. They called the ore boat back, but it'll be all right." I wondered why we should be worrying about an "oar boat" being called somewhere but drowsily accepted her reassurances and went back to sleep. In retrospect, I imagine my mother on that chilly March morning both trying to reassure me and seeking comfort to face what was ahead, even as she couldn't quite bring herself to tell me what had happened. The real news was that the recall of the ore freighter from the middle of Lake Michigan meant that Wisconsin Steel, the mill in Southeast Chicago where my father worked as a shear operator, had shut down. The mill's major lender, anticipating its imminent financial collapse, had reclaimed its rights to the iron ore in the freighter's hold—prompting the Coast Guard to meet the ship and prevent it from docking. The action spurred the mill's other financial lenders to foreclose, pushing Wisconsin Steel into bankruptcy. Although shrouded in confusion at the time,[1] this moment would mark a crucial rupture for myself and my family. It sharply divided our lives into a time Before the Mill Shut Down and After the Mill Shut Down. My mother, it turned out, had hesitated to tell me what had happened for good reason: the recall of the ore boat would set in motion momentous changes that would transform us all.

The abrupt shutdown of Wisconsin Steel on March 28, 1980, was a harbinger of things to come for the Calumet region of Chicago and northwest Indiana, once one of the largest steel-producing areas in the world. Beginning in the early 1980s, the other steel mills in Southeast Chicago—mills that had employed thirty-five thousand workers at their height—also began to close. A short distance across the Indiana state border, another fifty-five thousand jobs were lost. Even the pockets of the steel industry that survived in Indiana continued with vastly fewer workers. During the time that the region's steel industry was collapsing in the 1980s and early 1990s, my family and other stunned residents strove to make sense of what was happening. Some remarked bitterly that it was worse than the Great Depression of the 1930s. At least after the Depression, they said, the mills had reopened and people went on with their lives. This time, the steel mills were gone for good. Their closing would tear through a social fabric that had sustained generations.

I write this book as a middle-class professor now living in a comfortable college town. The journey that led me here began not long after Wisconsin Steel's demise. On my sixteenth birthday, I left Chicago to become a scholarship student at a wealthy East Coast boarding school with ivy-covered brick buildings and affluent classmates. While my family's situation was taking a dramatic turn for the worse, my own life was moving in what seemed like the opposite direction. This transition turned out to be a difficult one for a working-class girl from Southeast Chicago. Just as Wisconsin Steel's demise had upended the world as my family knew it, this later journey turned my life upside down yet again. In a country where many are reluctant to speak directly about social class, it was difficult to find language to describe the profound sense of rupture I experienced going back and forth between the radically different worlds of home and school, worlds that seemed to be actively growing ever farther apart.

Despite the American faith in the ability of individuals to remake themselves, I have found that it is not so easy to leave this kind of personal history behind. I continue to be troubled by the collapse of the world as I had known it in Southeast Chicago and by the impact that deindustrialization had on family and neighbors. I remain unsettled by the difficult transitions of my teenage years, when I shuttled between extreme ends of the US class spectrum that I previously only barely knew existed. I am conscious even now of how my class origins shape who I am: how I speak—or don't speak—in the world, my outlook on life, and perhaps even, as I discovered when diagnosed with a now-treated cancer, the chemical composition of my body.[2]

But the reason I can't let go of this history is not simply personal. It is because this journey illustrates in unusually stark terms something larger and more troubling. It reveals the costs of both the class divisions that have long existed in the United States and those associated with the increasing economic inequalities of more recent decades. My parents' generation came of age in the immediate post–World War II era, when America's middle class was expanding. They took for granted that greater economic equality was the wave of the future. In contrast, many observers now see this period as a historical anomaly. In recent years, levels of inequality in the United States have reached heights not seen since the 1920s or even the "robber baron" days of the 1890s.[3] Increasingly unequal lives have become one of the defining characteristics of our era. In the United States, conservatives and liberals have long debated the social implications of economic inequality. While liberals have tended to view high levels of inequality as inherently unjust and antidemocratic, conservatives have argued that inequality can lead to greater dynamism as long as it is accompanied by social mobility. Yet researchers suggest that social mobility in the United States has stalled. The chance to "move up" is now more common in what used to be thought of as class-bound Europe than in the United States, a country historically defined in terms of upward mobility and the "American dream."[4]

Should the post–World War II hopes for an expanding middle class, then, be simply dismissed as a historical blip between two Gilded Ages? I would argue that such transformations instead suggest the need to pause, take stock, and consider how the United States ended up heading down this path and at what cost. In this book, I explore these questions in two ways. First, I consider how rising economic inequality in the United States is linked to a phenomenon on the opposite end of the class spectrum from the financial excesses of Wall Street: the fallout of deindustrialization. And second, I ask what my own journey across classes suggests about how social class works more broadly in the United States.

In college classes, I teach statistics on deindustrialization, including the fact that, in 1960, one-third of all laborers in the United States outside agriculture had jobs in manufacturing, while in 2010, only a little over one-eighth had. It is even more striking that, in 1960, 62 percent of those jobs were unionized, while, by 2010, only 13.6 percent were.[5] As a social scientist, I spend time poring over literature that conveys what most workers know all too well: that the manufacturing jobs lost in the United States had better pay, more benefits, and far greater security than those that remain. The jobs that are left are far less likely to serve as a rung up the social ladder to middle-class life for working-class and poor people. As a result, the loss of such jobs has been a major contributing factor in the hollowing out of the American middle class.

What such statistics do not convey are the human realities behind these numbers. When I return home to visit in Southeast Chicago, the fallout of this transformation once again becomes real to me. When I was a child and the Calumet's mills were going full force, a thick dark haze hung over the region. Automobile travelers arriving in the area via the Indiana Toll Road were assaulted by the acrid smells and soot of the steel mills. Although the vestiges of Indiana's steel industry continue to produce steel with a tiny fraction of their once enormous workforce, the steel mills of Southeast Chicago are now all gone. The air is much cleaner, as residents ruefully note, but the sturdy prosperity of the region is also gone. Despite the deceptive glitz of Indiana's waterfront casinos and a few neighborhoods that cling to a semblance of middle-class lifestyles, much of the region is now pockmarked with boarded-up houses, empty lots, and deserted storefronts.

The highway exit ramp for Southeast Chicago's old steel mill neighborhoods is numbered "zero." My father once explained that since Southeast Chicago begins at the state line where the Indiana Toll Road meets the elevated Chicago Skyway, the exit ramp is literally located at mile zero. However, there is something about the big "0" on the sign that captures a sense that this is a passed-over region. Even when the steel mills were going strong and when Southeast Chicago residents lived in economically vibrant neighborhoods amid an industry widely understood as the backbone of the national economy, the region was largely ignored by the rest of the city. For most Chicagoans, it was a little-known place best sped over on the skyway. When I was living in Chicago and told people from other parts of the city that I was from the East Side, one of Southeast Chicago's neighborhoods, some would ask sardonically, "East side of what? Chicago doesn't have an East Side! You live in Lake Michigan?" This perception has only become more extreme in the wake of deindustrialization, as toxic brownfields have replaced taxpaying industries. The Exit 0 sign all too aptly sums up a sense of being caught in the limbo of a postindustrial no-man's-land, heading nowhere. Today, Southeast Chicago residents carry on with their lives below the exit ramp. While older residents often cling to memories of the past, newer residents bring alternative histories and hopes. However, the enormous abandoned industrial spaces, still empty decades later, serve as a visible reminder of how the past continues to dominate the present. The half-life of deindustrialization is turning out to be a very long one.[6]

I studied sociocultural anthropology in graduate school because it specialized in understanding human difference, and I needed to find a way to make sense of the extreme disjunctures between the different class worlds I had experienced during childhood and adulthood. Although I am now a professional anthropologist, I have chosen not to write this book in a clinical academic voice. Instead, it is a book of stories.[7] While some are stories of neighbors, friends, and others with whom I have engaged in conversation over the years, most of these stories are about my family. For four generations, members of my family lived and worked in Southeast Chicago's neighborhoods. Our lives have nearly spanned the rise and fall of the Calumet's steel industry, from my great-grandparents' generation, which was attracted to Southeast Chicago's expanding industrial economy, to my parents', which suffered the trauma of deindustrialization, to my own generation, which has since scattered in divergent directions. These stories are of passing generations collectively bound up with an industry and with a place that could be experienced as both stifling and a refuge. Understanding the subsequent transformations of this region offers a window onto broader changes in American society as a whole.

Personal stories, like those told in this book, are, of course, never just about individuals; such stories are also about the social worlds in which we live. Those in the United States who celebrate the ideals of meritocracy often believe that an individual's ability to transform himself or herself ultimately lies within. Such viewpoints ignore the fact that our lives only exist and take on meaning within the social worlds that have shaped us and through which we negotiate our paths in life. Our individual stories are also always communal ones. Consequently, telling personal stories means not only looking inward but also turning the self outward and tracing the links and relationships that shape and define not only who we are as individuals but also the broader social worlds of which we are a part.

Some stories, however, are easier to tell than others. Social scientists would say that certain kinds of story lines are "hegemonic"—they are linked to dominant ways of thinking, talking, and acting in the world that become taken for granted as "just the way things are."[8] Hegemonic narratives reach us through mainstream media outlets, in the classroom, on the political campaign trail, in economic textbooks, and countless other ways. They shape the possibilities we can envision for thinking about the world, how we interpret our own realities, and, often, the kinds of stories we choose to tell. In many instances, our personal stories are built upon, and given meaning through, references to more dominant social narratives. Of course, people also regularly challenge hegemonic interpretations, but our alternative accounts often carry less traction or feel awkward or unimportant to tell precisely because they fail to fit more familiar story lines.

In writing this book, I am drawn to the points of awkwardness and even conflict between the personal stories I want to tell and the more common story lines through which I and many others have been encouraged to make sense of our experiences. Carolyn Steedman's classic account of growing up working class in post–World War II London provides one example of what we can learn by paying attention to such tensions.[9] By pointing to the gap between assumptions about working-class experiences and the realities of women on the borders like her mother, Steedman's raw, personal account shattered romantic, mythical stereotypes of a close-knit British laboring class then dominant among the left that paid little attention to the experiences of women. Although the stories we tell about ourselves are of necessity built upon, and given meaning through, references to more dominant narratives, it is the points of tension and omission that I hope to convey. As we attempt to narrate our lives, where do we feel constrained? What are the discrepancies between our own stories and those that others wish to tell for us? What do such gaps reveal about our social worlds?

In each chapter of this book, I tell family stories that fail to "fit." By letting such stories wrestle with more dominant understandings, I try to suggest alternative ways of thinking. The first chapter chronicles the history of Southeast Chicago through the life stories of my great-grandparents and grandparents. Such stories both reproduce and challenge commonplace narratives of immigration and labor in the early twentieth century, underscoring what the more dominant accounts of both right and left ignore in the telling of such lives. The next chapter conveys the traumas of deindustrialization in Southeast Chicago through the experiences of my father and the rest of my family in the aftermath of Wisconsin Steel's shutdown. Instead of viewing the emergence of the nation's "rust belt" as part of an evolutionary transformation in which the short-term costs of deindustrialization would give way to a more dynamic and expansive "new economy," these stories underscore how deindustrialization has contributed to the far-reaching disenfranchisement of working people. This chapter calls into question the presumed causes of deindustrialization and asks who benefited and who lost from such transformations and why certain public responses won out over others.

In the third chapter, I explore my own experiences with upward mobility traveling between Southeast Chicago and an elite East Coast boarding school. Conservatives often respond to critiques of class divisions in the United States by emphasizing possibilities for upward mobility. They depict upward mobility as a relatively straightforward process at the heart of the American dream. Yet such assumptions downplay both the personal and familial ambivalence that can accompany upward mobility and fail to explain why the collective upward mobility that once characterized industrial regions like Southeast Chicago has been replaced by a narrower focus on isolated individuals getting ahead. The fourth chapter shifts the focus from stories about people to stories about place. It considers the environmental fallout of both industrialization and deindustrialization in Southeast Chicago and how its toxic legacy has become part of residents' bodies even as it also constrains possibilities for the region's postindustrial future. Although the assumption that a new economy must inevitably rise from the ashes of the old has proven to be a mirage in many formerly industrial regions like Southeast Chicago, community activists continue to work toward their own alternative vision of the Calumet's future. Such efforts are loaded, nevertheless, with contradictions and remain an uphill struggle.

In short, each of these chapters explores the tensions between more dominant interpretations of key changes occurring for working people in the twentieth century and the alternative viewpoints evident within the stories of Southeast Chicago residents themselves. Although the family stories told here were not originally intended as social critique, taken together, such stories become exactly that. Probing their points of tension suggests a larger perspective—perhaps even a counternarrative—that places social class in its many manifestations at its core. The stories told in this account aren't always heroic ones, nor do they articulate an easily identifiable politics. Nevertheless, such stories do suggest a complexity and richness to working-class lives that defies conventional stereotypes and opens up possibilities for the kinds of alternative understandings our contemporary period so sorely needs.

Acknowledging that deindustrialization has knocked out a rung of the social ladder for many does not, however, necessitate romanticizing industrial jobs. Mill and factory labor was and is difficult and life-sapping work. It is also work that continues to become ever more elusive in higher-wage parts of the world, not only because companies often move factory production to other regions, but also because of the ongoing role of automation and computerization in replacing workers. Revisiting questions of deindustrialization, in my mind, means paying attention to the *kinds* of jobs that have been lost: not whether such jobs were located in factories, but whether they were stable, decent-paying jobs around which strong working families and communities could be built. Acknowledging the impacts of deindustrialization does not mean indulging in an act of nostalgia, but rather the need to take part in a hard-nosed critical exploration of where we have come from as a nation and where we are heading.

## Defining Class

As a young person, I actively sought out a concept of "class" as a way to make sense of my life. But what does the concept of class come to mean in these pages? Observers have long noted that Americans across the economic spectrum tend to avoid overt discussions of social class. (This is one reason why some stories are harder to tell than others.) The fact that most Americans prefer to think of themselves as part of an amorphous and all-inclusive middle class is not surprising in a country that has long defined itself as the embodiment of a meritocracy. For poor and working-class individuals, admitting to being less than middle class opens one to charges of being lazy, a failure, or, in some other way, personally at fault.[10] For those who have inherited wealth, acknowledging an elite class status means that others may assume they have neither worked for nor deserve their own social position. For all such groups, claiming to be middle class can relieve awkward assumptions. Of course, people do talk about class, but they often do so in roundabout ways and through other kinds of language. Even though Southeast Chicago is a region with a long history of labor conflict, most people I knew tended to avoid talking about class too directly. Instead, people relied upon alternative vocabularies such as talk of "the little guy" or "fat cats" or such cultural markers of taste or lifestyle as someone's "trashy" clothes or "snotty" demeanor. Such tendencies are widespread in the United States. Even our quintessential national narrative of the American dream, in which the United States embodies the chance to get ahead for all who work hard, is a way to talk about class without really talking about it.

As anthropologist Sherry Ortner has observed, Americans often use other social categories such as gender and race as surrogate ways of thinking and talking about class.[11] In particular, class and race are often conflated in the United States, or treated as if the two were the same thing, with African-Americans, regardless of their backgrounds, symbolically associated with poverty. In the Southeast Chicago of my childhood, this tendency played out in a particular way.[12] Working-class whites, who were desperate to differentiate themselves from poor blacks living elsewhere on Chicago's South Side, used race as a kind of shorthand for the poverty they wanted to keep at bay and that seemed all too close both geographically and generationally given many whites' impoverished immigrant forebears. Conflating race and class in this way exacerbates the intensity of racism. However, it does other things as well. It makes it difficult to acknowledge the experiences of middle-class blacks or working-class whites who do not fit easily into such dualistic thinking. It also downplays class tensions *within* racial and ethnic groups, resulting in a polarizing perspective that makes it difficult to recognize other kinds of social fault lines.

In recent years, the tendency to avoid discussions of class and to deflect it onto other topics has been central to a highly dysfunctional early twenty-first-century American political culture. The failure to speak directly about social class means that, when class is acknowledged, it is often expressed in terms of cross-class cultural resentments that make it impossible to either understand or remedy the underlying causes of growing economic inequality.[13] Such avoidance of direct talk about class has, for example, helped to transform the class resentments harbored by working- and lower-middle-class whites in response to expanding economic inequalities into resentment against less powerful minorities rather than the more powerful figures who may actually be calling the shots. My point is not that people's economic interests are more real than their social and cultural outlooks. (As an anthropologist, I am all too attuned to the power of the latter.) Rather, as other critics note, there has been a cynical manipulation of the cultural in recent decades in order to obscure the economic and political, obfuscating the powerful interests and policies that underlie this nation's growing economic inequality. When serious questions are raised regarding who has benefited or lost out in the economic transformations of recent decades, it is summarily dismissed as envy or caricatured in hyperbolic terms as "class warfare."

Acknowledging that we need more direct discussion of social class in the United States does not imply that "class" simply exists "out there," an aspect of reality that we can take for granted. Like all concepts, ideas of class offer a particular *interpretation* of the world, rather than a mere description of it. Yet class as a concept *is* a compelling one that can offer penetrating insight into our contemporary world. It is a concept that I actively searched for as a teenager to make sense of what I experienced journeying between Southeast Chicago and a wealthy boarding school. It is a lens necessary to understand the history of both industrialization and deindustrialization in the United States. And it is a lens crucial to understanding early twenty-first-century American society. Class is crucial to our contemporary national conversation, not only because it addresses head-on the kinds of issues that Americans of all backgrounds so often avoid, but also because such issues are key to the contemporary dilemmas and choices we currently face.

The concept of class has been defined and used by academics in a variety of sometimes competing ways. For those working within the lineage of Karl Marx, class refers to the social divisions between people based on their economic location within the relations of a capitalist mode of production (capitalism itself being understood as continually in transformation, most recently from what contemporary theorists refer to as "globalization"). Class positioning, in this sense, stems from one's job or the economic capital one possesses, and conflict and exploitation between classes are at the center of historical transformation. Sociologist Max Weber challenged Marxian frameworks by arguing that class is crosscut by other kinds of status distinctions and social groupings not reducible to economic relations. For Weber, beliefs exerted their own form of causality—the economic need not be the prime mover of history—and multiple factors could bring about historical change. Weber's ideas created space for what theorists would later understand as "culture" and to explore the centrality of meaning in human lives, including how those within particular classes make cultural sense of the world. Weber's legacy also encouraged academics to consider how, for example, the consumption of material goods among the emerging twentieth-century middle classes helped to determine people's sense of identity and status, offering new arenas for understanding class beyond the realms of economic production.[14]

In the 1970s, French sociologist Pierre Bourdieu sought to wed the viewpoints of both Marx and Weber by considering how class is bound up with the cultural tastes, styles, habits, and linguistic accents we acquire based on education or work experiences or by living within certain communities. Such cultural proclivities are accorded different amounts of status, becoming what Bourdieu refers to as a form of "cultural capital," which helps reproduce our economic standing.[15] Other scholars have countered that although the social and cultural dimensions of class can reproduce its economic dimensions, for example, when having the "right" tastes or hanging out with the "wrong" kind of people perpetuates our class position, things are not always this neat. For example, individuals sometimes consciously appropriate the cultural styles of different classes. As some scholars argue, we *perform* class, not only in ways that signal our existing economic location, but through attempts to link ourselves symbolically with those "above" or "below" us in class terms, often as expressions of either social aspiration or rebellion. For middle-class white teenagers who wore workingmen's jeans in the 1950s or who, today, listen to hip-hop or date across class lines in ways that anger parents, such acts can be forms of cultural or sexual rebellion against the social expectations and constraints of their own class positioning.[16]

In short, rather than thinking of class as a rigidly defined group of people or even a predetermined social position within an economic order, we might do better, as historian E. P. Thompson long ago noted in a different context, to think of class as a *process*. Class, I would argue, is about the trajectories of our lives—individually and collectively—that often play out in ways that we cannot influence, but sometimes in ways that we can. Class is also about our experiences of who we are in relation to more or less influential others and is bound up with both the economic and the cultural. However, linking class and "culture" in the contemporary anthropological sense does not imply castigating the presumed bad habits of the poor that supposedly help keep them down, as the "culture of poverty" arguments of the 1960s suggested.[17] Rather, the "cultural" here refers to the dynamic, constantly changing, yet power-laden resources available to us that constrain our actions and beliefs *and* that we also draw upon in order to make meaningful lives.

Finally, I would argue there is also a different kind of materiality to class than is often assumed in economic discussions. Class can make itself felt in our bodies in an overtly physical sense. Here, I do not simply mean the ways that class comes to be "embodied," as anthropologists might say, in terms of our daily habits, tastes, and styles of living. Instead, I refer to how class can leave its mark on the actual chemical composition of our cells, organs, and biological processes as a result of environmental exposures to harmful pollutants and toxic substances, realities that are linked to the kinds of jobs that we do, the kinds of places where we live, and the kinds of food we eat. As environmental justice advocates and occupational safety experts recognize, some workers and communities experience considerably greater exposure to environmental hazards than others. Those most affected generally possess working-class jobs or live in working-class or poor neighborhoods, with people of color often, but not exclusively, most affected. In Southeast Chicago, environmental exposures have been historically widespread due to the nature of industrial work, the pollution found in air and water, and the proximity of homes to toxic waste. Such histories mean that we need to think literally about how our bodies are "classed."

In order for the concept of class to do justice to the realities of our lives, I would argue, it must be a multifaceted one.[18] Working with this kind of wide-ranging understanding of class, however, does not mean that class becomes everything and, thereby, meaningless, as some critics might worry. Class remains that form of inequality linked to our relative economic positioning in the world, even as it also carries social, cultural, and physical dimensions. Nevertheless, it is a form of inequality that takes on its meaning in relation to other forms of inequality. As some academics have argued, class, race, and gender are "mutually constitutive." In other words, each is generated not along independent axes of experience unrelated to the others, but simultaneously and in mutual interrelationship.[19] Specifying how each form of inequality works in relation to others remains a crucial task. In some instances, such inequalities may reinforce others, moving them in parallel directions. In other instances, such inequalities may work and be experienced in very different ways. In short, class is not a dominant variable that trumps others. Rather, it is one strand of inequality among others, with some being more salient in certain social and historical contexts, even as all of these strands come together to define who we are and our place in the world.

Although I had been obsessed with issues of social class for many years, I did not begin to fully explore these ideas until late in my schooling. Given my passionate desire for a concept of class as a teenager and young adult, I was excited to find that class represented a respected analytical framework once I arrived in graduate school. Yet I also experienced a certain kind of alienation during my studies. For someone with a profound need to find a mirror that could reflect back upon and help make sense of my own experiences and those of others in Southeast Chicago, I often found it difficult to recognize myself, my family, or my neighbors in the more abstract academic accounts of class that I read. Although I felt most at home in the anthropological literature that focused on the particulars of people's daily lives and their understandings of the world, it was the more theoretical literature that portrayed capitalism as a structural system or abstract logic in ways divorced from flesh-and-blood people that seemed to receive the most respect.[20] For a while, I worried that I somehow lacked the authority to offer my own interpretations of class, since in order to really understand "class," it seemed one first had to master seemingly esoteric theoretical accounts. This feeling of alienation alternated with one of resentment at the privilege implicit in creating such high barriers for the less educated and the more plainspoken to participate in academic conversations. Although as the years progressed, I found the ideas of these more abstracted academic works intensely stimulating and learned a great deal from them, I remained troubled by the irony that the more theoretically sophisticated a text seemed to be about class, the more inaccessible and distant it sometimes felt from the working-class lives it was intended to describe.

At the same time, I longed for more recognition of the meanings and analyses that individuals from working-class backgrounds could offer of their own class experiences.[21] Might there be, I wondered, a more inclusive meeting ground for thinking about class, where theory and experience could be revealed as false dichotomies and where conversation could happen on a more level playing field? Of course, many people have managed to forge such meeting grounds in union halls, church basements, community meetings, or even the give-and-take of ethnographers' fieldwork encounters. Here, I try to create a meeting ground of sorts through this book of stories. When I was a teenager and talked about "big issues" with my dad, something we both loved to do, my father would always respond to my questions with a story. When I asked him about the mills or politics, he would poke me with his forefinger on the leg and begin, "Let me tell you, Peanut . . ." and launch into some story that illustrated how he viewed the world. I didn't always agree with his stories; some I even found troubling. But it was clear that his stories were not mere anecdotes but a form of analysis of the world.

I have made this book a book of stories for a variety of reasons. Psychologically, I've had a deep-seated need to do so. Anthropologist Barbara Myerhoff in *Number Our Days* has described how people often feel a need to create a coherent narrative of their lives, whether through storytelling or writing, a process that allows them to piece together potentially disparate and conflicting experiences in ways that create a more unified sense of self.[22] In my own case, I have felt a similar need to tell my story and my family's stories as a way to heal the ruptures in my own life. Yet there are also other reasons. I see stories as forming a potential meeting ground, a space where both the personal experiences that go into creating theory and the analysis that is part of making sense of one's experiences can be equally recognized. Although stories may be an imperfect medium through which those from a variety of backgrounds can communicate, it is a better one than most.[23]

Stories are helpful because they are always told by someone and from somewhere. Storytelling about our lives forces us to acknowledge the particularities of how we are each, as anthropologists might say, "socially positioned" in the world.[24] We all live in space and in time, within particular social contexts and historical moments that shape who we are and how we think about the world. Recognizing the fact that we are all coming from somewhere in social and class terms can challenge the tendency of elites to make abstract and authoritative generalizations in ways that seek to define the world from their vantage point without appearing to do so. Personal narratives are also good at showing people and class in motion. After all, our life stories are bound up with the class trajectories our lives have taken (or failed to take), our hopes and fears for the future, and how we relate to our own pasts. Personal stories register the class-based frictions that appear as individuals within families, neighborhoods, regions, and even nations move "up" or "down," in unison with, or opposition to, others, altering the economic relationships that bind us together. And, finally, telling stories forces us to acknowledge how class is bound up with other dimensions of our experience. After all, in our personal stories, we also speak as women and men, African-Americans, whites, Mexicans, immigrants, natives, gays, and straights in addition to our class backgrounds.

Valuing storytelling does not necessitate romanticizing it. As scholars who focus on narratives note, the stories we tell are not a privileged form of understanding, nor do they offer any intrinsic insight into the world:

stories can be perceptive or lead us astray and can either contest or but-tress the viewpoints of the most powerful. And while stories are often a way that people attempt to convey their experiences, stories are not direct windows onto these experiences. Conveying stories always happens through the medium of language, through our choices about how to represent our experiences, and through the social conventions that guide our storytelling. What we share with each other are our *interpretations* of our experiences, not the experiences themselves. In short, it is as necessary to guard against the tendency to romanticize stories from "below" as it is to guard against romanticizing theory from "above."

The point of conveying personal narratives is not, of course, *just* to tell stories. When we tell stories, it's not simply the content that is important, but the context in which we speak them. To whom do we tell our stories? Why? Toward what ends? And, most crucially, to what effect? Our stories are meant to intervene in the world, to persuade others, to give voice to feelings and events, to make our lives meaningful. In this way, stories are not a mere *reflection* of the material world; they are a dynamic part of it. The kinds of stories that we tell about social class or deindustrialization, for example, help to actively create and transform the world in which we live. Because our stories are inextricably linked to the ways we act in the world, they are part and parcel of what scholars would see as broader "structural" concerns. We might well ask what kinds of storytelling aided the process by which certain categories of people in the United States came to benefit in economically disproportionate ways in recent decades, while other groups were repeat-edly hurt. And, what other kinds of stories made the loss of industrial jobs that offered decent wages, benefits, and employment stability seem inevi-table and even a form of progress? Thinking through these kinds of stories and the challenges to them, from an era in which deindustrialization still seemed unfathomable to an era in which it may seem inevitable, can help us make sense of a past that we need to understand both to comprehend the roots of our country's expanded inequality and to create alternative paths for the future.

## "The Struggle for Existence from the Cradle to the Grave"

When writing this book, I struggled with how to describe it. Was it a mem-oir, a social scientific analysis, or simply a book of stories? Anthropologists, who write ethnographies or in-depth descriptive analysis of the daily lives of the people with whom they work, might define it through the unwieldy term "autoethnography" or as a form of "intimate ethnography."[25] According to Deborah Reed-Danahay, an autoethnography is "a form of self-narrative that places the self within a social context." Others might clarify that the goal is not simply to *place* but to *analyze* the self in such a way.[26] An "intimate ethnography," in turn, explores the lives of family members, linking such lives to larger social processes, while also considering the methodological, emotional, and ethical issues that come into play.[27]

Regardless of the term used, this book has consciously mined a self entwined in family relationships for ethnographic material. Although all anthropologists rely upon the self as an instrument of research, I have done so in this book perhaps more overtly than usual. During the initial period, when I wrote the most personal stories found in this book, I would sit in my computer chair with eyes closed and attempt to turn inward, trying to channel my own feelings regarding the past. When it began to get painful, I knew I was getting close. Then, like the surrealists who used the tool of stream-of-consciousness writing as a window onto the unconsciousness, I would force myself to write without thinking. My training as an anthropologist was useful. Like a good fieldworker, I tried not to judge my own feelings and memories—instead they were ethnographic "data" to be respected. Once the stories were out, I combined them with the personal narratives of other family members captured, in most cases, on video or audiotape. I then created the shape of this book around these stories. In working with them, I tried to walk the precarious line between feeling emotions and analyzing them, in the process probing and challenging these ideas and feelings, trying to discover what lay underneath. I then cross-checked and contextualized these stories through references to a range of other material collected over many years, including additional audiotaped and videotaped interviews, archival research on Southeast Chicago, government reports, newspaper clippings, academic writings, and literary memoirs on related topics, and, most important, conversations with others. I used this material to work on these stories from different angles, turning them over in my mind's eye, viewing them from a variety of perspectives, trying to discover what could be taken away from them.

The book itself emerges from a kind of double consciousness, one that combines the viewpoints of a daughter of a steelworking family with the societal outlook of an anthropologist. The personal narratives offered here are part of an attempt to think and talk about social class in a way that feels like "home": a way that allows the "me" that I was Before the Mill Shut Down to still have a conversation with the "me" that I have become so many years later. No longer solely the daughter of a steelworking family but also a middle-class professional, I have felt that it is important for me to have such a conversation. These stories have offered a way to tack back and forth between these different parts of myself. They have provided a space to write and think in ways that refuse to artificially keep emotion at bay and that draw upon the ideas and experiences of both halves of my life. In short, the narratives in this book have been part of a personal quest to find a way to understand social class that "fits" in a context in which many available accounts have proven unhelpful. Of course, in our daily lives, all of us speak in different "registers," what linguistic anthropologists call those ways of speaking and acting that are appropriate for particular settings. The dissonance comes when these registers are perceived to be in opposition and rarely come into contact. My own experience of how distinct these two parts of my life have felt says something revealing about class—and about the United States.

Finding a way to speak that bridges these "worlds" is bound up with a desire to challenge such divides within the United States more broadly. In the end, I ponder these questions not only as a daughter of a steelworker, but also as a parent with a child whose generation will inherit a country deeply divided in both economic and political terms. Reconsidering the transformations at the heart of deindustrialization and their implications for the United States at large must be central to any discussion that seeks to challenge the growing divisions within our nation as a whole.

Although I have wanted to tell the stories found in this book almost to the point of obsession since I was a teenager, I found it difficult to do so at earlier stages of my life. I had watched other members of my family, including my father, struggle with doubts similar to my own: How does one find the confidence to believe that one's story is worth telling and that others should listen? How does one find the language to express such experiences or make the words stick to intended meanings? How does one keep one's meaning from being derailed or appropriated by the accounts of more powerful others?

Such quandaries were also apparent in another, much older, piece of writing by a family member. My great-grandfather Johan Martinsson wrote a memoir in 1967 that also had a hard time saying what it wanted to say and that didn't quite "fit." After his death, my grandmother found a paper bag hidden in their attic. It was stuffed with poorly typed pages that my great-grandfather had written at the age of seventy-five. In order to understand the English of this Scandinavian immigrant, it is helpful to read the text out loud with a Swedish accent. Then it becomes clear that "vont," for example, signifies "want" or "fju" means "few." On the front of the paper sack, my great-grandfather had scrawled in pencil the dramatic title "The Strugle for

Existence from the Cradle to the Grave" (plate 1). Clearly, he wanted to tell his story, but the fact that he hid his writings in the attic to be found only after his death suggested a deep ambivalence both about describing painful family events and about telling a life story that so bitterly contradicted mythic portrayals of immigrants eager to land on American shores. Presumably, he hid his writings in order to both *tell* and *not tell* things that were difficult to say. Although the points where our own personal narratives come into conflict with more dominant ones can make it difficult to speak, I want to suggest that these uncomfortable spaces are the most important ones from which to try to do so. Sometimes one has to point to one's own life and announce, "See! This is why my view of the world doesn't fit." In such a context, to tell one's story is to call attention to a reality ignored—in this case, to the class realities central to our lives that often remain unspoken.

On the morning that Wisconsin Steel abruptly closed, my mother hesitated to tell me outright what had happened presumably because she suspected the momentous impact it would have on our family. And, as this book suggests, it did so, in ways that it has taken decades of my life to understand and learn to say. However, this account holds out hope that the act of telling stories that don't "fit" can contribute, in however small a way, to redefining how we think about our changing class relationships with each other and the kinds of collective futures to which we might aspire.

# A World of Iron and Steel:
# A Family Album

When I was a kid, I liked to take long drives with my dad around Southeast Chicago. We lived in an area east of the Calumet River. Known simply as the East Side, our neighborhood lay on the opposite bank of the river from South Chicago's massive US Steel–South Works plant. My father worked as a shear operator at Wisconsin Steel, a mill located in an adjacent Southeast Chicago neighborhood originally known as Irondale and later renamed South Deering.[1] Beyond these neighborhoods, the part of Southeast Chicago most removed from the rest of the city was Hegewisch, a region cut off from the East Side by the wide industrial spaces of what was then Republic Steel. Some elderly residents suggested the neighborhood's isolationist streak by obstinately writing their addresses as "Hegewisch, Illinois." My older relatives would also casually mention smaller subdivisions within these communities that carried such colorful names as Slag Valley and Millgate, although I had trouble keeping straight exactly which section of old wooden frame houses they meant. At that time, during the late 1960s and early 1970s, the steel mills of the Calumet region were still in full swing. My dad, like other steelworkers, did shift work; and so, during the hot weeks of summer when he was "on nights," and when the sounds of kids and cars kept him awake during the day, he would sometimes take me for a car ride around the neighborhood and point out the places that marked the boundaries of our world.

On these occasions, we would drive past the steel mills and other industry, and he would name the mills by those we knew who worked there. My uncle Don worked alongside my great-uncle Leland at Interlake Steel; my grandfather, who spent decades working as a craneman, was at the Valley Mould iron foundry; Great-Uncle Arley labored alongside my dad at Wisconsin Steel, and so on. In between the mills, and often hidden from view except for the telltale cattails along the roads, were the remaining wetlands, or "swamps," as we referred to them when I was growing up. The highly industrialized Calumet River, with steel mills and other industry positioned along both banks, also crisscrossed the region and connected Lake Michigan with the heavily polluted, fenced-off remains of Lake Calumet, which was completely inaccessible and hidden from the sight of both residents and passing motorists. Lake Michigan itself also bordered the mill neighborhoods. Although we could feel the lake breezes and see the seagulls flying overhead, our view of the great lake was blocked by the Edison power plant, a series of enormous granaries painted like giant Falstaff beer cans, and an elevated expressway known as the Chicago Skyway that allowed motorists to pass high above the mill neighborhoods. From the air, the defining features of the landscape would have been water and steel mills.

The residential areas of Southeast Chicago lay scattered among the region's mills and waterways. Historically, the neighborhoods bordered the mill entrances so that people could walk to work in the days before cars. Cut off from each other by industry, water, train tracks, drawbridges, and vacant lots we called "prairie," these neighborhoods resembled (and often functioned like) small islands. Their most striking visual features were the church steeples that soared above the sturdy brick bungalows and old wooden houses. There seemed to be a church for every ethnic group that had migrated to work in the steel mills: Catholic churches for Poles, Italians, Croatians, and Mexicans; Orthodox churches for Greeks and Serbians; Protestant Lutheran and Methodist churches for "old timer" groups such as Swedes and Germans; Baptist and other evangelical churches for southern whites and African-Americans, and so on. The commercial strips were lined with mom-and-pop shops, ethnic specialty stores, and storefront taverns, many of which catered to steelworkers finishing their shifts.

If my dad and I could have driven out onto the restricted promontory in South Chicago that formed part of US Steel–South Works, we would have had a dazzling view of downtown Chicago on a clear day. The promontory, built from slag, or waste left over from the steelmaking process, juts far out into Lake Michigan. It offers stunning views of the Loop's skyscrapers ten miles to the north. It was only as an adult, however, that I learned about the places, well known to historians, that existed in those ten miles between Southeast Chicago and downtown. Just west and slightly south of the Loop, for example, lay the Near West Side. A heavily immigrant manufacturing area in the late nineteenth century, the Near West Side was also the site of the infamous 1886 Haymarket bombing. In the midst of struggles for an eight-hour workday, an anarchist bomb thrower attacked the Chicago police in retaliation for the shooting of two workers a few days prior. In the resulting melee, seven police officers and unknown numbers of civilians died. Although the identity of the bomb thrower was never determined, seven anarchists and labor leaders were charged with the crime and four were hanged. The event provoked an international outcry and became a defining event in nineteenth-century history, even as it dealt a crippling blow to Chicago's emerging labor movement.[2]

Further south of the Loop lay the historic expanses of the Chicago stockyards, which had begun operations in 1865 and closed around the time that I was born, a hundred years later. As part of an increasingly commercialized food economy, massive numbers of hogs and cattle were transported to these stockyards for slaughter from areas outside the city and further west and were later transported as meat by railroad to the east.[3] The Chicago stockyards would become infamous for their labor and sanitary conditions through Upton Sinclair's 1906 muckraking account, *The Jungle*. On the opposite side of Lake Calumet from Southeast Chicago's steel mills lay Pullman. Built by industrial magnate George M. Pullman in 1880 as a social experiment to create ideal housing conditions for workers and their families, Pullman was known to historians as the quintessential "company town." Critics, however, argued that the planned town also attempted to unjustly control workers, and after George Pullman cut workers' wages in 1893 but refused to reduce workers' rents, the town of Pullman became another famous site of labor struggles.[4]

Growing up, I knew nothing of these places and events. Even the occasional trips to downtown Chicago on a school field trip or on an excursion with my mother were like a visit to another world, an "outside" world that my grandfather and many other area residents assiduously avoided for decades at a time. Our world was instead bounded by the neighborhoods of Southeast Chicago. What connected this world together was not the kind of history recounted in textbooks, but the social ties forged in the shadows of the steel industry and its satellite businesses, as well as the nearby churches, ethnic organizations, unions, and schools that gave meaning to residents' daily lives. When we did look beyond Southeast Chicago, it was not toward Chicago but towards the steel mill towns across the Indiana border. Northwest Indiana, linked ecologically to Southeast Chicago by the Calumet's waterways, was also the historical spillover point of Chicago's explosive nineteenth-century industrial growth. It was the tendrils of the expansive steel economy itself that bound the two sides of the Calumet together.

During our drives together through Southeast Chicago, my dad told stories that turned the region's neighborhoods into a living landscape. His history was not an "official" one readily recognizable by a historian, but one told through anecdotes, the stories of people we knew, and personal experiences. When he pointed out the brick bungalow on the East Side where Al Capone once had a "safe house" in the 1920s and which was still rumored to have bullet-proof glass, it triggered a humorous recounting of how one of my great-uncles had quit his job as a night watchman because of Capone. Great-Uncle Leland had to hide in a hole in the ground to escape from Capone's men, who showed up at his workplace one night and told him not to report to work the following evening. Passing the plot of land where the seminal labor event known as the Memorial Day Massacre occurred in 1937, my father would reminisce about how his own father had marched through this bit of "prairie" alongside locked-out Republic Steel workers and got shot at by the cops. Or, passing an area in South Deering known as Trumbull Park, my dad might describe how he had to walk rather than drive to work at Wisconsin Steel when the area was locked down because of the race riots that occurred there in the mid-1950s.[5] Presumably it was these riots that in 1966 led Martin Luther King, Jr., to hold marches on the streets of Southeast Chicago to protest the area's deep-seated racial hatred and housing segregation, much to the consternation of many of the neighborhood's white working-class residents, including my father and some other family members.

On these drives, we also often passed the homes of extended family members, and, if it looked like they were home, we might drop in unannounced to "bullshit" a bit or have a cold drink. In the mill neighborhoods, dense networks of family ties were at the root of social life, and many families, like my own, had lived in the mill neighborhoods for generations. It was unremarkable when I was growing up that my grandparents lived across the alley from my parents' house, and that nearly all my cousins, aunts, and uncles were a few short blocks away. My sisters and I attended the same grammar school as our parents as well as several of our grandparents and even great-grandparents. The interconnectedness was so extreme that at times it reached near comic proportions. For example, my mother's mother, a widow, married my father's father, a widower, a year before my own parents were married. Despite perplexed looks when I explained that my mother and father had become step-brother and step-sister as adults, the situation seemed an oddly appropriate expression of the dense social bonds that knit together the mill neighborhoods. At other times, the interconnectedness took on darker overtones. I remember my parents reminiscing about trying to decide as newlyweds whether it was appropriate to attend the funeral of my father's aunt after she had been killed by a distant relative on my mother's side. The relative, who had become mentally unstable after serving in the Korean War, exploded a bomb in a local department store that had killed a number of neighborhood residents, including my uncle Don's stepmother.

This tightly knit world was the one my family and I knew Before the Mill Shut Down. As I think back on these years in Southeast Chicago, I'm filled with a desire to document this way of life both in order to understand what it was and to understand what it would later become. Even as a kid, it was a place that I found both enthralling and troubling. On those drives with my father, I was fascinated by the way a landscape could be so saturated with history. For my relatives, every place, every building, every piece of ground in Southeast Chicago seemed to hold a meaning or story, stories that might be spontaneously bestowed upon us children or that might have to be coaxed with effort. It was through these stories that we came to be tied to this place across generations.

In an embarrassingly cliché preoccupation for a future anthropologist, I was also fascinated by the quotidian diversity of daily life in Southeast Chicago. I relished the chance to eat homemade noodles at the Serbian New Year celebration of a classmate, to stand in the midst of icons and incense in a Greek Orthodox church as a friend's baby brother was baptized, or to get drunk for the first time on the homemade wine from the backyard grape arbor of an Italian-American neighbor. Yet this world could also be a harsh one. The neighborhoods of Southeast Chicago were a patchwork mix of racial and ethnic enclaves. At that time much of Southeast Chicago was what is often labeled "white ethnic,"[6] although other areas were predominantly Latino and a few were increasingly African-American. There was a strong sense of insularity in the midst of this diversity: a constant emphasis upon the need to draw boundaries in a landscape populated by people and groups to whom you either did, or did not, belong. Challenging such boundaries could mean provoking not only outrage, but also violence, and whites in particular jealously guarded their neighborhoods against those ethnic and racial groups perceived to be on a lower social rung, whom they saw as threatening their own recent and hard-won respectability.

In later years, when I was a young adult and after the demise of the mills, my fascination with Southeast Chicago took on a new, almost obsessive form. The need to make sense of this place and the loss of the world I had known as a child was like scratching an itch or salving a wound that had opened years earlier and wouldn't heal. The desire was heightened by the fact that Southeast Chicago was rapidly becoming someplace different. During these years (when I was also becoming someone different), I would jot down stories and anecdotes in bits and pieces on the backs of envelopes, collect family photos, or coax taped interviews from sometimes hesitant relatives. Home on vacation from graduate school, I would visit the Southeast Chicago Historical Society, a community-run museum in a single room in the Calumet Park field house. Crammed to the rafters with memorabilia donated by elderly residents, it was the beloved attic of Southeast Chicago. There, I could rummage through unpublished histories of the mills by labor activists and industry employees, find home movies of Labor Day parades and Miss East Side pageants, peruse steel industry brochures from the 1950s extolling how American steel would overcome communism, and discover photos of buildings and places long gone that allowed me to put an image to the stories of family members. The search for such bits of history became part of a quest to make sense of the rupture that had occurred in our world when the mills shut down, the point when what had long been taken for granted in Southeast Chicago began to disappear.

The following pages offer one account of Southeast Chicago's history: a history that emerges through family stories just as my father's accounts on our drives did. My family's history is both typical and entirely unique in the way that the particularities of history usually are. My relatives' stories are inseparable from the history of industrialization in the Calumet region at a time when heavy industry was at the core of both the United States' economy and its self-image. It is necessary to begin with this history in order to understand what Southeast Chicago meant for many of us who lived there, why it could feel both restrictive and like a refuge, and what deindustrialization would signify for the region as a whole. In telling my relatives' stories, I am struck by how their narratives echo classic tales of American immigration and labor that have been central to understanding US history in the late nineteenth and early twentieth century. As I repeat these stories, they feel almost stereotypical in the telling, veering toward the well-worn grooves of tales of hardworking, upwardly mobile immigrants or of feisty laborers seeking their share of the American dream. In the United States, variations of these classic narratives have long been told by both the political right and left as part of a broader understanding of what it means to be an American.

Yet such classic tales of immigration and labor leave other aspects of my relatives' stories untold, or fail to capture their ambivalence or points of tension. It is the often-ignored aspects of these stories that suggest a complexity to people's lives that defies such mythic tellings and makes them recognizable as the human beings I knew growing up. At the heart of such stories is Southeast Chicago itself. Some scholars suggest that experiences of social class are often tightly bound up with a sense of place.[7] Certainly, this was the case in Southeast Chicago. Instead of speaking of abstract forces like "class," we acted as if the forces shaping our lives both emanated from the place itself and were deflected by it. In a region where so many residents shared similar histories of migration, work, and family ties, it was Southeast Chicago that bound our narratives together.

## Stories of Immigration and Labor

The stories of the four generations of my family members who lived and worked in Southeast Chicago span much of the history of steel in the Calumet region. Their stories also underscore many of the divisions historically found among the white working class. Anthropologist Sherry Ortner has argued that when Americans think about other classes, their first reaction isn't antagonism (as some on the left might assume). Rather, she argues, Americans tend to see in other social classes projections of their own hopes and fears for the future: those they aspire to be like, and those from whom they seek to differentiate themselves.[8] This is just as true within social classes as between them. After all, the "classes" to which we belong are never static, and our own positions are under constant negotiation. While sociologists tell us that people's class positions often remain remarkably stable over time, psychologically it does not always feel that way. After all, our status and position in relation to others is never truly assured. While some may take their positions in the world for granted, for many others it remains a constant question: something we might hope to change, be desperate to maintain, or resign ourselves to perpetuating. It is something that may be challenged by life developments and passing generations, by the twists and turns of local and far-off events, and by broader changes in the social and economic landscapes we share. "Class," in this sense, is about the constant negotiations, large and small, of the relationships of inequality in which we find ourselves, some of which we can shape, and many of which we cannot.

In my own family, my mother's side approximated the classic immigrant narrative of (modest) upward mobility, while my father's family reflected the far-less-commonly-told story of long-term white poverty in the United States. Although the immigrant narratives of my mother's family are valorized, stories like those of my father's family's are often swept under the collective national rug. Both sets of accounts, however, simultaneously build upon and contradict the classic American mythology of a modern industrial "melting pot" society. This mythology, bound up in a male-centered account of industrial labor and immigration, transforms the stories of my mother's great-grandfather or my father's father into seemingly archetypal ones. Other stories, however, like those of my maternal grandmother, suggest another reality: one in which women are central and the social networks they maintained were at the core of life in the old steel mill neighborhoods. As a small child, I grew up living across the alley from this great-grandfather, grandfather, and grandmother, all of whom shared a single small house on 105th and Avenue G on the East Side. In retrospect, I can see how their lives represented the various class fractions that existed in the old mill neighborhoods, even as they bumped elbows in their small, shared home.

## The Immigrant's Tale

I begin with the immigrant's tale. It was my mother's grandfather Johan Martinsson who came to Chicago from Sweden in 1910 and was renamed John Mattson in the process. It was this great-grandfather who had written the memoir *The Struggle for Existence from the Cradle to the Grave* that had been found hidden in the attic by my grandmother after his death. In this account, my great-grandfather's ambivalence about both wanting to convey and being afraid to convey a life story that often bitterly contradicts ideals of what one's life was supposed to have been on American shores is palpable.

John, or as I knew him, Big Grandpa, tells a story that simultaneously references and contests the classic immigrant narratives that were intended to make sense of experiences like his. At the beginning of his memoir (fig. 1), he recounts how, as a child, he grew up on a farm north of Göteborg in Sweden. In the family photo albums that my mother inherited from her mother, there are pictures of Big Grandpa and his family later visiting relatives in Sweden. My grandmother, who labeled the photos, jokingly scrawled a "a lot of Swedes" on one (see fig. 2). In contrast to the more prosperous times depicted on these visits back to the "old country," Big Grandpa's life as a child had been a difficult one. He was apprenticed to a blacksmith at the age of eight. Later, he alternated odd days of school with hard labor for neighboring farmers. Part of a large and impoverished family of thirteen, he decided to leave his community in 1910 at age seventeen along with a group of other Swedes, including the father of his future wife, in order to find work in America. In the decades around the turn of the nineteenth century, nearly one quarter of the population of Sweden emigrated to the United States, nearly all leaving from the port city of Göteborg. The peak came in the decade before Big Grandpa arrived, when vast numbers of immigrants were leaving regions throughout Europe. Big Grandpa's destination was unsurprising, given that Chicago during this period boasted the second-largest population of Swedes in the world after Stockholm.[9] When my teenaged mother visited relatives in Sweden in 1951, her uncle showed her a pier in

(I)

This Is the tru story of my life,written after
my 75th birthday.Its the trught,amd nothing
has been exagerated,just written as i remember
it,and to the best of my knowlege.

## Chapter I

I was born in Sweden April 28-1892 in Göteborg
and Bohus Län,Kville församling.my name in the
Parich books was Johan Albert Martinsson,and
from that litle place on thim earth,my fight
for existemce and the daily bread started for
me.We were 13 kids in a small house and a fju
acres land,we had a cow and a pig and some
chickens.I hawe seen all the kids come to this
world,exept 2 the where gone before i arived.
My Parets name was Martin and Adolphina Adriansson
My mothers maden name was Kristiansson and she
was born on Rörvik Hamburgsund.I drowe the horse
and flat farm vagon,widt his coffin to the *my grandfather*
Church Cemetary 1901 I think it was,iwas onley
a small boy i remember.His name was Kristian
and now 1967 his doghter Eva my mothers syster
died and is laid in the same grave,he had gone
back to mother earth compliteley in 66 years.
My parents is laid to rest in the same Cemetary
litle bit east of the north entrange to the
Church.I wendt to this Church,an was Confimed
there 1906.

1. The opening page of Big Grandpa's memoir

*9 Lot of Swedes*

2. Photo of family in Sweden as labeled by my grandmother Ethel

Fjällbacka, the fishing town close to the family farms north of Göteborg, where you could still find ships that would take you directly to 95th Street in South Chicago.

Growing up, I had no conception of what Southeast Chicago would have been like when Big Grandpa arrived in 1910. I took for granted that the Calumet region had always existed in the form I knew. In later years, however, I grew increasingly curious about this early twentieth-century world. As a graduate student home on break, I would dig through obscure historical articles about the region, some unpublished, during repeated visits to the Southeast Chicago Historical Museum.[10] From such articles, I learned that the winding footpaths of Native Americans, who had been pushed out of the Calumet region around the 1830s, would set the template for major transportation thoroughfares in the future, following the higher ground of this marshy area.[11] Later, during the mid-1800s, the wetlands and small lakes of the Calumet became known as a hunting and fishing paradise for Anglo residents of the growing city of Chicago to the north. I still find it hard to imagine that the dusty site of Interlake Steel, where my uncle Don had worked for decades, was once the grounds of a popular hunting lodge. Although railroad tracks were laid throughout the area during the mid-1800s, it was only later, after the post–Civil War economic boom known as the Gilded

Age, a time when American society was being widely transformed by industrialization, that this sleepy area on the fringes of Chicago would become something recognizable to later residents. The region's existing network of railroads, cheap unoccupied land, "swamps" suitable for industrial waste disposal, abundant water for steel production, and waterways that allowed raw materials such as iron ore from Minnesota to arrive and finished products to depart were a powerful magnet for the heavy industry that would soon define the region.

Reading the yellowed, hand-typed historical articles located in the Southeast Chicago Historical Museum makes it possible to imagine the rough late nineteenth- and early twentieth-century world of old Southeast Chicago neighborhoods like Irondale. There were wooden boardwalks over swamp waters, boardinghouses, and taverns that lined streets running with raw sewage. As young men like my great-grandfather flocked to the region to work in the burgeoning metal industries, a largely male-centered world emerged, with cockfights and wrestling matches as primary forms of entertainment. When I described to my mother the early accounts of Southeast Chicago found in articles from the museum, she nodded knowingly. She told me how her Great-Aunt Jenny, the wife of her father's uncle, had run one of the many boardinghouses that catered to young steelworkers. For the few women who lived in the mill neighborhoods in the early days, this was a common occupation. Even those with tiny apartments often took lodgers into their homes. The photo my mother showed me of Great-Aunt Jenny's boardinghouse shows her lodgers wearing coats and ties while she serves dinner (see fig. 3). Perhaps it was a holiday, although as an elderly family friend put it, "Everyone dressed up back then." I find myself wondering whether these clothes also signaled the hopes for respectability and dreams for the future that the wages in the steel mills seemed to hold out for immigrants and country boys. Articles from the Southeast Chicago Historical Museum describe the darker things that the photographs do not. The young men who lived in boardinghouses customarily worked twelve-hour shifts or longer, often seven days a week. It was common for the men to share a bed with another steelworker. While one slept during the day, the other worked. At night, they would trade places.

When Big Grandpa arrived in 1910, he would have found a dynamic, bustling, and harsh world in a Southeast Chicago that had only recently emerged from the wetlands as a result of the growing steel industry. The steel industry itself had begun to boom in earnest around the turn of the nineteenth century, and mills soon lined the Calumet River. The first mill,

3. Great-Great Aunt Jenny's boarding house

Joseph H. Brown Iron and Steel, was built in 1875 in an area subsequently dubbed Irondale. (In 1902, this mill would become International Harvester's Wisconsin Steel Works, where my father would work many decades later.) In 1881, the North Chicago Rolling Company expanded to the south of the city and built a mill known as South Works in South Chicago. South Works was followed by Iroquois Steel, located on the East Side and the industrial predecessors of what would later become Acme/Interlake in Irondale.[12] The mills that were converted into the precursors for Republic Steel were built in the "swamps" between the East Side and Hegewisch. Like Irondale, the other local neighborhoods were built to house steelworkers and other industrial laborers and their families. The East Side, for example, was originally known to surveyors as the Iron Workers Addition to South Chicago, while Hegewisch was built as a planned industrial town by Adolph Hegewisch, a less successful industrial competitor to railroad magnate George Pullman.

At the time of Big Grandpa's arrival, South Works was the largest of all the steel mills lining the banks of the Calumet River. Around the time this photograph was taken in 1910 (see fig. 4), it employed eleven thousand workers, and, later, in its heyday, it would employ twenty thousand. Almost a decade before my great-grandfather's arrival, the parent company of South Works, Illinois Steel, had been absorbed within the newly formed US Steel Corporation (although the mill would still be known locally as Illinois Steel). J. P. Morgan and Elbert Gary had founded the mammoth US Steel holding company in 1901, bringing together their own steel-related enterprises with

Noon Hour, Illinois Steel Company, South Chicago, Ill.

4. Postcard of lunch hour at Illinois Steel (South Works) around 1910. Courtesy of the
Southeast Chicago Historical Museum.

those of Andrew Carnegie and others in Pennsylvania, Ohio, Illinois, and
beyond. At its inception, US Steel became the largest business enterprise in
the world.

Chicago's growing steel industry and other industrial concerns quickly
spilled over into the Calumet region on the other side of the state border.
In northwest Indiana, Inland Steel had begun operations in East Chicago in
1893. A few years later, John D. Rockefeller's Standard Oil Company built
what would become the country's largest oil refinery in neighboring Whiting, Indiana.[13] Attracted by Indiana's laissez-faire business climate and limited by available space on the Calumet River near its Chicago South Works
plant, US Steel soon followed. In 1906, it would begin to build an entire
planned industrial city. The city would be known as Gary after Judge Elbert
Gary, one of US Steel's founders and presiding judge in the notoriously
antilabor Haymarket bombing trial. Dwarfing the planned industrial communities of Pullman, Hegewisch, and Hammond, Indiana,[14] the lakefront
city of Gary would become home to the world's largest steel mill, spanning
four thousand acres. US Steel's Gary Works would employ thirty thousand
workers at its height. In short, Big Grandpa arrived in the Calumet region at
the pinnacle of these transformations. By the 1920s, the region had become
not only one of the largest iron and steel producing locations in the United
States, but one of the largest concentrations of industry in the world.

5. Postcard of Iroquois Steel in the early 1900s. Courtesy of the Southeast Chicago Historical Museum.

6. A 1918 World War I bond rally for Pressed Steel workers in Hegewisch. Courtesy of the Southeast Chicago Historical Museum.

In his memoir, Big Grandpa conveyed a sense of the vulnerability of newly arrived immigrants like himself as well as the importance of ethnic ties in this expanding industrial setting. At the turn of the nineteenth century, heavy industry was attracting tens of thousands of immigrants from Ireland, Sweden, Germany, Bohemia, and, later, Poland, Croatia, Serbia, Lithuania, Italy, Greece, Mexico, and elsewhere into the greater Chicago region. Between 1890 and 1920, 2.5 million European immigrants arrived in the city. In a 1910 government survey of twenty-one industries across the United States, it was noted that 58 percent of all industrial workers were foreign born. The percentage in Chicago was even higher. According to historian Dominic Pacyga, by 1910, immigrant stock residents made up nearly 80 percent of the population of Chicago.[15]

Big Grandpa arrived in Chicago after traveling across the Atlantic by boat from Liverpool and then by train from Boston to Chicago. Despite the booming industrial economy and the large number of Swedish immigrants already in Chicago, settling in was not easy. He described the situation he found upon arriving in Southeast Chicago in his memoir:

> [It was difficult to get a job] when you can't speak the language. I had to look for Swedes to ask for me. So I found a Swedish Saloon on 86th and Greenbay [in South Chicago near South Works] and the owner knew my parents in the old country. And he told me to come back at 6 o'clock when the whistle blows in Ill Steel co [South Works] and he will help to talk to some Swedish bosses that comes in there and try to get me a job. He did and I got a job in the Rigger gang.

At that time, it was customary for laborers to work in "gangs" with members of the same ethnicity and for well-located foremen and local power brokers to procure jobs in the mills for those they knew, making would-be steelworkers dependent upon such ties for work.

In Big Grandpa's case, another Swedish immigrant to whom he had turned for help either intentionally or inadvertently revealed my great-grandfather's true age to the mill's operators. Being underaged, Big Grandpa was forced to obtain his parents' written consent before he could begin work. In the interim, he found himself alone and penniless:

> Well now I had a job, but could not go to work until the papers come from Sweden and that took 6 weeks at least. So my first problem and my new worries was only a few $ in my pocket, no place to stay, no place to eat. So in a few days I went back to the Saloon and the nice owner that got the first job

for me. I told him what had happened. He put a beer in front of me and some free lunch. He said to me, "I know you are broke by now. I was in a fix once myself. So this is on me and I won't be around here tonight [so you can sleep here]. I will get you a labor job, something to get you started until the papers get back from Sweden." He made me acquainted with a man from Wisconsin Steel Co. He took me to the office and spoke for me and he took me in to the gang I was to work in: all Polish. Here I learned to run the wheelbarrow steady day in and out bringing fire brick to the Blast Furnaces. For this I got 16 cents pr hour. We worked 7 days per week, no extra pay for Sunday.

As was the case for so many others, it was the ethnic compatriots with whom one lived and worked who provided support in a new, seemingly friendless, world.

Big Grandpa's memoir (see fig. 7) emphasizes the hardship of the steel mills and the various turns of luck he experienced in his early years in the United States. He relates:

I worked labor [in Wisconsin Steel] until the papers came back from Sweden. . . . So I go to my Polish boss and scratch in my hand with my fingers, he nodded his head, he understood that I wanted to quit. . . . The next day I started as a Rigger in Illinois Steel Co [US Steel–South Works] in an all Swedish gang. I got 22 cents per hour here. We had Sunday off unless we had a breakdown. I had to work on top of the blast Furnaces on booms and rigging high up all the time and I seen many young men get gassed and fall down and die.

Put off by the notoriously high death toll at South Works,[16] he and a friend quit their jobs and took off for the Dakotas in an unsuccessful attempt to follow the harvest as farmhands. Upon returning to Chicago and finding himself completely broke, he received a lucky break and obtained his first carpentry job on one of the steel mill railroads. From then on Big Grandpa worked as a carpenter, sometimes within the steel mills and sometimes on buildings throughout Southeast Chicago. After decades of periodic hardship, the ups and downs of the building trade, and the loss of his home during the Depression, he would take a three-year correspondence course with a technical college and become a building project foreman and a contractor of small houses in Southeast Chicago. Eventually, he retired with a small pension from the carpenters' union, an apparent immigrant success story of modest upward mobility. As a widower late in life, he bought a tiny cottage in rural Michigan. He painted it white with red trim in the style of houses in

(II)

But I had to work amd the first Payment on the
loam i had to take to get here, was due my Father signed in the Eank in the old country for
the ticket here.The price was about $50 i had
$25 to showe Emigrant Inspectors before i could
get in to this country,its the law.I worked
at the Blast Fornaces in the sumer of I9I0, in
the fall me and another young fellow quitt our
job,we had seen maney young men,get killed in
our gang.So we taught it most be another way
to make a living that was not so dangerus,and
we took of for So Dacota farms for the Harwest
But we where to late,and the farmers had all
the help the neded.So we had to go back to Chicago while we had money for the Train fare.
we was now back in Chicago again and looking
for ajob,and we was broke,and winter was cog-
ming,But i had credit on the boarding house,
and in 2 months i found a temporary job that laste
to spring this was I9II a bad year.I loafed the
streets all summer looking for work,anykind
anything so i could eat,but without success.
In the maintime the boby that was with me to
the farm,got sick he had T B and the Viking
Lodge sendt him back to Sweden,where he died.
Amd inthe fall of I9II i walked the tracks
of N Y Central R R toward Grand Crosing,holes
in my shues from —

7. Big Grandpa's description of working at South Works

8. Big Grandpa riding a paddleboat on Wolf Lake

Sweden and stayed there, increasingly a recluse, until ill health forced him back to my grandparents' home in Southeast Chicago in his final years.

In contrast to mythic accounts of immigration in the United States, however, Big Grandpa referred to his decision to leave for the United States as a "mistake" and one that "I should never had made if [I] had known what I know today." He complained bitterly that, "Sweden had peace for 150 years and do not meddle in another nation's affairs. That's more than I can say for my adopted country where I raised my family and worked hard since 1910. I was drafted in the First World War and had a son in the 2nd World War and now a grandson soon of age for Vietnam. When are this going to stop?" In addition to expressing his regret that he ever left Sweden, his story dwells in bitter detail on the hand-to-mouth existence of his early years in the United States, the utter vulnerability and dependence upon others of those like himself who were without resources, and the cruel insecurities of the life of a laborer.

In my childhood memories, I remember my great-grandfather as an enormous, taciturn man who always wore suspenders and occasionally still played the accordion. In old family movies from the 1940s, Big Grandpa can be seen riding a paddle-boat-like contraption built by his younger brother Gust (see fig. 8). Wearing a suit and hat, he stares at the camera from the industrial wetlands amid the steel mills. In this and other images, I try to locate the inner turmoil revealed in his writing beneath its impenetrable surfaces. Family lore has it that Big Grandpa tried to move back to Sweden in later years but found himself too heavy to ride a bicycle and came back to the United States. I have always taken the story of the bicycle to symbolize the immigrant's inability to go home, the dilemmas of a life transformed unalterably by the journey and caught betwixt and between.

## A Life of Labor

In contrast to my Big Grandpa's story, the story of my father's father cannot be made sense of through classic immigrant narratives of upward striving. His family represented yet another fraction of the American white working class: those with roots among the long-term native poor. His wife, my father's mother, was the child of Czech immigrants from Bohemia—Bohemians being common among the early immigrants to Chicago. Her story, however, is largely missing from the family album. Since it was the women who passed on family histories, her death when my father was barely more than a teenager meant that I grew up knowing almost nothing about her. According to her baptism certificate, her parents' names were Rosalie and Vaclav Dvorak and her father was a boilermaker. In this photo (fig 9)—one of the few we have of her—she is standing next to my grandfather, whom she married shortly after he arrived in Southeast Chicago and when they were both very young. They are surrounded by their sons, including my dad on the right. In contrast, the family of my father's father was—I surmise— originally from Appalachia. Before coming to Chicago to work in the steel mills, they were tenant farmers and coal miners in central Illinois, where my grandfather was born in 1908. I never knew where they were from before that. When I asked my grandfather (who was known to us as Little Grandpa to differentiate him from our maternal great-grandfather), he would answer angrily that we were "American, goddamn it," and tolerate no further questions. Later, I learned that he had asked his own father this same question upon arriving in Chicago and had received the same answer. In a place where nearly everyone was an immigrant from somewhere and in which ethnic affiliations, churches, and organizations were powerful institutions of social life and upward mobility, to be without an ethnic group was a form of deprivation. I only then realized that being "American, goddamn it," was not simply a statement of ethnic antagonism, but of the defensiveness of poor whites denigrated as "hillbillies" who were viewed as socially inferior to the incoming immigrant groups and who clung to their Americanness as one of their few badges of status.[17]

In other ways, my grandfather's story parallels classic tales of the transition from rural to city life and the rise of American industrial labor. A family crisis occurred when my grandfather's father, ill with "sugar diabetes," was forced off the land where he had been a tenant farmer. My great-uncle Arley,

9. Little Grandpa and Emily surrounded by their sons

then a teenager, rose to the occasion in the early 1920s by leading the family to the north in search of opportunities for labor in heavy industry. Arley went first, hitching rides on freight trains and dodging the gun-toting railroad detectives commonly known as "dicks" on his way to Detroit. He then sent the fare for my grandfather who went to work as a water boy in the car factories at the age of fifteen or sixteen. My Grandpa told me how later he and Arley took the train back to Central Illinois for a visit, this time with Arley as a proper passenger. They were so scared of thieves that they hid their wages in their socks. Little Grandpa grinned as he recalled his mother's delight when they handed over the earnings that were so essential to the survival of their family of eleven. Over the next few years, nearly all of Little Grandpa's family would relocate to Southeast Chicago, drawn by the possibility of what seemed to a country family like irresistibly high wages in Chicago's expanding industries. Little Grandpa's father, still struggling with diabetes, would find work laying sewer lines on the East Side. Six months after arriving, he was decapitated when he was hit by a trolley as he emerged from a manhole. His wife, Great-Grandma Nellie, too kindhearted to sue the trolley conductor responsible, returned south to remarry and became a farm wife yet again. When I was a child, my family occasionally visited her in the tiny central Illinois town of Arcola. My very first memory is of being woken up by the clanging cast iron stove that she still used in the 1960s as she cooked sizzling breakfast sausages for an ever-changing retinue of visiting children, grandchildren, and great-grandchildren.

When Little Grandpa arrived with his family in Chicago in the mid-1920s, he found work in a newly established iron foundry called Valley Mould. The foundry, where he would labor for more than forty-five years, lay directly across the heavily polluted waters of the Calumet River from Wisconsin Steel. Most of his brothers and brothers-in-law joined him in the steel mills that had come to dominate the Calumet region. There was a sense that they were contributing to important things. Steel from South Works would be used to build skyscrapers in downtown Chicago, including the Prudential Building, the Hancock Building, and, later, the Sears Tower,[18] while metal from Wisconsin Steel built the tractors and combines that helped mechanize America's farmlands. Steel was at the core not only of the US, but of the world economy. And it was transforming workers' lives as thoroughly as the steel itself was transforming skylines and marketplaces.

In the years before the unions ameliorated labor conditions, my Little Grandpa, like many Chicago steel and iron workers before him, worked twelve-hour shifts, seven days a week, with one day off a month.[19] When someone didn't show up for work, he sometimes worked twenty-four hours straight. One day, a crane operator, who was working a twenty-four-hour shift, fell asleep at the controls as workers were extracting an ingot from an enormous, red-hot casting mold. My grandfather barely managed to scramble out of the way of the swinging tons of hot steel, and he lost part of two fingers of the hand he had thrown up to protect himself. According to my father, my grandfather's severed fingers were placed in a paper sack, and he was given a nickel for the trolley and told to take himself to the hospital. "Can you believe it?" my dad would say, offering this story repeatedly over the years as an archetypal example of how the "little guy" got screwed. My grandfather himself scoffed at this account and asserted his own respectability by insisting that he had been brought to the hospital in a proper ambulance. I was never sure which story to believe. Either way, Valley Mould was nicknamed "Death Valley," and my grandfather could tell stories of men he had seen die. One friend of his had fallen when walking across a plank catwalk over an enormous vat of hot sand. The man succeeded in grasping the chain that my grandfather threw down to him but suffocated before they could pull him out. My grandfather said that the man's body shriveled up from the heat. My father said that it had taken a long time for my grandfather to get over it.

Not surprisingly, Little Grandpa was an ardent supporter of the unions. "You better believe it," he'd say. When my father was six years old, my grandfather would take him to meetings at a former tavern called Sam's Place on 112th Street. There, locked-out steelworkers from Republic Steel and supporters from other mills who, like my grandfather, were fighting for the right to unionize what was then known as "Little Steel,"[20] gathered for planning meetings in the days just before the Memorial Day Massacre. On that day, May 30, 1937, a protest march to the gates of Republic Steel was broken up when police on the payroll of the mill management killed ten people and wounded nearly a hundred. Although newspapers originally sided with the police, images from newsreel footage such as the one shown in figure 10 helped encourage a federal inquiry. Although the strike was broken, subsequent legislation resulting from this tragedy was a milestone in contributing to US workers' rights to unionize.

Little Grandpa's stories, however, were just as challenging to beliefs on the left as my great-grandfather John's were to those on the right that celebrated America as an unprecedented land of opportunity. While he fought passionately for his scrap of the pie, Little Grandpa had no time for social causes or political ideology that went beyond a decent wage and a measure of respect. Unions were important to him because with the "big boys" in control "you need a little something to show," a statement with an implicit

10. Newsreel footage of the 1937 Memorial Day Massacre. Courtesy of the Southeast Chicago Historical Museum.

hint of violence. When I tried to get him to talk about the terrible conditions in "Death Valley" and the other mills which I had been reading about in historical articles, however, he impatiently insisted that "it was all right" and took me down to his workroom to proudly show me the gadgets he had forged with scrap metal in his downtime at the foundry. He was far more interested in discussing the intricacies of ingot molds than issues of social justice in the mills. My grandfather's stories were also shorn of idealistic notions of bravery and patriotism that laced the mythic narratives of both right and left in the United States. When I asked my grandfather what he did on the fateful Memorial Day when the police started shooting, he looked at me as if to determine whether I was an idiot and spat, "What d'ya think I did? I turned around and ran like hell!" When I asked him why he hadn't fought in World War II, he boasted that, after receiving an induction letter, he conspired with his superintendent at Valley Mould to get shifted to the job of crane operator, a category of worker for which the superintendent could claim a deferment. "Hell yes!" he snorted. "What would I want to go to any shitting war for?!"

Like many in Southeast Chicago, Little Grandpa never lost the profound ethnic and racial hatreds that characterized the mill neighborhoods, and he never privileged the plight of "the working man" over such prejudices. Over Sunday dinner, he banged his silverware and told how in the old days if you were dating a girl whose families were "bohunks" (Bohemians) or "hunkies" (a generic term for Slavs)[21] and you strayed over to the wrong side of Ewing Avenue, you'd "better watch out, you'd better believe it!" When I went to say good-bye to my grandfather before leaving for a college study abroad program in Greece, his parting words were, "You watch out for those dagos over there." I smart-mouthed back that there were no dagos in Greece. "Dagos, spics, whatever, they'll get you every time," he glared ferociously at me. In a place where ethnic animosities had long been fed by company practices of hiring the most recent immigrant arrivals en masse as strikebreakers or using them to lower the wages of existing mill workers, ethnic divisions were a profound source of contention as well as of identity and support in my childhood world.[22] As my grandfather's stories suggest, it was various factions of European immigrant and native workers who fought among each other before they turned on Mexicans and, later, African-Americans as the latest entrants into the mill neighborhoods. Ethnic and racial prejudice are at the heart of stereotypical depictions of the white working class, yet it is necessary to understand how such divisions came to be so symbolically loaded. In an older industrial world, where workers and their families depended upon ethnic ties as their primary social safety net and where industrial leaders encouraged and exploited ethnic and racial tensions in a deliberate attempt to keep laborers divided, the reality of such antagonisms ends up seeming less than surprising, even as we acknowledge their destructiveness.

Such destructiveness was all too apparent in the Southeast Chicago of my childhood, and some groups suffered much more viscerally from it than others. My first distinct memory of a black person suggests the bitterness of such divides. I imagine I was about four or five years old at the time and holding my mother's hand. Two white neighborhood boys were chasing an African-American teenager with a pipe near the Swedish Lutheran church we attended, and they clearly intended to beat him senseless for daring to cross neighborhood lines that were as rigidly enforced as any national border. It was the same hatred that in later years would cause a troubled teenage cousin from my father's side to go off into the woods with his biker buddies and machine-gun portraits of Chicago's first black mayor, Harold Washington. In writing this, I struggle with the question of how to talk honestly about such hatreds without reproducing simplistic stereotypes of the white working class.

For years, I tried to lash together an understanding of my seemingly contradictory Little Grandpa, a man who could both spout vitriolic hatred and be reduced to tears watching television reruns of *Little House on the Prairie*, TV dinner sitting on his lap, transfixed by nostalgic memories of his own impoverished rural upbringing. During college, I valorized the parts of my grandfather that accorded with romantic leftist labor narratives—his work in the foundry, his union activities, and his presence at the Memorial Day Massacre. It was convenient for me to ignore those parts of his character that would make my liberal college friends cringe. Secretly, I doubted whether most of my college friends would actually like "labor" if they met them in person. Yet I also enjoyed talking to my grandfather. It was almost like stepping into a time machine. He often spoke and acted as if it were still the 1930s. And it wasn't simply a sign of old age; from what everyone said, he had been like that his whole life, as if his world had stopped at some point when he was in his twenties. Once in the 1990s outside a neighborhood restaurant on one of Southeast Chicago's main drags, he only half-jokingly pushed my future husband into the shadows of a storefront as a police car drove by. "Watch out. It's the flivver squad," he said in an undertone, as if it were still the Al Capone era and they were a couple of young punks afraid of the cops catching them and knocking their heads together.

My grandfather remained irascible until the end. My mom called me once when Little Grandpa was in his eighties and told me in an exasperated voice how he had been banned for life from the local Ace Hardware store for pulling a penknife on a smart-mouthed employee. Suffering from lung cancer at age ninety-two, he expressed his impatience to see deceased loved ones again in the afterlife. One afternoon, he instructed my sisters and myself to help him put on his best suit, and he lay down on the bed to await his death. To his intense annoyance, however, he lived for another six days and would spend his final hours venting his frustration by berating and throwing slippers at family members attempting to care for him. Thinking back on my Little Grandpa's life, I am struck by how mainstream narratives of both right and left fail to account for the unvarnished complexity of such a life.

## The Place of Women

My maternal grandmother, Ethel, the daughter of Big Grandpa and, later in life, the wife of my Little Grandpa, was the link between the two sides of my family. In this picture (see fig. 11), my grandmother is on the left. At the time, she was a young woman, recently married and having fun at an event in Calumet Park with her new husband and a friend. Like her own mother and unlike my Big Grandpa, my grandmother Ethel was a playful, fun-loving woman who liked to surround herself with people. Somewhere, I have a grainy photograph, taken when she was in her sixties, showing her

11. Grandma (*left*) with her new husband La at Calumet Park

dressed up like a tomato for Halloween. Unfortunately, I don't have any stories in her own words in contrast to her father, who left his memoir, and my
Little Grandpa, who left taped conversations about his early life. Although I
asked my grandmother for an interview, she refused. She was nervous about
being tape-recorded and claimed she had nothing to say. Perhaps because I
framed my project in those early days as being about the "steel mills," it left
women like her who never worked in the mills feeling as if they had little
to contribute. She died shortly after, while I was in graduate school. When I
think back upon growing up, however, it was always women like my grandmother who seemed most at the center of things in Southeast Chicago. In
my own mind, this was because women were the linchpins in a multigenerational world of kin and neighbors, as well as within the churches and
social and ethnic organizations that were at the heart of life in the old mill
neighborhoods.

In most accounts of labor and immigration in the early twentieth century,
it is the stories of men like my Big and Little Grandpas that take center stage. In
such accounts, the overwhelming focus is on the roles that male workers and
immigrants played within an expanding industrial economy—a tendency
as common among observers on the political left as on the right. Although
historians have increasingly offered accounts of women's activities during
the late nineteenth and early twentieth centuries (particularly accounts of
women who were themselves industrial workers or wage laborers), the focus

on industry as the center of theorizing about class has long worked to place attention disproportionately on men. For many people, the term "working class" itself is synonymous with heavy industrial jobs and, often, with men (and particularly white men) who worked those jobs. In contrast, sociologist Julie Bettie, herself from a working-class background, has argued that much of our sense of ourselves in class terms develops within what she calls "nonwork" spheres of life—as part of families, schools, or other institutions. Although Bettie published her work in 2003, when industrial work had already waned in much of the United States, such insights hold a broader validity. Although industrial work *was* central in early twentieth-century Southeast Chicago, people's sense of self-identity in class terms was similarly created in varied settings. Recognizing such "nonwork" settings can help make sense of the lives of women like my grandmother.

I do not, however, want to downplay the economic roles that women played in steel mill regions like Southeast Chicago. It is true that, within the steel industry, it was nearly always men who labored in the mills (unlike the situation in nineteenth-century textile mills, cigar-making factories, or sweatshops, in which women often dominated the labor force, or, in later years, in industries like automobile manufacturing, where a sizable number of women worked). Although women labored temporarily in the steel mills during World War II and a relatively small number of women entered the permanent steel labor force beginning in the 1970s,[23] it was overwhelmingly men who were steelworkers. Growing up during the 1970s in Southeast Chicago, I had heard of a few women who worked in steel mill offices, but I didn't know a single female steelworker. Nevertheless, women played other important economic roles throughout the history of the old mill neighborhoods, in addition to domestic labor as wives, mothers, daughters, and grandmothers. In the early years of the steel industry, steelworker wages were low even in comparison to other industries, a situation that lasted until the rise in steelworkers' wages after World War II. Because male steelworkers as fathers or husbands did not make enough money to provide for the needs of their families and because mill work was erratic, families relied upon the financial contributions of a range of family members, including women.[24]

The life stories of many women in my family are filled with accounts of work for pay both inside and outside the home, even if such stories were often downplayed when I was growing up. As mentioned earlier, one of the most common ways that women, and particularly married women, earned money in the early years of the old steel mill neighborhoods was by taking in boarders, as my mom's great-aunt Jenny did. Others, like my father's Czech immigrant grandmother, took in laundry in their homes. Others took in sewing. Some did domestic work in other parts of the city. Still others held jobs in the expanding service economy that emerged alongside a growing industrial one. Some service jobs were located in the steel mills, such as the job my father's great-aunt held in a steel mill cafeteria; others were in the restaurants and stores that served steelworkers and their families and that represented a growing consumer culture within the United States. Over time, working-class women also increasingly came to work in offices.[25] My grandmother Ethel over the course of her life did all of these things. As a young woman living with her family in South Chicago, she worked cleaning houses for rich families further north in South Shore and as a waitress in the Swedish-American restaurant on the East Side where she met her future husband. In later years, as a widow, she worked as a cashier for a grocery story and as occasional catering help in the evenings, again for wealthy South Shore families. For many years, she was also a dental office receptionist. In short, although paid work for women might be more common at certain stages of the life cycle, for example, when many were either young adults or widows, the lives of women in Southeast Chicago were frequently, if erratically, interwoven with paid labor.[26]

Men's monopoly on the more highly paid steel mill jobs and their links after the 1930s to powerful unions did give men strong economic and political advantages in relation to women. Why, then, was it women who were always at the center of life in my memories of growing up in Southeast Chicago? Some might link this to the fact that families took on an enhanced importance in industrial settings as people looked to the mutual assistance found in kin and ethnic ties to deal with the uncertainties and stresses of immigration and industrial work.[27] I would also argue that given the alienating nature of so much industrial labor,[28] ultimately, it was the social worlds of kin and neighbors built up over generations—more than people's jobs—that gave life its deepest meaning in Southeast Chicago. In either case, it was overwhelmingly women who were in charge of these social networks. They were the ones who bound together kin groups, nuclear and extended, and it was women who often maintained the church, school, civic, and ethnic organizations that were crucial to marking ethnic identity and creating community life in Southeast Chicago. While men might mark ethnicity with belligerence and, occasionally, violence, the women in the area could just as definitively draw ethnic boundaries, in my family's case, through such acts as making Swedish holiday glögg and sausages, managing the Santa Lucia pageants in which we girls dressed up in white robes and silver tinsel, and organizing potlucks for organizations like the BahusKlubben and the Viking Lodge. In a working-class world in which who you were was based as much on the people to whom you belonged as on the job you did, women as the keepers of identity, of family, and of belonging were at the core of the steel mill neighborhoods.

In some ways, I acknowledge the central position of the women I grew up among with a certain reluctance. Growing up in Southeast Chicago, I often felt boxed in. Although the focus on families in Southeast Chicago could offer strong sources of support, the roles expected within families could also be experienced as profoundly confining for those who didn't "fit" or who longed for alternatives.[29] In my own case, I nursed grievances from the time I was a child because my dad didn't want me to throw a ball overhand (he was afraid I would get hurt), because he wouldn't let me touch any of the tools or electronic buttons in the house, and because he told me I should be a nurse when I said I wanted to be a doctor. However, the policing of such gender-segregated norms came as much from the women I knew as from the men, if not more. The women who raised me valued a "traditional" gendered division of labor. Such realities are symbolized for me by the anti–Equal Rights Amendment button that my mother hung on a bulletin board next to the family phone and which remained there throughout my adolescence. As a young college student taking women's studies classes, I often found myself frustrated—as were my professors—that so many working-class women in neighborhoods like Southeast Chicago seemed actively antifeminist. Why did so many of the women I knew growing up value "traditional" gender roles even while other women were contesting them?

The answer, I would argue, lies partially in late nineteenth- and early twentieth-century history. Scholars describe how the Victorian middle classes espoused a "cult of domesticity" emphasizing the need for women as mothers to stay home to care for children, thereby providing their families with a domestic haven in a harsh world of expanding capitalism (and, not incidentally, simultaneously differentiating themselves in class terms from women who labored). Working-class women often did not have such opportunities, and much of their time was taken up with working out of economic necessity whether inside or outside the home. Progressive Era reformers—some women from middle-class and elite backgrounds associated with Chicago's settlement houses like Hull House—often couched their critiques of capitalism in terms of the need to protect working-class women from the extreme conditions of turn-of-the-century industrial labor.[30] The inability of working-class women to stay home as mothers was often linked in the popular imagination to the presumed degradation of working-class and immigrant families. In reaction to such historical arguments, many women of my mother's generation in Southeast Chicago saw the post–World War II ability to "stay home" as men began to earn "family wages" as a privilege rather than a constraint, a sign of upward mobility for working families. Ironically, it was just at the historical moment when working-class women were gaining the ability to achieve the middle-class nuclear family ideal that had long eluded them that growing numbers of middle-class women began chafing at their own domestic confinement and seeking work outside the home (albeit in far more fulfilling jobs than those available to working-class women). Such historical debates also suggest why women in steel mill communities, including the women in my own family, often sought to emphasize the more "traditional" ideals of staying at home and systematically downplayed their own histories of paid labor, a phenomenon noted in other steel mill communities as well.[31]

Like my mother, my grandmother Ethel was a strong woman capable of holding her family together when things got tough. She raised my mom and uncle on her own after her first husband, my mother's father, "La" Hansen, died when my mother was twelve. La's own immigrant father had labored in an East Side brewery located on the lakefront. However, La was a diabetic who had to be careful of his health and avoid heavy work, a reality that pushed him into what I, as a kid, envisioned as the more genteel occupation of running a newspaper delivery business. Many years after La had died, my grandmother, then in her fifties, met and married my father's father—my Little Grandpa—and brought him to live with her in the house on Avenue G, where my mother had been raised.

In some ways, my grandmother reminded me of a psychologically stronger version of the working-class but Tory mother in Carolyn Steedman's account of English working-class life, *Landscape for a Good Woman*. Like Steedman's mother, many of the women on my mother's side of the family also gravitated toward cultural styles of "classiness" which they associated with refinement and upward mobility. Anthropologist Sherry Ortner has suggested that among the American working classes, women are often culturally coded as being of a higher class than the men in their families. In Southeast Chicago, this was particularly the case for those women who performed low-paying clerical jobs, an increasingly common phenomenon over the course of the twentieth century. While such women would dress up to work in offices alongside those from middle-class backgrounds, their husbands and male relatives continued to do manual work, dressed in dirty workclothes and swearing and cussing in the style customary to the historically confrontational nature of labor relations in the steel mills. Although the men made more money, it was the women who showed a greater degree of class.

In contrast to Steedman's mother, my grandmother expressed her desires for upward mobility via claims to respectability played out in a dense world of overlapping ties with extended family members and long-term neighbors. I suspect that women like my grandmother and mother also supported the gender norms that I, in my own life, found so confining in part because of this class-tinged sense of respectability. As a college student, I remember reacting with outrage when my dad approvingly described how in earlier decades women had been banned from drinking alone at bars on the Indiana side of the border. When I turned to my mother for support, she instead supported my father, explaining how such rules kept away "loose" women and chastising me for not understanding how "nice" it had been. Although such ideals of respectability felt repressive to me, it offered women like my mother the moral authority that they felt placed them at the center of family and community life.

This sense of respectability, as strong for my grandmother Ethel as for my mother, was bound up in churchgoing. In the Southeast Chicago of my childhood, attending church was as much about maintaining ethnic and social networks built over generations as finding religious solace. Historically, in Southeast Chicago, people joined churches based on their ethnic affiliation (although the sharp edges of these ethnic divisions would soften as the children of immigrants intermarried). Bethesda Swedish Lutheran Church was built in the 1890s for a mere $236.95, because, like so many churches in Southeast Chicago, its working-class male congregants built much of the church with their own hands when they weren't working in the mills. This church was at the center of my grandmother's and mother's social worlds and connected them to the multigenerational, upwardly mobile world of Swedish immigrants that was at core of their personal history and self-identity.

My siblings and I would trail after our mother and grandmother as they went to church and positioned themselves at the center of the teeming social activity there. While they were busy organizing coffee hours, pancake breakfasts, charity auctions, and holiday events or attending meetings of women's groups like the Dorcas Society or the Eunice Priscilla Circle, I would play with my siblings and other children in the church basement. We loved looking through the heavy glass cases that held the church's confirmation photos, ranging from the seemingly exotic black and white photos of the late 1890s, when immigrants were entering Southeast Chicago in large numbers, to the photographs of my grandfather La's generation in the 1920s to the color photos of our own. We would rummage through the old bibles stored in the basement that were printed in an unfamiliar Swedish language and try to recall the words to the mysterious songs, now rarely heard, that women in the choir still sang in Swedish for midnight candlelight services on Christmas Eve. Like the stories my father told on our drives around Southeast Chicago, the photos, artifacts, and songs of earlier generations found in this church bound us to historical worlds on distant shores that became part of the crucible—the patchwork mosaic—of life in Southeast Chicago.

Being a committed churchgoer did not tame my grandmother's feisty streak or relegate her to the moralism that some of my friends with leftist leanings associate with religion. If anything, my grandmother's self-image seemed to have crystallized around being the kind of daring, modern young woman who wore fashionable clothes and acted in the cheeky style of Hollywood starlets of the 1930s and 1940s. As an adult watching old Hollywood films, I had a jolt of recognition when I saw my grandmother's mannerisms perfectly mirrored in a young Claudette Colbert mixing it up on the screen with Clark Gable. In later years, my grandmother's fun-loving streak continued to surface in acts like buying lawn ornaments of brightly painted wood cutouts of kids peeing on the lawn or wearing bloomer-clothed bottoms. Somehow the bawdiness and respectability came together to form a seamless package.

It was the politics of material desire that Steedman so astutely analyzes that, I believe, made my utterly apolitical grandmother a Republican in the midst of this quintessential Chicago Democratic machine ward.[32] Desires for upward mobility, after all, might not only be associated with gendered ideas of respectability but also with political parties, as they were for Steedman's Tory-voting working-class mother. On election days, my grandmother would meet with other women from our neighborhood, mostly children of immigrants like herself. Dressed in bright, even gaudy, polyester clothing of red, white, and blue, with enormous plastic earrings and flag pins stuck to their shirts, my grandmother and her friends volunteered to work every year at the polling stations. My grandmother was proud to take up such civic responsibilities, but she was, as far as I could tell, completely agnostic toward larger intellectual and political debates. Although she graduated from high school and read Harlequin romances (unlike the more hardscrabble working-class women on my father's side, who never read books), her desires for upward mobility were not overtly linked to education. Instead, the manifestations of these desires, like those of Steedman's mother, were material and concrete. They emerged through wearing her neat and brightly colored pantsuits, not swearing in public (in contrast to those women others might describe as "trailer trash"), and creating a clean home with plastic on the sofa seats to keep it that way.

As Maria Kefalas describes in *Working Class Heroes*, her ethnography of white working-class residents on Chicago's Southwest Side, homes are more than the primary economic asset of many working-class families or the even symbolic markers of status and respectability that separated immigrant families from their own more precarious pasts. Homes were also spheres of control for women, who used material displays of cleanliness and color-coordinated home decorations and holiday displays as tangible statements of their own moral worth. According to Kefalas, the work and care that went into such home presentations were used by women to differentiate themselves symbolically from other presumably less worthy women. My own mother's house was dominated to an unusual degree by early twentieth-century family furniture and wood moldings. Although the wood my mother and I had always found beautiful did not signify classy antiques to East Siders, the way it might have to my college friends (more likely, it suggested a lack of money during the 1950s and 1960s to turn the house into a "modern" one), the careful attention that my mother put into maintaining the house's decor strongly supports Kefalas's analysis. Just as clearly, I recognize my own habitual messiness as a form of rebellion against the fetishistic focus on cleanliness that defined what it was to be a good woman in the social world of my childhood.

Yet, there was more than one set of gender ideals found among women in Southeast Chicago. Just as recent immigrant groups might hold different beliefs about what it meant to be a proper woman or man, there were different gender ideals found among the various class fractions that filled the neighborhoods of Southeast Chicago. The ideals espoused by my grandmother or by my mother's childhood friends who eventually married "up" and out of the old steel mill neighborhoods were more common among the more upwardly mobile. Although some have argued that the Aryan phenotypes of Swedish immigrants eased their assimilation into US society,[33] there were equally blonde, white women on my father's side of the family whose lives followed very different trajectories. For those from poor white or US "hillbilly" backgrounds, there were different models of gender shot through with class. To the disapproval of the more "respectable" neighborhood women, these women sometimes chained-smoked, played poker, paid less attention to dress, and yelled louder and more often at their kids. Education was not considered to be important. Even though my grandmother Ethel herself was staunchly anti-intellectual, graduating from school was, nevertheless, something respectable to her. This was not the case for my Little Grandpa or many of his relatives. (When I needed a few hundred dollars to tide me over during college, my grandmother intervened to borrow it from my grandfather, refusing to tell him that it was for college, since, as she put it, "you know your grandfather doesn't believe in education.")

Some of my cousins and second cousins on my father's side had lives that some academics would call "hard living" as opposed to "settled" models of working-class life.[34] A number of these female cousins had children outside marriage and dropped out of high school. Some lived in trailers and were single moms or had steady male partners who couldn't be married because it meant losing welfare payments. Yet on my father's side of the family there was little of the moral disapproval that emanated from my grandmother's and mothers' social circles, which were intent upon respectability. My father's older brother, my uncle Bill, made a comment that brought this vividly home to me. One day in the mid-1980s, when my sister and I were home visiting from college, he only half-jokingly criticized us for not having babies, comparing us disparagingly to my female cousins who had dropped out of school and become teenaged mothers. For him, being married or in college was irrelevant. The kids were what mattered and what conferred adulthood, creating bonds across generations. Children were a source of power in a world where people had little, as well as a welcome source of distraction and entertainment for the adults around them. Education, in this worldview, was not only beside the point but could be potentially negative, holding out possibilities of moving outside the neighborhood and rupturing relationships. In contrast, placing priority on having kids—not first on having jobs or education, as in middle-class worlds—was the key to social continuity. In short, there were different class-inflected models of what it meant to be a man or a woman in Southeast Chicago, and these models were impossible to disentangle from the histories that brought particular groups there.

In the economically modest but people-rich social world in which I was raised, I was accustomed to women like my grandmother who ran their families and sometimes their husbands. My far more passive father acerbically acknowledged such realities when he jokingly labeled the senior women in our family the "Swedish Army." Some scholars suggest that Swedish women immigrants in Chicago drew upon historical traditions of strong women with an unusual degree of control over their homes.[35] Yet, in thinking of neighbors or in-marrying relatives hailing from a range of ethnic groups—or at least those with equally long histories of assimilation into the mill neighborhoods—I can see similar patterns. The strength of such women, I believe, didn't come simply from individual personalities or from the influence of ethnic backgrounds, but from the centrality of families and the women-dominated neighborhood institutions of Southeast Chicago in giving meaning to working-class lives.

In challenging lopsided hegemonic portraits of white working-class women, I do not want to overstate the case. In addition to men's strong economic advantages over women in Southeast Chicago, there was an ethos of steelworker culture that provided models of masculinity that some men with forceful personalities could readily translate into domestic dominance. Jack Metzgar's account of the tension-filled relationship between his steelworker father and the rest of his family offers one telling example. Such stories were also present in my own family's history. My father told the tragic story of his uncle by marriage—a "big mean Polack," in my father's description—known for his alcoholism and violent temper. This man continuously got into drunken brawls with other men in the steel mills and, at home, beat his wife, my father's aunt. While the doctor's certificate said she had died of natural causes, my father and other family members suspected internal injuries after a beating. My mother also told the story of how my grandmother Ethel, not long after her second marriage to my Little Grandpa when she was in her fifties, had come across the alley to my mother's house in tears. My Little Grandpa had expected her to shine his shoes, a request she had refused. The story cut both ways: my grandfather's assumption that she should do such a thing; and my grandmother's refusal, as a woman who had headed her family as a widow for years, to do so. In the end, however, although men in Southeast Chicago might have had various bases for power, economic and otherwise, both inside and outside the steel mills, women in the old steel mill neighborhoods also had their own rich social institutions that they had built and within which they found sources of strength. In more mainstream narratives that depict working-class women largely as the victims of working-class men, such sources of strength often go unrecognized, making it impossible to explain what gave birth to the powerful women I knew as a child.

In retrospect, I recognize that the ideals of womanhood that had appeared confining to me growing up were sources of strength to my grandmother and mother, who valued the centrality conferred upon female lives by the thick networks of social and familial relationships found in places like Southeast Chicago (a reality that feminist anthropologists have noted about women in many other parts of the world as well). I also recognize that my frustration was partially based on the refusal of my grandmother and mother to validate what I valued and their tendency to dismiss my bookishness in favor of a social dominance over family to which I never aspired. Understanding my mother's and grandmother's views, however, requires thinking about class as well as gender in ways that my college women's studies classes did not always help me to recognize. Although for much of my life I may have been profoundly ambivalent about the ideals of womanhood common in the Southeast Chicago of my childhood, I can testify to the power of the lives they might generate.

## Conclusion

Growing up in Southeast Chicago, class was, for me, about the tensions and rumblings, not only between "us" and those my father referred to as the "richy rich" who lived in far-away suburban neighborhoods, but also among ourselves, as I and my relatives sought to redefine ourselves and to cobble together a sense of identity that both linked us to a past and gave us hopes for the future. Class, then, was not only about economic production; it was also about how economic inequalities intersected with gender and ethnicity and how individual and collective histories came together to create the buzzing social world that I knew as a child. It was about northern Europeans who distinguished themselves from poor "hillbilly" whites and southern European Catholics, all of whom distinguished themselves from darker people who lived in the outlying areas of Southeast Chicago neighborhoods.[36] It was about how the meaning of being a good man or woman was linked to the kinds of families that people kept, the kinds of attitudes they displayed toward work, and how they related to one another.

In retrospect, I can't help but be fascinated by the "family" of people who lived in that frame house of my grandmother's during my childhood. It brought together those three very different individuals: my grandmother, the respected member of the Swedish ladies of the Lutheran church, a Republican, a woman who bossed her family and wore the makeup and earrings that signaled her youthful aspirations to be a smartly dressed "classy" woman; my Little Grandpa, a man with a grade school education raised with the cultural habits of the rural "white trash" poor, a strong union man and Democrat with a stable working job (and, later, a generous "middle-class" pension) who possessed right-wing anti-intellectual sympathies; and the most enigmatic of the three, my grandmother's father, Big Grandpa, a taciturn, bitter man, a Freemason with socialist sympathies, an individual with a grade school education who drank too much and sought to better himself by taking correspondence classes in engineering and who secretly aspired to write.

Nevertheless, no matter what one's life trajectory might be, it was also understood that no one needed to look farther than Southeast Chicago; ours was an insular world differentiated within, yet tied together by the economic bonds of a common enterprise. Although the economic realm failed to determine the breadth of our social world, in other ways it could not be escaped. Antagonism towards the "big boys" in steel mill management had a long history in Southeast Chicago, but it was the union wages in the years following World War II that allowed many of my parents' and grandparents' generations to redefine themselves as economically middle class. They demonstrated this newfound respectability through neat bungalows and tidy lawns with colorful lawn ornaments that showed off their industriousness and worthiness in contrast to "poorer" others. In part because African-Americans were symbolically coded as poor (despite the middle-class steelworker wages of some), many white homeowners in Southeast Chicago desperately, even viciously, tried to keep African-Americans out of "their" neighborhoods in the 1950s and 1960s. Perceiving class through the lens of race, whites attempted to shore up a social respectability they perceived as under siege, while their unmarked category of whiteness gave many an unacknowledged boost in accessing jobs, homes, and other necessities in the competition for respectability. In short, both the rumblings within homes and among different ethnic and racial groups in Southeast Chicago cannot be separated from these kinds of class-based resentments and aspirations, even if class is unable to explain them all.

In the world in which I was raised, the steel mills were at the economic center, creating the conditions out of which our social lives and communities were forged. Even though the mills failed to determine who we were, in the end it must be recognized that the mills brought everyone together, and it was the steel industry (and the industries and businesses that served it and its workers and families) that provided the backdrop for most of our daily lives. Even much of the dry land in this swampy landscape had been created by the slag generated by the steel mills. Like a domineering family member about whom one feels profoundly ambivalent, the mills were both frightening and something upon which nearly everyone either directly or indirectly depended. As a child sitting in the backseat of our family car, I would crane my neck as we drove past the steel mills, trying to catch a glimpse of the fires blazing in their innards. There was a stark beauty to the enormous industrial scale of the mills, with vats the size of houses pouring molten rivers of glowing steel, while gas jets flared through the nighttime sky (fig. 12). As a teenager skinny-dipping with friends at night in the industrial lakes of Southeast Chicago, I found the vista almost overwhelming. We paid far less attention to the sooty air, and virtually none to the invisible toxic waste that

12. South Works at night in 1947. Courtesy of the Southeast Chicago Historical Museum.

seeped from heavy industry into the surrounding ground, rivers, wetlands, and lakes—and into our own bodies.

With historical hindsight, it's clear just how much Southeast Chicago served as a social crucible during the time various generations of my family lived there. It brought together respectability-seeking immigrants and the hardscrabble native poor. The steel mills and post–World War II union wages raised members of both these groups to a stable, almost middle-class prosperity. Even African-Americans, relegated to the worst jobs in the mills until the 1970s, were able to use steelworker wages to create communities like those in neighboring Gary that offered many a bridge from poverty to the middle class. Despite my Big Grandpa's supposed regret about emigrating to the United States, he too would have to admit that he enjoyed a degree of economic security in the second half of his life that contrasted sharply with the hardships he had known as a child. In retrospect, it is possible to recognize that places like Southeast Chicago were not simply locations to live and work, but rungs on the American social ladder.

Although the stories my relatives told sometimes resonated with and sometimes challenged the dominant societal narratives that threatened to overshadow their own, there was a continuity and stability to the world of my childhood. For my parents' and grandparents' generations, there was a widespread belief in future prosperity for oneself and one's family both in the Calumet region and in the United States as a whole. There was a sense that factory owners and workers were bound together in a common enterprise that linked them indelibly to each other and to places like Southeast Chicago. Growing up in this world, it seemed unfathomable that this would ever change.

# It All Came Tumbling Down: My Father and the Demise of Chicago's Steel Industry

The world we thought would never change did change, and with shocking speed. In 1980, when my father's mill Wisconsin Steel closed, words like "deindustrialization" and "globalization" hadn't yet become part of the collective vocabulary.[1] Pundits and scholars were only just beginning to offer explanations for what was happening that would become the dominant interpretations of future years. While Southeast Chicago's steelworkers were used to long periods of layoffs and the mills' erratic ups and downs, the permanent closing of heavy industry—the reason why everyone was there in the first place—was simply unfathomable. The closings, not surprisingly, were met with bewilderment and disbelief, and they set in motion profound shifts within economies, families, and individual psyches.

In later years, my own efforts to try to make sense of deindustrialization would center on the need to glean some meaning from the fact that the world in which I had been raised had been turned upside down. Did this transformation ultimately defy explanation, one of the vagaries of history that one can suffer but never fully understand? Or was there something to be discovered, some way of thinking about the world that might throw light on what had happened and perhaps even suggest a course of action for the future? At the time the steel mills in Southeast Chicago began closing, most commentators attributed deindustrialization to global competition and the supposed inability of US industries to keep up. But if one looked closely at what actually happened in countless places like Southeast Chicago, it became clear that there was far more to the story than this. Deindustrialization—a phenomenon as symptomatic of the economic restructuring of recent decades as the "excesses" on Wall Street—was also about other kinds of pressures, logics, and choices only dimly hinted at in these more dominant accounts.

I recall my father's attempts to challenge arguments, popular in the 1980s, that reduced the causes of the demise of the American steel industry to overpaid and lazy workers, outworked by global competition and getting their comeuppance. I remember him making such challenges unbidden at family gatherings or in infrequent chance encounters with individuals who lived outside Southeast Chicago. Anthropologist Kate Dudley, as part of her 1994 study of the downsizing of the auto industry in Kenosha, Wisconsin, spoke with many middle-class professionals who had resented the strong paychecks of autoworkers, their union protections, and the seeming injustice of the fact that, even though industrial work didn't require advanced education, it could lead to middle-class livelihoods.[2] Perhaps the individuals from outside of Southeast Chicago with whom my father struck up random conversations were, beneath the politeness, similarly unsympathetic? Certainly, many of the accounts we heard on the news conveyed similar assumptions. Over time, my father gradually sank under the weight of trying to contest such narratives and retreated into himself.

The counternarrative regarding deindustrialization offered in this chapter is not only about the extent of the human fallout of deindustrialization—a fallout that my family knew only too well—but also about those pieces of the story that were left out of more dominant accounts and that pointed to different kinds of economic, social, and political logics. When looked at from these alternative angles, it becomes clear that deindustrialization's costs have not been limited to the pain of industrial workers and their families in places like the Calumet, the Monongahela and Mahoning Valleys of Pennsylvania and Ohio, the area around Detroit, Michigan, or other "rust belt" regions, but have been exacted more broadly upon wide swaths of the nation as a whole.

In my own life, I have associated the destruction of the steel mills with my father's destruction. I always identified with my dad. I looked like him. I was sensitive like him, and also, like him, I could throw what my husband refers to as "dagger eyes" on those occasions when I became angry. When I was a child, my mother always told me, "You are your father's daughter," her voice laced with exasperation that I wasn't more like her. Continuously told that I was a Walley (with all the low-class positioning that name implied to her), I had taken a special interest in my father's family, about whom my mother was profoundly ambivalent. I was also fascinated by Wisconsin Steel, the fiery place where my father disappeared while working endless night shifts, and where he had to wear long underwear under his workclothes as protection from the heat even in the summertime. In later years, I was annoyed when fellow feminist academics assumed that girls primarily identified with their mothers. Paying less attention to the relationship between daughters and fathers, some assumed that if girls identified with men it was ultimately because males were more powerful. In my own case, it was the opposite. I identified with my father because we were both in some ways rebellious outsiders in a domestic world dominated by the senior women in the family.

My father's own personality was contradictory. On the surface, he had the macho veneer that easily fit stereotypes of white working-class men of his generation. Born on the dining room table during a snowstorm in the depths of the Depression, he had been a rowdy but playful neighborhood boy. My grandfather once caught him and his older brother, my uncle Bill, hiding in a ditch in the "prairie" near one of Al Capone's speakeasies,[3] trying to catch a glimpse of the action. When he was a teenager, my mother, who was several years younger, admired him from afar. He hung out at the school playground, where he was known as an ace Ping Pong player, then a popular pastime. When they froze the schoolyard, he proved to be a beautiful ice skater as well. My mother relates that he courted her neighbor, an older girl, and he would sit with her on her lawn for long hours "picking four-leaf clovers." Yet he was also a "bad boy," sent to a special high school for "juvenile delinquents" (he insisted it was only for ditching school, although I was never fully convinced). At sixteen, he quit school and went to work pumping gas at one of the gas stations that lined the Indiana state border. He also devoted himself to drinking and being unruly with his friends, most of whom were known by nicknames, including "Inky" (who had been put in an incubator as a baby) and "Peg" (who had lost a leg hopping rails and who is pictured in fig. 13, standing next to my dad in my father's backyard). He hopped freight cars himself and sometimes ended up in places like Kentucky with no way to get home. It was on a drinking binge in downtown Chicago with his buddy Big Russ that he got the tattoo that I loved as a child. All my male relatives, nearly all steelworkers and veterans, had tattoos. I liked to admire them when they wore undershirts and smoked cigarettes in kitchens at family parties or on the porch in the summertime. My father's tattoo was of a black panther crawling up his arm, with red dye drops of blood dripping from where the claws appeared to penetrate his skin. When he was in the hospital with lung cancer at the end of his life, his chemotherapy nurses looked at his sagging panther and teased him about how he "really must have been a thing back in the day!"

Yet underneath the tough-guy exterior he was a sensitive, even fragile man, one wounded in so many places that it was impossible to patch him up. A difficult life as well as his own father's harshness had fatally damaged

13. My dad (*right*) and "Peg" in the family backyard

him. After he married my mother, he often chose to stay home during his free time. Figure 14, a photograph taken at Christmas, shows me sitting on his lap surrounded by my mother, sister, and an aged Big Grandpa. I suspect that, secretly, my father longed for a quiet, even reclusive life—having to live up to a veneer of self-assured masculinity was a heavy weight to bear. As a kid, I would try to extract stories of his younger days from him. His early life seemed glamorous to me, an exciting contrast to the churchgoing respectability of my mother, yet to him, it was a source of embarrassment. When I tried to get him to recount thrilling tales of riding the rails, he would instead tell the bitter story of how one time, when he had ended up in Kentucky and phoned his family for help, his father had refused to pay for his fare home.

I liked the times when instead of going out to play poker with his older brother and in-laws, he stayed home and played cards with my sisters and me. It was while playing cards or Ping Pong in the basement that the joking demeanor of his youth would occasionally reappear. At such times, my sisters and I sometimes managed to extract a good story from him, like how he had lost his corporal's stripe when he was in Germany immediately after World War II. He and a buddy of his went AWOL, ended up drinking in a

14. Our family with Big Grandpa at Christmas

tavern, and had to be hauled out by the German police after a fight broke out. At such times, my dad would jokingly intone *Nicht rauchen in der barren* (No smoking in the bar), the few words of German he had acquired while in the army. Although it was clear that respectability was important to my mother, it was only later that I realized that it was important to my father as well. Perhaps he had seen marrying my mother as a form of upward mobility, an escape from the tumultuous family life of his own relatives. As if to keep us from the fate of those nieces and female cousins on his side of the family who became unwed mothers at a young age (shamefully in the judgment of some, unremarkably for others like my uncle Bill), my father ferociously told us at adolescence that if we got "knocked up," we would be kicked out of the house.

In his married life, my father lived on the periphery of my mother's social world. Like a number of neighborhood women, she had worked in an office as a young woman while my father did manual labor; in her case, it was as a bookkeeper in a real estate office in South Chicago. Although she stopped working when she had kids, she claimed never to have missed it. She was (like my grandmother before her) president of our school's PTA, headed and served on a variety of women's church and volunteer groups, and was part-time secretary at our church. Even when she was not involved with various women's organizations, my mother's world was a full one. When I was a kid and my sisters and I walked around the neighborhood on errands with my mother, it seemed like she knew everyone on the East Side. It seemed that every ten feet she would bump into a friend, relative, or acquaintance and stop to chat: one might be a childhood friend from Avenue G, another a former school classmate, yet another a fellow church member or maybe a distant relative of either hers or my father's. After the housework was done, we kids would accompany my mother on her social rounds, often protesting that we were tired of all the grown-up talk, as she dropped off newsletters at the home of a fellow PTA officer, stopped to visit a childhood friend, or ran errands for a church group. As children, we were minor players in the multigenerational adult world of thick social bonds that swirled around us, an inversion of contemporary suburban lives where mothers (and some-times fathers) organize their lives around the playdates, soccer matches, and violin lessons of their children. My mother had an astounding memory for social details, and we used to joke that she could list the names, birthdates, addresses, spouses, children, relatives and life histories of everyone she had ever known in Southeast Chicago across multiple generations. She was like a living East Side social registry, a testament to the density and centrality of social ties in the old mill neighborhoods.[4]

Although my father also had been born and had grown up on the East Side, his world was a much more socially attenuated one. He would occa-sionally stop to bullshit with friends from elementary school or from the mills when we ran into them "up the street," as we referred to Ewing Avenue, the East Side's main business thoroughfare. He also had bonds to coworkers in the mills to which we, his family, were not privy, a camaraderie heightened by the fact that mill workers depended on fellow workers for their physical safety in a highly dangerous job. In general, however, my father, like the other men we knew, left the maintainence of social relationships, or what anthropologists refer to as "kin work," up to my mom. He preferred to stay at home quietly watching a ballgame on TV, inevitably complaining about all the cleaning, cooking, and hubbub before gatherings with extended family. He occasionally followed my mom to church when some activity was hap-pening: Easter egg hunts in the church basement, Christmas Eve pageants, or Father's Day, when the men were given boutonnieres. Mostly, he would sit in a corner of the church basement, finding an occasional "old timer" male to bullshit with, while my mother was at the center of the activity.

It was my father's paycheck from the mills that was his source of manhood and self-respect. Going into the mills soon after World War II, he never suffered the long hours or low pay that my grandfather had. Instead, he was of a generation that watched the expansion of powerful unions and their representatives with a cynical eye.[5] After the mills went down and newspaper accounts blamed it on US workers wanting "too much" or lacking the work ethic of the Japanese, he made a point of stressing that the average steelworker never made very much money; it was skilled workers who worked long hours of overtime that made the "big money" in the mills.[6] My memories support his contention. A climate of anxiety over money permeates my childhood recollections. When I was about five, I remember my dad coming home from the hospital after a hernia operation from a mill-related injury. I recall drawing him a "get well" card with crayons and taping my own pennies on it in an attempt to prevent him and my mom from fighting over money. Practical and down-to-earth like her own mother, my mom was skilled at stretching to make ends meet. Nevertheless, despite the fact that we had a home, a used car, and food, it was never easy for her. I hated the hand-me-down clothes that I was given by a neighbor's grandchild who now lived in the suburbs, and I remember my disappointment at getting a toy guitar Christmas ornament instead of the real one I had asked for—a disappointment she sensed as well. I also hated the fact that my father used his role as male family provider to ground his own authority. I remember how he punctuated arguments with my mother with the refrain that since it was he who "paid the bills," he should make the decisions. Although, in retrospect, I recognize his bravado as an attempt to buttress his own losing domestic position, the injustice of it still rankles and has underwritten my own determination never to live without a wage of my own.

## The Closing of Wisconsin Steel

Given that his role as family provider was central to his identity, as it was for many men in the area, the closing of the mills devastated my father. Wisconsin Steel was the first mill to close in Southeast Chicago (see figs. 15 and 16). If not the largest mill to go down, its closure was certainly the most abrupt and chaotic. It was also the mill shutdown that would be most closely documented by scholars and other observers.[7] Nevertheless, at the time, however, there was a great deal of mystery about what had actually happened. My father told the story of how, after being assured only the day before that their jobs were safe, he and other workers who were ending a shift were simply told to go home without further explanation. The gates were padlocked by armed guards. They weren't even allowed to clear out their lockers; a pipe fitter neighbor from across the street lost a locker-full of expensive trade tools he had accumulated over a lifetime. It turned out that bank creditors, suspecting an imminent shutdown, had hired the guards to ensure that they were at the front of the line to enforce their claims to mill property, even though workers hadn't even been notified of the closing yet.

The shutdown of Wisconsin Steel would later be challenged in the courts.[8] At the center of the dispute was the fact that, in 1977, International Harvester, the owner of Wisconsin Steel for the previous seventy-five years, had sold the mill to Envirodyne, a tiny California technology company with almost no assets, a transaction detailed in David Bensman and Roberta Lynch's book *Rusted Dreams: Hard Times in a Steel Community*. As Bensman and Lynch noted, headlines in the financial news had characterized the sale of Wisconsin Steel as "Minnow Swallows Whale."[9] Critics of the sale argued that International Harvester had deliberately sold the steel mill to a company that lacked both the experience and assets to run it in order to avoid paying $62 million dollars in unfunded pension obligations. By selling the mill, Harvester transferred its pension obligations to the new company, which

15. Wisconsin Steel after it closed. Courtesy of the Southeast Chicago Historical Museum.

16. A shuttered Wisconsin Steel yard in 1982. Courtesy of the Southeast Chicago Historical Museum.

set up a limited liability subsidiary to minimize its own risk in the event of a mill shutdown. If Wisconsin Steel declared bankruptcy, the government body that guarantees pensions, the Pension Benefit Guaranty Corporation or PBGC, would be obliged to pick up the tab, and both Harvester and the purchasing company would be off the hook. The PBGC would later charge that the sale of the mill was a "sham" transaction.

My dad, like other Wisconsin Steel workers, had long had suspicions about what was happening. Once considered a "gem" in the industry, Wisconsin Steel had been allowed to fall into disrepair by an International Harvester plagued with management problems. After the mill was sold, workers were even more frustrated by the failure of the new company to plow money back into maintaining the mill. It turned out that when Envirodyne bought Wisconsin Steel, the sale agreement stipulated that the company could use mill earnings to finance a wholly unrelated business venture.[10] In short, Envirodyne hoped to milk Wisconsin Steel of revenues, treating it as a "cash cow" for the benefit of the parent company in its years of ownership.[11] In the aftermath of the shutdown, Wisconsin's closing gained notoriety as an egregiously unethical (and, by some measures, illegal) plant closing. Although such dealings were considered shocking at the time, Harvester and

Envirodyne acted in ways that would become increasingly common in the corporate world of the 1980s and 1990s. As the years progressed, these kinds of bare-knuckle tactics would become familiar ones as America's corporate landscape was transformed. An age had dawned in which mergers and acquisitions were cynically used to milk companies of profits and to increase short-term stock values, regardless of the destructive, even cannibalistic, impact on the acquired companies.[12] In addition, as Steven High has argued, many US-based corporations had deliberate policies of not reinvesting in industrial infrastructure and of diverting funds elsewhere.[13] As a consequence, the planned obsolescence of industries like steel, in which the decision was made to intentionally let them fall into disrepair and then move on to greener pastures, served as the silent counterpart to the more publicized phenomenon of "runaway" shops, in which factories moved from higher-wage to lower-wage regions.

Many residents of Southeast Chicago were distressed that International Harvester, which had long proclaimed its commitment to Wisconsin employees and to the region, had not only fled its obligations to workers but also seemed to deliberately provoke Wisconsin Steel's final collapse. When my mother told me on that fateful March morning in 1980 that "they called the ore boat back," the "they" she referred to was International Harvester and a series of complex machinations that I would only come to understand years later.[14] When Envirodyne had bought Wisconsin Steel, it had put down almost no money and taken on little risk. It borrowed $35 million from Chase Manhattan and $50 million from International Harvester itself, allowing Harvester to retain rights to the mill's ore and coal mines as collateral. Harvester also agreed to continue buying steel from Wisconsin Steel for its other operations. As Wisconsin Steel teetered on the brink of bankruptcy, some claimed Harvester deliberately delayed settling a strike at other facilities that it owned. Since Harvester was a major purchaser of Wisconsin Steel's output, the strike starved the mill of much-needed funds. Even though Wisconsin Steel's new management was actively negotiating for federal government loans to keep it afloat, Harvester made the decision to call in its legal claims on its loan collateral, including the iron ore boat traveling across Lake Michigan that March morning. Harvester's unilateral move pushed the struggling mill over the edge into bankruptcy. My dad and other Wisconsin Steel workers speculated that Harvester actively wanted Wisconsin Steel to fail so it would no longer be obligated to buy its steel and could search out cheaper alternatives.

When bank creditors froze Wisconsin's payroll accounts, workers' last paychecks bounced even when the checks had already been deposited in the bank.[15] Adding insult to injury, my dad and his coworkers became liable for a cascade of bounced-check fees as well as bills they thought they had already paid. Not only wages but also pensions and health insurance benefits were abruptly cut off. Even steelworker accounts at the employee credit union were frozen. In addition, workers were contractually owed millions of dollars in severance pay, vacation pay, and supplemental unemployment benefits. Corporate and bank lenders, however, ensured that they were paid back first as the remains of the defunct mill were sold to reimburse creditors, while Wisconsin's employees were pushed to the end of the line. Although Harvester and Envirodyne had carefully insulated themselves against suffering a major impact from the mill's shutdown, the plant's 3,400 employees and the surrounding community were not in a position to do the same.

Such realities contributed to a profound sense of betrayal among Wisconsin Steel workers. Although the steel mills had been a dominating force in Southeast Chicago, the mills were also, as countless employees and residents put it, "like family." The steel industry, over the course of its long history in the region, had encouraged such ideas. In an effort to manage unruly labor, the industry had emphasized its own commitment to place and community and of the need to work together for the patriotic causes of war and social and industrial progress.[16] International Harvester, as the owner of the Wisconsin mill, had done so even more than most companies. Providing electricity to churches in South Deering, funding adult sports teams, and even paving streets, it sought to create a sense of identification and common purpose between workers and the mill.[17] In the end, the sense of obligation connoted by "family," however dysfunctional, would backfire, contributing to the profound sense of betrayal and anger among mill workers and other residents. Family, as we all knew in Southeast Chicago, were those you could depend upon.[18]

## The Aftermath

Immediately after the mill shutdown, there was hope that the mill would open again, although, over time, this hope dissipated. While some politicians sincerely tried to help steelworkers, others cynically manipulated hopes that the mill would reopen in order to gain votes.[19] After Chicago's mayor, Jane Byrne, erroneously assured steelworkers that the mill would find a new buyer and that workers would have turkeys on their tables by Thanksgiving, Wisconsin Steel workers picketed her posh Gold Coast home on Thanksgiving with signs reading "Where's our turkeys, Jane?" In the meantime, Wisconsin Steel's independent steel union, the Progressive Steelworkers Union, did little to help its members. It turned out the union's lawyer, Edward Vrdolyak, known in the media as "Fast Eddie" and a man who was also the old-style political "boss" of the Tenth Ward, had been taking campaign contributions from Envirodyne, Wisconsin Steel's new owner.[20] Eventually, a grassroots activist group of former rank-and-file Wisconsin Steel workers called the Save Our Jobs Committee filed a class action suit against International Harvester. In 1988, eight years after Wisconsin Steel closed, their suit would lead to a partial settlement. For my father, this meant that a small fraction of the pension that he was owed was restored. However, the settlement was too little and too late for most workers.

In an area where neat lawns and never going on public assistance were quintessential points of pride, the stigma of being out of work was deeply traumatic for many. In the aftermath of the mill shutdown, my dad became increasingly depressed, eventually refusing to leave the house. Too wounded to show his face to the outside world, he gradually stopped shaving or changing his clothes. He would sit on the couch or at the kitchen table, with a cigarette continuously poised in his fingers, his fingertips dyed orange from the cheap butts. As my mother yelled about the wasted cigarette money and searched for odd change in the sofa cushions, the acrid smoke killed the house plants and turned the white ceiling orange. Coming home late at night, I'd find him watching the white fuzz on the TV set. Yet, in retrospect, our family considered itself lucky, and, comparatively, we were. My father was one of three Wisconsin Steel workers who lived on our block; after the mill closed, one of the others became an alcoholic and died a few years later. The third attempted suicide. In later years, I would read studies that documented the toll of the mill shutdowns in Southeast Chicago and that offered painful statistics regarding depression, suicides, illness, and broken families to back up the personal, lived experiences of those we knew. The numbers for Wisconsin Steel were staggering. In 1989, the *Daily Calumet* newspaper reported that in less than ten years since Wisconsin had been shut down, nearly 800 out of 3,400 workers had died, mostly from alcohol and stress-related illnesses, compounded by the lack of health care and high suicide rates.[21] For those who came of age in the post–World War II era, in which the future was assumed to be one of an expanding middle class and of growing prosperity for all (wasn't that supposed to be the *point* of modern society?), the unprecedented phenomenon of permanent mass shutdowns and countless people unceremoniously ejected from the American dream was more than many people could bear.

The shutdowns caused untold social devastation, but they also caused neighbors to band together. Some said the situation reminded them of how people depended upon each other during the Great Depression. While the dense social ties and animosities of Southeast Chicago could be stifling and insular, those same ties could be activated in times of trouble, providing a last-ditch social safety net for the working class and poor. The wife of the unemployed Wisconsin Steel worker across the street would bring over tomatoes from her backyard; her husband got my dad an off-the-books job for a few days emptying out a warehouse. Another neighbor, feeling sorry for my mother as she struggled to hold things together, secretly left an envelope with fifty dollars in cash in the mailbox; it was anonymous, so as not to hurt my mother's pride.

For those workers with no other adult wage earner at home to fall back upon, such as the handful of women steelworkers, who were often single moms with kids, the situation was the most dire. In our case, my mother joined the wives of many other steelworkers who went back to work to support their families. After a number of dark and uncertain days immediately following Wisconsin's shutdown, she became part of a growing army of temporary workers. In short, she became a cog in the economic logic of what geographer David Harvey has referred to as "flexible accumulation."[22] After several anxiety-filled years of bouncing between temporary jobs and scrambling to find friends and family to help with rides when there was no money to fix the family car, she found a "temp" position in Whiting, Indiana, doing clerical work in the blueprint room of the Amoco oil refinery.[23] She would work more than a quarter century at the same "temporary" job, much of that time without benefits for herself or the rest of our family.

Although media accounts presented the movement of women like my mother into wage labor as a "new" development in the traditionally gendered division of labor in Southeast Chicago, for many, the trend was actually more of a "return." It was not unusual for women in the early years of the mill neighborhoods, such as the older female relatives described in the previous chapter, to work, sometimes in formal, sometimes in informal economies. In the 1980s, as the mill shutdowns became more widespread, many of the stay-at-home wives of former steelworkers went back to work as waitresses, hairdressers, cashiers, salesclerks, bank tellers, receptionists, and clerical workers. Some worked informally out of their homes, making household crafts, holiday decorations, and cakes for extra cash. Although my mom had enjoyed staying home and the social centrality this gave her, the chance to "get out" and earn some money increased her self-confidence, even as my father's crumbled.

Over the course of the 1980s and early 1990s, it sometimes felt as if our entire world was collapsing. The other steel mills in the area closed one by one. US Steel, which had once employed twenty thousand people, would partially close South Works in 1981, permanently laying off fifteen thousand workers, and eventually closing entirely in 1992. In the early 1980s, Republic Steel, which had once employed six thousand seven hundred workers, laid off half its employees. In 1984, it was sold to LTV, which declared bankruptcy and then reorganized a few years later, shedding more workers. (Part of the mill was also sold to workers in an employee buyout scheme that would later fail.) When the remnants of the LTV mill shut down entirely about a decade ago, it would throw its last few hundred employees out of work. Interlake/Acme and the other smaller mills followed similarly checkered paths. In Southeast Chicago, where the population of the combined old steel mill neighborhoods of South Chicago, South Deering, the East Side, and Hegewisch numbered fewer than one hundred thousand people in 1980, approximately thirty-five thousand steel mill jobs were lost during this time. Over the border in Indiana, fifty-five thousand steelworkers out of a workforce that had once numbered seventy-five thousand would also find themselves unemployed.[24] In addition, there were what economists refer to as the "multiplier" effects of the shutdowns. The service and supplier businesses that depended upon the steel industry and the paychecks of their employees also began to close, and many of the women and men who labored in the industries subsidiary to the steel mills as well as at the local stores, restaurants, and taverns would also find themselves out of work. Even retirees, many of whom in this deteriorating environment helped support extended family members, worried about cutbacks to their pensions and health insurance.

In short, the impact in this highly condensed geographic region was devastating. While market enthusiasts touted the "new economy," such idealistic-sounding pronouncements did not help those who had been restructured out of their jobs in places like Southeast Chicago. Instead, residents were left with whatever often unstable and poorly paid jobs could be found, many in the service industry. Immediately after the mill shutdowns, former steelworkers also suffered active discrimination in hiring, as the steelworkers' union legacy often made service employers uncomfortable. Middle-aged workers like my father had the most difficult time of all. Although my father found occasional work during these years, he would never hold a permanent job again. Looking back, it seemed like a cloud of depression and despair hung for years, not only over our house, but over the entire region.

A few steelworkers, family members, and activists did try to protest the mill shutdowns (see fig. 17). Strikingly, the most cohesively organized

17. Wisconsin Steel workers protesting in downtown Chicago in 1980. Copyright
Chicago Tribune.

steelworkers in Southeast Chicago (and the central figures in the Save Our
Jobs Committee) were African-American and Latino.[25] Such individuals
were more likely to support extended families, and, as a consequence, the
loss of their jobs had an even more devastating effect upon their communities. Some were also of a generation that had watched, or taken part in,
the civil rights movement and were comfortable with political organizing.
Those like my father, who had traded in the fighting spirit of my grandfather's generation for a shot at middle-class respectability and who came of
age disillusioned with the hierarchy and perceived corruption of unions,
were often left at loose ends. Perhaps protesting seemed too much like the
1960s-style rabble-rousing they hated. For a region that had sent large numbers of young men to Vietnam and applauded Mayor Richard J. Daley for
cracking the heads of college "hippies" during the Democratic Convention
in 1968, there was room for little other than individualized despair and bitterness at being ejected from the American dream. Years later, I would hear
my father mutter, more to himself than anyone else, "Yeah, we thought we
were middle class there for a while. We were almost middle class."

## Remembering What Happened

When I think back upon this time from my adolescence, these are the memories I recall: I remember local community groups, like the East Side Lions, bringing my family and those of other unemployed steelworkers free turkeys and care baskets during the holidays. I recall the inedible government-issue free cheese given to steelworkers after the mills went down, the thought of which, even now, makes my stomach turn. And I remember how, at a time when the waves of plant closures hitting the Midwest still seemed unfathomable, a newly elected President Ronald Reagan (a man many steelworkers had voted for) would seek to cut back unemployment benefits, including those for the victims of deindustrialization.[26] When Reagan died in 2004, I was shocked by the resurgence of bitterness that I felt toward the man. It was not the resentment of an adult calculated from an abstract political philosophy, but the painful disillusionment of a fourteen-year-old. I remember thinking as a young teenager, with a sudden realization like the stab of a knife, that those in power did not care about me or about my family: our lives were meaningless to them. It was a harsh lesson that would stay with me.

I also remember trying to help relieve my parents' burden of providing by trying to take care of myself. I did odd jobs after school and even went to the office of the local ward boss to ask for an age exemption so that I could work on the government's jobs program for poor youth under the Comprehensive Employment and Training Act (CETA). Although my father explained that I might have to distribute political flyers in return for the favor, the summer job helped me buy my own school clothes and supplies. When I later read the literature on deindustrialization, it was easy to recognize myself in the accounts of those children who tried to grow up quickly in an attempt to help shoulder responsibilities that could offer their careworn parents some relief. However, I am embarrassed to admit that my most powerful emotion during these years was the desire to escape. After an unlikely series of events, I would end up leaving home at age sixteen, a year and a half after Wisconsin Steel's shutdown, to attend an elite East Coast boarding school. As I describe in the next chapter, this radical life change would raise a whole new set of issues for a working-class girl from Southeast Chicago.

When I returned home on school vacations during the 1980s and 1990s, my father would sometimes be working, but more often he was unemployed. After a harrowing period of competing with legions of other unemployed steelworkers for even an application for a job (any job), he briefly found work as a tollbooth attendant on the Chicago Skyway. One day, he made a sarcastic comment to a higher-up who asked him to work when he was officially on break. Part of the legacy of being a unionized steelworker was being trained not to grovel; the price, however, was the job. He then found an assembly-line job at a paper cup factory but, given his lack of seniority, was laid off again a few months later when that factory too began shedding workers. A few years later, he landed a job as a night janitor at a suburban elementary school. He liked the independence of working the night shift, but after a year or so the school closed due to declining enrollments. Finally, after years of unemployment and depression (interrupted by occasional off-the-books jobs as a driver illegally hauling hazardous chemicals down south in the back of a pickup truck), he found the job that lasted the longest of all. He became a security guard in a building in downtown Chicago that had offices filled with lawyers and the staff of a wealthy nonprofit foundation. Like my mother's job, it was through a temp agency; a neighbor who already worked there had put in a good word for him. Ironically (or not), the agency was owned by the brother of Edward Vrdolyak—the politician who, as a lawyer, had been accused of selling out Wisconsin Steel's independent union.

After my father landed the job, I remember both the excitement and the worries. Since there was no money, how could the family afford to buy the guard uniforms and shoes he was required to purchase in advance? And would our friends and relatives be willing to take turns dropping him off at the South Chicago train station every day so he could get to the Loop (our own family car having long since died)? Once he started, however, my father enjoyed the job. He liked chatting with tourists who visited the building's art deco entry hall in order to look at mosaics depicting the history of Chicago. My father would remember interesting facts the tourists had gleaned from their guidebooks and would pass them on to the next round of visitors. He even bought a blank notebook that he kept at the front desk and had the visitors, particularly those from Europe, write down where they were from and what they thought of Chicago. After six years of relative stability, however, the building management decided not to renew the contract for my father's temp agency. If they had, they would have been legally mandated to pay a twenty-five-cent-an-hour raise to the security guards. My father was hurt that the well-heeled professionals in his building who stopped to chat with him every day failed to protest management's decision. "All for a lousy twenty-five cents," he kept repeating in disgust. Although when the mills were running my father used to make sarcastic comments about lefty college kids eager for revolution who sometimes arrived in Southeast Chicago as labor activists, he would have been deeply grateful for someone to take up his cause then. After this job ended, he largely stayed at home. When those he didn't know asked what he did, he replied that he was "retired" even through he was only in his late fifties. He took naps on the couch, watched the neighbors out the window to make sure they didn't park their cars in "his" spot, scrubbed the kitchen sink till it gleamed, and perhaps watched a ball game on TV. Although the intense depression that followed the mill's shutdown had lessened over the years, he continued to exude the deep-seated bitterness of a man who felt that life had passed him by.

My father retained this bitterness for the rest of his life, just as he retained a sense of identity as a steelworker. Once, when he was still working as a security guard downtown, he found an abandoned painting in the garbage. It was an acrylic rendering of an early mill with furnaces aglow. My dad dusted it off and brought it home where it hung in our dining room for years, a fitting reminder of a lost world. Another time, I brought home a college friend whose father was a wealthy executive at Navistar, the latter-day incarnation of the International Harvester Company. While driving us around the neighborhood, my father took a roundabout route that threaded past the abandoned steel mills and offered a quiet but running monologue about the hard times that had befallen the region. Although my friend obviously had no control over his father's company's actions, it would be the closest my father would ever get to having a conversation with those who had made the decision to end his livelihood.

My father's bitterness at how his life had turned out, his lack of confidence that a place still existed for him in the world, emerged in small expressions of anger that surfaced on a regular basis. He gave ferocious looks to the neighbors' children who dared to ride their bikes on his grass or chase a ball under his porch. He would strike up conversations about politics with friends and acquaintances that usually ended in outrage expressed through some conspiracy theory. Yet his kind and sensitive streak also continued to surface in small ways. When he worked as a security guard downtown, he sometimes complained about the homeless people who built cardboard box shelters alongside the building. It soon became obvious, however, that his complaints stemmed from the fact that he had been assigned to "clear" the area. "You can sleep here at night," he would tell the people living in the cardboard boxes. "Just stay away during the day when the building's open so you don't get me in trouble." He would then give them the Wonder Bread sandwiches from his lunchbox. I suspect that he saw in these homeless people a future that might have been his after the mills closed if he hadn't had a family to support him during his downward spiral.

In the years before his death, my father enjoyed watching a family of sparrows nest in the air vents above the walkway between our home and our neighbor's. I think he somehow felt that by watching the baby birds he was contributing to protecting them (his own ability to protect his family was one that he, as an unemployed man, doubted in his day-to-day life). He seemed to feel that there was almost a magical power in "keeping an eye on" the nest. My father enlisted Reuben,[27] our next door neighbor, in this task. Reuben is Mexican-American. Immigrants from Mexico had been coming to work in South Chicago's steel mills since the 1920s. However, far greater numbers of Mexicans had begun arriving during the 1990s, and many settled on the East Side, which seemed a safer place to live than South Chicago. Tensions between this new wave of immigrants and remaining white residents (as well as older Mexican-American immigrants, some of whom labeled newer neighborhood arrivals as "ghetto Mexicans") were palpable. When my father, shortly before his death, walked to the corner to buy a newspaper, his own animosity toward the new arrivals was paid back with interest by a Mexican-American youth who asked, "Hey, old man, what are you doing in my neighborhood?" Despite his bravado, my father was cut to the quick to be symbolically displaced from the neighborhood in which he had been born and spent his entire life.

Reuben had been raised in South Chicago, however, and he and my dad were buddies. He had a good union job killing rats in the alleys for the city of Chicago. He laughed and drank a lot and had colorful tattoos that dwarfed the panther on my father's arm. I think Reuben reminded my dad of himself when he was a rowdy young man. When I came home to visit in later years, I had to smile at the apparent incongruity of my dad and Reuben—Reuben with his muscle shirts, chains and tattoos and my dad in the flannel shirt and baseball cap that constituted the standard uniform of the old steelworkers—laughing it up in the gangway between the houses. They would compare notes on the baby birds and, like a couple of doting fathers, would debate whether the hatchlings were warm enough. Masculinity, middle-class commentators have often implied, was at the core of the old steel mill neighborhoods. Yet that masculinity was inextricability bound up with a particular class position and entailed vulnerabilities as well as privileges. Deindustrialization had exposed the often unsuspected fragility beneath the bravado of men like my father.

## Analyzing What Happened

During my trips home from school, it was often difficult to see anything other than the death throes of Southeast Chicago's steel industry. Although some steel production continued on the Indiana side of the border, the entire steel industry collapsed in Southeast Chicago. As the large mills closed, some spectacularly, some incrementally, "mini-mills"—tiny mills that made cheap steel by heating scrap and that offered reduced wages and benefits to work-ers—sprouted up in a few places. However, even these eventually died. I have watched home videos that former mill workers made documenting the final expiration of Southeast Chicago's steel mills. The videos are now housed in the overstuffed room of the Southeast Chicago Historical Museum. One video captures the dramatic demolition of much of the old Republic Steel site as building after building went down in a heap of rubble and smoke. An-other video shows the last day of work at the historic US Steel–South Works plant in South Chicago. On an April day in 1992, seven hundred workers, the remnants of a once vast workforce, were left to shutter what remained of the enormous steel complex. In these home videos of the last days of the steel industry in Southeast Chicago, the camera passes, with little narration, lovingly, almost caressingly, over each section of the enormous mills where these workers had spent a good portion of their lives. It is a tender visual good-bye from a generation of men who were not expected to express emotions through writing or flowery speeches. In this final farewell, the harshness of the steel mills is all but forgotten; what the camera instead conveys is an over-whelming sense of loss, an emotion still palpable to viewers across the years.

As I was growing up, my mother always told me that I was like my father. When I grew older, however, I realized that I was like my father in another way. Like him, I was unable to leave the demise of the steel industry behind. For the twenty-five years between when Wisconsin Steel shut down and my father's death in 2005, he and I both remained obsessed by the closure of the mills. We were each psychologically unable to get past the trauma of what had happened. After entering graduate school in anthropology, I decided to write my master's thesis about the deindustrialization of Southeast Chicago in what I hoped would be an act of catharsis. During the early 1990s, I con-ducted taped interviews for my thesis with numerous people in Southeast Chicago, including my family as well as many neighbors, family friends, acquaintances, and community leaders. I wanted to hear the voices of those I knew from earlier in my life and how former steelworkers and their family members had made sense of what had happened. I agreed with an area resi-dent who later told me that such stories were a way to "keep it real."

Perhaps inevitably, our discussions veered toward the question of where to lay the blame for what had happened in Southeast Chicago. Some steel-workers vented their ire in equal measure upon the government and the steel companies. Hadn't the corporations, which had preached ideas of a corpo-rate "family" that promised ongoing commitment to the industrial commu-nities where they were located, sold them out for a cold profit when convenient? And hadn't politicians also failed to defend them? Others turned their worries inward. Perhaps, as the newspapers suggested, they hadn't worked hard enough after all; could this, somehow, have been their own fault? Were they greedy to have wanted to be middle class? Many whites turned their anger on more socially vulnerable others. Some men asked how, after they had fought in world wars, the government could abandon them while it helped welfare moms (read: African-Americans) who didn't want to work? Even the working-class African-Americans and Latinos I knew joined in a variation on this chorus: why, they asked, should the United States spend so much money on international aid helping countries "over there," when there was such need at home? Yet hidden beneath the apparent selfishness of these bitter complaints was a common demand for respect: "We are good citizens; we are human beings; how can we be abandoned as if our lives mean nothing?"

In their most pensive moments, a few people wondered whether the demise of the steel industry wasn't simply inevitable, part of an evolutionary transformation, much as newspapers and academics often suggested when they used the language of globalization. One neighbor and former US Steel employee followed an angry diatribe against government and corporations with a defeated sigh of resignation. "Was it just the end of an era," he asked, "like the passing of the steam engines or horses and buggies?" There was something appealing in the possibility of historical inevitability. Part of me also longed for the rest promised by such a perspective (after all, if there was no one or nothing to blame, then there was nothing to be done except pick up the pieces and go on with one's life). Yet I was troubled by the fact that in my most intellectually honest moments, those moments when I tried to distance myself from both my anger and my intermittent desire to escape from the ties that bound me to Southeast Chicago, this sense of inevitability failed to describe what had happened to area mills. It failed to acknowledge all the choices that had been made and the calculated decisions of which my father and other steelworkers were all too well aware. It failed to acknowledge that particular social groups, with American leaders at the forefront, had played a central role in creating the domestic and international laws, institutions, and market dynamics that had underwritten the destruction of communities like Southeast Chicago.

## Challenging Dominant Narratives

In between my trips home, I tried to gain a broader perspective on the loss of Southeast Chicago's steel industry by reading analyses and commentary on deindustrialization and how it played out in other areas across the

United States. The dominant narrative offered by many pundits and business analysts to explain the shutdown waves of the 1980s, as well as deindustrialization more broadly, was that the US steel industry and other heavy manufacturing had become lazy and inefficient and could no longer keep up with growing foreign competition, such as that of the highly disciplined Japanese.[28] In later years, as more and more US firms moved their factories to parts of the world with lower wages and environmental standards, such transformations were increasingly described in terms of the phenomenon of globalization. Conceived in quasi-evolutionary terms, globalization appeared to be an inevitable process in which American businesses were forced to restructure in order to become "global" players in a new way. In order to compete internationally, the narrative went, they had to make difficult decisions like shutting down unprofitable and inefficient manufacturing facilities at home. The future for the United States, as business observers saw it, lay in a knowledge- and service-based economy, or one that emphasized high finance. Although painful in the short run, this perspective held that such transformations were ultimately about "progress" and would, in the end, benefit all workers by keeping the American economy dynamic. Some even argued that deindustrialization was ultimately positive, in that it represented a stage on a developmental ladder of progress toward a more advanced kind of economy.[29]

After living through, and learning more about, the collapse of Southeast Chicago's steel industry, however, I was most struck by what was left out of such commonplace explanations. Certainly, some of these popular accounts contained elements of truth. As other countries outside the United States industrialized or rebuilt destroyed industry after World War II, the easy (and inequitable) economic dominance of US companies in preceding years was inevitably challenged.[30] Some commentators emphasized the allegedly widespread "mistakes" made by steel industry management and the long years of antagonistic relationships between labor and management that hobbled the industry.[31] A family friend in Southeast Chicago, whose husband was one of the few white-collar workers to live in the area, resented the high wages of less educated steelworkers. As Dudley has shown, such resentments were not uncommon among the middle class.[32] This friend told stories about a steelworker neighbor who thumbed his nose at the oppressive heat of the mills by sneaking out for beers during work hours, suggesting such abuses were the cause of the steel mills' demise. Nevertheless, crucial aspects of what happened, not only within the steel industry but more broadly, are entirely missing from such explanations.

It was too simple, for example, to label Southeast Chicago's steel industry "inefficient." Although Wisconsin Steel (once described as a "gem" in the industry) had become antiquated and was losing money after years of neglect by International Harvester, parts of US Steel–South Works had been recently modernized, and it was a profitable mill when massive layoffs began.[33] In fact, despite the aging infrastructure common across the industry that Steven High identifies as a policy of planned obsolescence or deliberately allowing mills to age in order to close them, US steel businesses were more profitable than the Japanese steel industry at the time. According to Bensman and Lynch, during the crucial years of 1968–77 that preceded many mill shutdowns, America's integrated steel mills made a profit of 6.7 percent in comparison to 1.7 percent for the Japanese and even less for European mills.[34] Much of the US steel industry met its demise during the 1980s, not simply because most steel industries worldwide were nationally subsidized (Japanese firms had been selling steel below what it cost to make it in a national drive to increase market share) or even because the US dollar was wildly and deliberately overvalued—a move designed to curb inflation but one that made American exports prohibitively expensive on the world market.[35] Although both were crucial factors, the key to understanding deindustrialization more broadly lay in considering the larger context in which US firms were competing, not simply globally, but internally, within the United States.

Even if steel mills in the United States were profitable, they weren't profitable *enough*, in comparison not only to other manufacturing firms or even "sunrise" industries like high technology, but also to high finance, which was increasingly able to make greater profits than businesses that manufactured things.[36] In the years after the shutdown of Wisconsin Steel, it would become more and more common for companies to buy manufacturing enterprises in leveraged buyouts, strip them of assets (including in many cases large pension funds), direct cash flows toward more lucrative enterprises, declare bankruptcy of the acquired businesses (forcing the government Pension Benefit Guaranty Board to cover unfunded pensions), and then reemerge as a new unscathed corporate entity. In other words, what happened at Wisconsin Steel would no longer be perceived as an outrage but as a commonplace way to do business in the United States. As ethnographers and journalists of the business world in recent decades have widely noted, raising corporations' stock prices for short-term gain through a growing reliance upon downsizing or mergers and acquisitions, rather than investing in and building a product or company, had become a way of life for American firms. Within the steel industry, the famous declaration of US Steel chairman David Roderick that his company was "in business to make money, not steel," was iconic of such trends. Equally iconic were US Steel's purchase of Marathon Oil in 1981, the crippling interest payments that ensued, the forced downsizing of steel operations, and the firm's 1991 makeover into USX.[37] The trouble was not so much one of corporate leadership as one of growing pressure from Wall Street to increase the short-term profits of shareholders rather than the long-term stability of corporations.

If US supporters of what some call economic restructuring were correct in arguing that the "short-term" pain caused by deindustrialization would lead to a more dynamic economy that would ultimately benefit all, then it has yet to be explained why certain categories of people have been consistently hurt by such transformations, while other categories of people have benefited so inordinately. Why *have* the wealthy become so much wealthier? If US companies, more broadly, could not afford to pay "high wages" to factory workers and remain globally competitive, how is it that the same companies could pay increasingly astronomical salaries to top executives (executives who also increasingly owned a large percentage of company shares and who would benefit from the spike in share prices associated with downsizing)? The newspaper clippings I have kept over the years on such topics underscore these broader trends within the United States (trends that only belatedly generated widespread outrage, with the economic crisis of 2008). One newspaper clipping notes that in 1965, the average American CEO was paid 24 times as much as the average worker; by 2007, it was 275 times.[38] Another informs the reader that in 2005, the top 1 percent of the US population received the largest share of national income since 1928. Another magazine article states that by other measures, levels of economic inequality have reached heights only found during the late nineteenth-century's Gilded Age. Another, based on a 2011 Congressional Budget Office report, declared that the top 1 percent of earners had more than doubled their share of the national income over the last three decades.[39]

My need to make sense of the transformations in Southeast Chicago also took other forms. Around the time I began contemplating writing this book, my filmmaker husband and I started working in fits and starts on a documentary about Southeast Chicago. In 2003, we received permission to film inside US Steel's Gary Works, once the largest steel mill in the world and still the largest old-fashioned integrated steel mill left in the entire Western Hemisphere. It was my only opportunity to experience the kind of fiery world that my father and grandfather had labored in for years. We filmed from catwalks high above the red-hot strips of steel rushing along conveyor belts, and across from gigantic ladles that poured two hundred tons of molten metal at a time. Even on the catwalks, the air was so hot that our video camera periodically shut down, and we would have to go outside to let it cool. As we filmed, I was struck by the monumental size of the mills and their raw mix of heat, noise, and fiery, overwhelming beauty. I was even more struck, however, by how few people there were inside the now largely automated plant. An occasional face, looking out from a Plexiglas-enclosed control tower, was all that remained of the thousands of steelworkers who had once labored inside this place. The pervasive mechanization allowed the mill to produce as much steel as it did back in the steel industry's heyday, with only a small fraction of a unionized workforce to deal with. I tried to imagine my father and grandfather laboring in such a mill, but the place was so devoid of people I found it impossible.

The more recent academic literature explains that manufacturing output in the United States has largely remained the same, despite the apparently widespread reality of deindustrialization. Even though manufacturing jobs in the United States have declined from representing one-third of the total workforce in the post–World War II period to one-eighth, the increased use of technology in mills like US Steel–Gary Works (euphemistically known as "increases in economic productivity") has played a central role.[40] While this has led some observers to question whether deindustrialization is, in fact, a "myth," posing the question in this way, of course, only makes sense from the point of managers, owners, and economists concerned solely with the output of goods. From the point of view of workers and their communities, the effects are entirely the same.

The only functioning steel mills left in the Calumet are now all located on the Indiana side of the state border, once the historical spillover region of Chicago's vast industrial muscle. Not coincidentally, Indiana has lower taxes and notoriously lax environmental regulation. These remaining steel mills, however, represent more than just the remnants of a "dying" industry. The mills instead challenge commonplace assumptions that deindustrialization is a historical, even evolutionary, phenomenon. Indeed, in recent years, globalized business models have been repatriated to the old steel areas of northwest Indiana. While working on our documentary in 2004, my husband clambered aboard a small helicopter with a video camera attached to the nose that took striking aerial shots flying over Inland Steel, one of the last remaining functional steel mills in the region outside of the US Steel–Gary Works complex. Inland, like LTV and Bethlehem, the other remaining mills on the Indiana side of the border, had recently been bought by Lakshmi Mittal, the head of Mittal Steel (later Arcelor Mittal). Around the time of our shoot, the news media had declared Mittal to be the third-richest man in the world. He had managed to make a personal fortune by forging a globalized steel industry and buying up distressed steel mills in deindustrializing parts of the world. Journalists noted that, in 2003, Mittal purchased a mansion near London's Kensington Palace described as the single most expensive private residence in the world; the following year he spent 55 million dollars on a five-day wedding celebration for his daughter.[41] Such have been the radical disparities generated by a new form of globalized economy.

In Mittal's new global steel business model, one goal has been to jettison "legacy costs" such as pensions and benefits owed to retirees and to shift responsibility for former workers and environmental cleanup to government bodies. In 2002, in the name of making the global steel industry "competitive and allowing some steelworkers to keep their jobs," Mittal's company had workers in East Chicago, Indiana, agree to such concessions as the return of the twelve-hour workday—the same twelve-hour workday that my grandfather had protested in the lead-up to the 1937 Memorial Day Massacre. The company even cut the so-called widows pension, the sixty-two dollars a month that was historically paid to the wives of deceased steelworkers, which was reinstated only after a spate of bad press.

Antiglobalization advocates have often focused on the threat posed to workers by factories moving production overseas. Even if companies do not actually move production facilities overseas, however, many companies strategically dangle the possibility over their heads. Broader pressure within corporations to restructure and to pare labor and production costs to raise stock prices has meant that, even for factory jobs that remain, there is often intense pressure for employees to "give back" concessions relating to wages, benefits, and work rules in order to keep their jobs.[42] It is not coincidental that between 1985 and 2000, unionized jobs in manufacturing in the United States plummeted by 40 percent.[43] The issue, then, is not one of industrial jobs going abroad in an evolutionary historical transformation, but of a checkerboarded heightening of inequality at home as well as elsewhere. The goal of globalizing companies has never been to simply leave particular regions, but rather to rework labor relations between management and workers in ways that benefit company shareholders. With marginalized or nonexistent unions and wage and benefit givebacks, it no longer matters where these jobs are located.

Deindustrialization, then, is not so much about evolutionary historical transformations in which, as some would argue, one abstracted kind of economy (an industrial one) turns into another (a service- and knowledge-based one). Rather, it's about the reworking of social relationships in moments of historical flux in a way that benefits some at the expense of others. But, some might ask, hasn't deindustrialization in richer countries like the

United States benefited workers in other parts of the world? During the 1980s and 1990s, some well-off Americans made this argument, countering critiques of deindustrialization by arguing that sending factory jobs abroad brought development to other parts of the world. I remember a Thanksgiving dinner with my college friend's father, the man who was a top executive at Navistar, International Harvester's successor. At a fancy Manhattan restaurant in the Plaza Hotel, as waiters carefully laid white napkins across our laps, my friend's father characterized moving US-based jobs offshore in precisely such terms.

Yet, such celebratory accounts ignore an underlying circular logic. The global logic of a worldwide search for low wages as a means to heighten profits and for businesses to compete, as antiglobalization critics rightly point out, means that both foreign and domestic companies must keep shifting jobs to even lower-wage areas in order to stay competitive. Although steel companies in the United States did not necessarily "run away" to less developed countries like some other industries (they could also leave the playing field through planned obsolescence or failure to reinvest in existing mills or by shifting their interests to other kinds of enterprises), this more general critique is worth repeating. The factory jobs that have sprung up in Mexico may not stay there, but leave for China, while those in China, in turn, leave for lower-wage areas in Bangladesh and Vietnam. This global model can even be brought home to countries like the United States in the form of entrepreneurs like Mittal who seek to rediscipline old, unionized labor areas like those in northwest Indiana. Just as the downward spiral of the search for ever-cheaper wages has punched gaping holes in the American dream, it holds out the possibility, not just of "development" or higher standards of living in other parts of the world, but also of similar traumas of "creative destruction" and heightened inequalities.

After wading through the various literatures that deindustrialization touches upon, it becomes clear that the changes coded as globalization have not been simply economic in nature, nor have they operated outside human control. Although variations of these transformations have appeared throughout the world, the United States had not been simply pushed toward such outcomes in evolutionary fashion, but had led the push. This push came in the form of countless decisions whose outcomes were tied to the deregulation of US rules governing corporate activity and finance, the lack of antitrust enforcement, the rewriting of bankruptcy laws, and other policy decisions.[44] As Southeast Chicago steelworkers who simultaneously criticized governments and corporations were aware, these shifts were also thoroughly political in nature. In the World War II and cold war periods, investment in heavy industry in the United States had been viewed as an intrinsic part of national security, one which the national government dared not simply leave to market forces. In a post-cold-war climate, however, the link between heavy industry and patriotism was severed, and manufacturing came to be symbolically conceptualized as a backward, old-fashioned part of the economy. With the exception of a few politicians with large manufacturing constituencies, political leaders seemed ready to jettison manufacturing for sunrise industries that were depicted as the wave of the future and the key to heightened economic prosperity.

These changing economic logics have also been part and parcel of broader cultural shifts within the United States. Karen Ho in her insightful ethnography of Wall Street makes clear that "economies" and "economics" do not refer to abstractions but the actions of all-too-human people caught up in the context of particular social institutions and cultural worlds. As Ho has noted, the cultural shifts at the core of "economic restructuring" in the United States have included the savvy appropriation of populist language by Wall Street and business conservatives in ways that valorized shareholder profits at the cost of employees and even the long-term interests of corporations. In a country like the United States that has been historically reluctant to embrace the language of social class, such developments have further undermined the desire to think through the class implications of deindustrialization and related economic transformations. In this post-cold-war climate, with few alternative political visions out there to buttress workers in their downfall, and with no cold war fears to push Western democracies to level their social playing fields, inequality was reconceptualized as inevitable or even as a virtue. In the decades leading up to the economic debacle of 2008–9, instability increasingly came to be portrayed as a stimulus to greater dynamism, one that supporters believed would place the United States at the forefront of this evolutionary shift, riding high on the wave of the capitalist future. Capitalism's tendency toward what Joseph Schumpeter called creative destruction had increasingly embraced the side of pure destruction.

Just as terms like "collateral damage" hide the reality of the violence done to bodies during times of war, the naturalized language of globalization as an explanation for deindustrialization has been used to downplay the pain, destruction, and inequalities at its heart. The language of the "new economy" has worked in similar ways, as its celebrators have ignored the fact that the people being hurt by "restructuring" have not been the same ones who have benefited from a new economy. There has been a deliberate cruelty in the disembodied nature of such language. Those living in Southeast Chicago have not had the luxury of seeing this new economy in such abstracted terms. Steelworkers who could analyze like Monday morning quarterbacks the minute details of decisions made by their former companies not to plow profits back into a mill or to maintain plant infrastructure, were often very clear about what was happening. The working class, formerly known as the middle class, was, as my father would have put it, the ones being screwed.

Some readers may acknowledge the sad consequences of deindustrialization in places like Southeast Chicago, but may still ask whether all this wasn't ultimately inevitable. Even if linked to US policy decisions, doesn't the fact that similar dynamics have happened in other parts of the world suggest a certain inevitability? Aren't the origins of these transformations ultimately part and parcel of global economic realities that by definition extend far beyond the United States? Doesn't the fact that other "advanced capitalist" countries have been affected by deindustrialization prove that this historical transformation, linked to shifting relationships between different parts of the world and growing economic competition in a post–World War II era, suggest as much? Aren't I, in the end, tilting at windmills?

Historically, there is no doubt that the overwhelming US economic dominance of the immediate post–World War II era was challenged and that this resulted in shrinking profits for US businesses faced with growing international competition during the 1960s and 1970s. Changes in technology also clearly played a central role in allowing companies to become more mobile, to split production over multiple locations, and to exercise control over increasingly far-flung operations. Yet the decision to respond to such transformations by disinvesting in industry was not inevitable, and government policy strongly affected what direction companies would take. Policies similar to those in the United States led to similar outcomes in England. In Germany, however, different institutional frameworks regulating relations between unions and companies preserved a core of highly skilled and well-paid industrial workers.[45] In the United States, rather than being an inevitable evolutionary transformation, deindustrialization has been bound up with a range of conscious choices, from the decision to fight inflation through overvaluing the dollar and encouraging high interest rates despite its destructive impact upon US manufacturing in the 1980s to the decision to deregulate finance in ways that encouraged the destruction and cannibalism of manufacturing companies to the refusal to create a coherent industrial policy that could help preserve the stable jobs upon which so many working people depended.[46] These were deliberate policy choices that contributed to the jettisoning of an industrial base (or at least those parts of it that were unionized and paid decent wages) with nothing to replace it and with profound consequences for working-class people.

A graphic illustration of the fact that there were multiple ways to respond to these widespread pressures existed across the United States' northern border, as outlined by Steven High. At the time during the 1980s when the steel mills in Southeast Chicago and elsewhere in the United States were hemorrhaging jobs, very different dynamics were at work in Canada. Canada, which had many industrial-branch plants owned by US companies, experienced economic pressures similar to those experienced by the United States during the 1960s and 1970s. Although deindustrialization occurred in some Canadian industries like textiles, not a single steel mill or auto plant closed between 1969 and 1984, when mill shutdowns were at their peak in the United States. Over a ten-year period, the US economy shed 269,000 steelworkers.[47] According to High, differing legal and political frameworks as well as cultural interpretations within Canada led to different ways of dealing with these pressures. Canada's legal framework prevented companies from using old mills as "cash cows," milking them of profits, deliberately running them into the ground, and then moving on to new mills. The Canadian government also gave generous tax incentives for older mills to modernize, preventing the aging industrial infrastructure that so saddled US heavy industry. In addition, according to High, many Canadians culturally interpreted the threat of mill shutdowns through a nationalistic rhetoric that saw American foreign businesses as threatening Canadian stability through shutdowns of plants on the Canadian side of the border. Rather than a language of inevitability and rust belt decline that made the fate of US steel mills like those in Southeast Chicago seem sealed, such cultural interpretations led the Canadian populace and policy makers to actively prevent shutdowns. Although Canada has also lost industry in recent decades, during the core years of deindustrialization in the United States, it maintained a stronger manufacturing base than many wealthier economies.[48]

Although governments and corporations are not exempt from the exigencies of global economic logics (even as they participate in their creation), they do have choices, not only in how they respond to such pressures, but also in how they deal with those most affected. Herein lies another central question. Have we in the United States sought to respond to the economic and social fallout of deindustrialization in ways that have paid attention to those made vulnerable in the process, or have we instead embraced such transformations, and even forced them upon ourselves as well as other parts of the world? Have we allowed the presumed inevitability of deindustrialization to disguise the fact that economic rewards were being increasingly channeled toward the well-off rather than toward working families and communities? And, in the aftermath of deindustrialization, have we paid attention to those whose lives were battered in its wake? Did we even look for alternative paths? Once again, what has been at stake has not simply been particular kinds of jobs—my father, grandfathers, and other relatives would not have romanticized work in the steel mills—but rather jobs that paid living wages that supported families and communities and that allowed whole categories of people to perceive themselves as having become middle class.

## Conclusion

Although my father and I both obsessed about the demise of the steel mills, we each had difficulty expressing the object of our obsession in our own way. As I look back upon the master's thesis I wrote, I now realize how the use of academic jargon offered a convenient way to distance myself from the adolescent pain and anger I had experienced. It was a pain that I couldn't leave behind, but also didn't want to relive. Using the academic language of others was easier than trying to discover a language of my own, a process that threatened to reopen old wounds. When I formally interviewed my father for that thesis in the early 1990s, I discovered that he had also found a way of not speaking. For a man who spent more than a decade talking incessantly and with unmitigated bitterness about how they should have put him in his grave when they shut the mill, my father had little to say. In formal interviews, he answered in monosyllables or brief sentences with no elaboration. Perhaps he was afraid that putting himself on the record would get him into trouble with some authority, the vague powers-that-be that existed in the world beyond Southeast Chicago that he both respected and that oppressed him. Yet, in retrospect, I think he was even more scared that he had nothing of value to say. For a man whose self-respect was pummeled by the mill closings decades before, he had no confidence that his words were worth listening to.

My father's odd relationship to speaking emerged even more forcefully years later when my husband and I tried to interview him for our video documentary about Southeast Chicago. When my husband would pull out the camera, my father would at first demur and say he didn't want to be on tape. Then, unbidden, he would start talking to the camera, telling it his story and justifying his view of the mill shutdowns. Perplexed at first, we gradually realized that he liked the feeling of validation that having the camera listen to him gave, yet he did not have the confidence to make it "official." So, we videotaped him with minimal equipment, all of us upholding the pretense that we weren't really doing anything. When my father later saw an early cut of the video, he asked to replay it and nodded in vigorous agreement with his on-camera persona. It proved to be an odd sort of conversation with himself. It was my husband who spotted the pattern and the irony. Like my great-grandfather who hid his memoir in the attic, my father couldn't escape his own ambivalence about speaking. In many ways, neither could I. We all shared a common desire and an inability to speak—fears and thoughts that could be named and those that escaped naming. Perhaps this struggle to recount my own story—and theirs—is an attempt to break free of a legacy of such fetters. In the end, doing so entails constructing a counternarrative that matters, not only in relation to my family, but for those similarly relegated to the margins by deindustrialization and by the dominant narratives that have enabled it.

## CHAPTER THREE

# Places Beyond

My father spent much of his life contending with the economic, emotional, and psychological fallout of deindustrialization, a trauma in which my entire family shared. This trauma was more than just personal or familial; in retrospect, it took place in the eye of the storm of the changing class landscape of the United States. In my own life, I have contended with another set of class issues emerging from a wholly different quarter: the path of upward mobility. On the surface, these issues are positive ones and are, certainly, very distant from the kind of hardship unemployed steelworkers like my father experienced. Nevertheless, this alternative trajectory also reveals something of the tensions surrounding class in the United States and how such tensions can play out in ways unrecognized within commonly accepted or "hegemonic" accounts of upward mobility.

The possibility, even the probability, of upward mobility lies at the heart of what the United States has symbolized as a nation both for its citizens and for others. In the "rags to riches" Horatio Alger stories of the late nineteenth century that were so beloved in American history, it was hard work, a sense of fair play, and enough pluck to seize opportunities that could set even the lowliest street urchins on an upward path. Later conceptions of the "American dream" emphasized the ability of hardworking individuals and families to be become part of an expansive American middle class in which children could expect their lives to be more prosperous than their parents'. In such formulations, the act of upward mobility itself appears relatively straightforward. After all, we all want things to be better for ourselves and for our children. Consequently, once opportunity presents itself, the path should be clear.

Of course, the ideal of the American dream does not always accord with reality, as critics have long noted. Despite the very real experiences of upward mobility for many groups in the United States during, for example, parts of the nineteenth century or after World War II, other groups found themselves excluded from such trends. In more recent decades, many have noted that, regardless of widespread opportunities for class mobility in the past, upward mobility in the United States has also stagnated as class inequalities have expanded.[1] Both critiques are ones that this book shares. However, there is yet another critique to be made. Upward mobility, when it does occur, may not be the straightforward phenomenon our national mythology suggests (at least, not if the stories of many middle-class professionals from working-class backgrounds, those whom Alfred Lubrano refers to as class "straddlers," are any indication).[2] Instead, the path of individual upward mobility may be strewn with conflicting emotions, painful shifts in relationships with family and friends, and disorienting conflicts of identity.

It is only when we reduce class solely to material factors or to the relatively straightforward matter of unequal opportunities that one can assume the experience of upward mobility to be unproblematic. Such assumptions, however, leave out myriad other aspects of how social class works.[3] Although class is most often understood as our positioning within a broader economic field, it is not reducible only to this. Class is also about our sense of identity—who we understand ourselves to be and the unequal ways in which we perceive ourselves and are, in turn, perceived by others in relation to those from different class backgrounds—and what these experiences mean to us. Class is about the links that exist between our economic positioning and the ways that our beliefs, tastes, and lifestyles come to be judged in the world. It is embodied in how we walk, talk, speak, and dress. It is something that we "perform" and that we may try to mold in our daily lives. Class is also bound up with the places where we live and how we live in them, and it helps determine who our friends are, how we argue or choose to raise a family, and what we decide to read or watch on TV. In the end, changing how one lives in the world, despite the seemingly straightforward narrative of upward mobility, is not such an easy thing.

For many kids, rich or poor, discovering their class position is often a moment of revelation. For me, this moment happened when I was in grammar school. I was in fourth or fifth grade, and my class was studying the history of Chicago. I remember opening a thin, brown book with a hard cover that we were told to read at our desks and coming across a section about tenements and the urban immigrant poor in Chicago at the beginning of the twentieth century. Reading about the hardships of these people, I felt sorry for them and tried to figure out where in Chicago these poor areas might be. It was the same kind of pity that I remember feeling in church when they took collections in special boxes for starving children in Africa. Then, I flushed hot all over as it suddenly dawned on me that the book was describing old industrial areas like Southeast Chicago, where we lived. Initially, I was bewildered. "But we're just average here," I thought. Then again, I conceded, they were talking about the past and, certainly, things had been different back then. But my great-grandparents and grandparents (as well as the relatives of my friends) had lived in the area in the past. Were they the poor people the authors were talking about? When reminiscing about the old days, my relatives had talked about hard times, but they had not presented themselves as helpless objects of pity in the way this well-meaning account did. My mind continued to race. If this was "our" history and most of our dads were still laborers, what did that make us? Weren't we middle class now? The book offered no answer. Thinking back on this moment, I recognize a deep confusion about class that at the time I didn't know enough to articulate. I also could not have foreseen that life circumstances would lead these once inchoate questions to remain at the forefront of my consciousness in the years ahead.

In hindsight, I now recognize that my family and I experienced two very different kinds of upward mobility over the course of our lives, two very different versions of the American dream. My grandparents' and parents' generations experienced a form of economic upward mobility *as a community* in a post–World War II era of strong unions and high wages. In this shift, most (if not all) boats were raised together (even as other aspects of people's social lives remained relatively unchanged). It was this form of upward mobility that the collapse of the steel mills later destroyed. My own experience of upward mobility began when I was a teenager and was a decidedly more individual and lonely one. It is the kind of mobility almost exclusively emphasized in the more contemporary versions of the American dream. This experience of upward mobility was based on a form of education that brought me out of the community in which I was raised and into a very different world. It allowed me to peer into the lives of elites that I had only known as caricatures on TV. And it transformed my habits and outlook on life and put me in a position to write books rather than to simply be the subject of one.

Yet this process of upward mobility was the opposite of straightforward. I was entirely unprepared for the new world I entered as a teenager, and the abrupt transition left me unsure how to relate to my own past, to family members who remained in Southeast Chicago, and to a childhood world increasingly littered with brownfields and industrial ruins. Who, exactly, was I and where did I belong? In the years immediately after leaving Southeast

Chicago, I would often feel overwhelmed by this clash between disparate worlds. In later years, after I had largely assimilated into middle-class culture, I would continue to be surprised by moments of awkwardness and a sense of being ill at ease that I found difficult to articulate (and that often made little sense to others).[4] Eventually, I was forced to acknowledge that being raised working class wasn't simply something one left behind. The need to articulate this persistent sense of unease led me to search for a way to talk about the *experience* (and not just what academics might refer to as the structural realities) of class. Just as my great-grandparents', grandparents', and parents' stories challenged dominant narratives of immigration, labor, and, later, deindustrialization, my own story contradicts widespread assumptions about upward mobility. For me, telling this story offers a chance to rebel against the meanings that others would attribute to my life. It also represents my own struggle to find a language and concept of class that "fits," one that begins from the inside and works its way out (rather than being an analytical category imposed from above), one that acknowledges the workings of social class, not only in how we are economically positioned in a highly unequal world, but also in our identities, the existential crises of our souls, and, as discussed in the next chapter, the physical composition of our bodies. In the end, it also forces me to ask what we in the United States have lost by thinking of upward mobility solely as an individual rather than a collective project.

## A New World

After the demise of Wisconsin Steel in 1980 turned my family's world upside down, my overwhelming desire as a fourteen-year-old was to escape. I wanted to run away from the clouds of depression hanging over my father, my parent's home, and Southeast Chicago in general. My long-standing habit of reading and daydreaming turned out to be helpful in searching out escape routes. On a whim, I sent for a brochure about a girl's boarding school on the East Coast. I can't remember how I even thought to do this, since boarding schools were unheard of in Southeast Chicago—perhaps I saw a flyer on a neglected bulletin board in my public high school or the local library. I remember staring longingly at the brochure's photos of rich and athletic-looking girls who sat around reading books on neatly manicured lawns. It was merely fantasy literature, however, like the catalogs we received and never bought things from. Yet, a little later, a chance encounter offered an unlikely means for turning it into something more. A friend, the daughter of a neighborhood firefighter, had a brother who was attending the University of Chicago after graduating as a star student at the local Catholic high school. His college roommate told her about the New England prep school he had attended, called Phillips Exeter Academy. He encouraged my friend to apply, and she encouraged me, more for company in such an unlikely activity, I think, than anything else. During the application process, my mom humored me by taking me for a required standardized test in downtown Chicago. The test was given in a wealthy private school, where I sat intimidated and frightened by the alien environment and well-off students. Nevertheless, months later, a heavy piece of stationery with official Exeter letterhead arrived, informing me that I had been awarded a full financial scholarship. In retrospect, I am uncomfortably aware that it was my father's fall that unexpectedly made me a candidate for elite schools concerned with increasing the diversity of their student bodies.

Although my friend did not go to Exeter, I was determined to seize my chance. My parents, however, refused to let me go. The idea of sending a child away to school, and halfway across the country at that, seemed like an act of cruelty to them and to many in Southeast Chicago. But there were deeper reasons as well. When I yelled at my father, who was then working as a janitor, and demanded that he tell me why I couldn't go, he responded, almost in tears, "Because when you come back, you'll look down on me for being a janitor!" His words and the pained look on his face remain imprinted in my memory. Yet I was fixated on making an escape and refused to back down. My mom, convinced that I was simply causing trouble, complained about me to our sympathetic family doctor. He knew of Exeter and insisted she should let me go. At the time, I attributed the fact that my parents finally relented to his intervention. Yet, once again in retrospect, I suspect that the real reason was both more mundane and more troubling. At a point when my parents were fearful of losing their house and openly worried about the possibility of having to send me and my sisters to live with relatives, the brute economic fact that my expenses would be paid for and there would be one less mouth to feed at home was critical. In the days that followed, two kindhearted former teachers of mine took me shopping and generously bought me some new clothes, a winter jacket, and a portable typewriter. My uncle Bill, whose job was still safe at a local GM factory that built railroad cars, lent my father his blue pickup truck, and the entire family drove me across the country to New Hampshire.

I made my escape almost exactly on my sixteenth birthday, although it was a far rockier and more painful trek than I could have imagined or than is commonly found in the American mythology of upward mobility. It left me saddled with lifelong feelings of guilt. At a time when my little sister at home was making extra visits to my grandparents' house in the hopes of getting something to eat besides the hot dogs that had become my family's daily fare, I was catapulted to the other end of the American class spectrum. I found myself sitting in classes in imposing buildings of brick and marble alongside students with names like Getty, Firestone, Packard, and Coors. My euphoria at escaping soon disintegrated into a profound dislocation. In a country where the language of race and ethnicity are highly elaborated categories but class is not, there was no recognition that the transition might be difficult for a white working-class girl. While the outward appearance of the few African-American students then attending Exeter marked them as "different" regardless of their class origins, we few white working-class students simply faded into the background.[5] I often wondered whether my African-American classmates from middle-class backgrounds resented their inability to escape assumptions that they were different as much as I resented the inability to have my differences recognized. If, according to American mythology, all I had previously lacked was opportunity, now that opportunity had presented itself, I should have been fine. Yet the radical disjunctures in this transition—the profound social differences that I had no way to articulate—created an almost unbearable sense of rupture.

The sense of dislocation, and at times humiliation, that I felt at Exeter emerged in countless small incidents. In classes, I was startled by the self-confidence of my classmates, their belief that their words mattered, their relish in articulating abstract ideas in a mode I found foreign. I tried to contribute to class conversations, taking an entire class period to work up the necessary bravery. Red in the face, heart hammering by the time I managed to get something out, I was constantly afraid that I would speak in the grammatically "incorrect" English that was my first language or be judged insufficiently smart. I remember sitting one afternoon on the well-tended lawns outside my dorm with my housemates, including a classmate from Greenwich, Connecticut, who was dressed in expensive, preppy clothing. She stared in perplexity at an unfashionable, polyester-clad "townie" from the working-class town of Exeter who happened to be walking past (a woman who to me bore a comforting resemblance to my own mother) and wondered aloud, "What is wrong with people in this town?" Trapped in my own insecurities, I cringed inside and said nothing.

I remember dormmates good-naturedly telling anecdotes of their families, and when I would try to reciprocate, revealing a bit of what was happening with my family, there would instead be an awkward silence. My story was a "downer" that simply made people feel uncomfortable (and perhaps secretly guilty); I quickly learned to remain silent. At the end of such days,

I would go to the music practice rooms on campus where I was learning to play the harpsichord and would cry in the only truly private space I could find. My sense of dislocation eventually turned to anger. How could there be places where privilege was so utterly taken for granted? By what right did some people enjoy such ease when others' lives were being torn apart in places like Southeast Chicago? For a while, I even tried to hate my class-mates and their parents. After all, weren't their parents among the business elite who made decisions such as closing my father's mill? Weren't they the ones who stood to profit as the value of their investment shares in the conglomerates that owned the mills rose? But, it didn't work; I was forced to admit that I liked many of my classmates. When the father of one classmate, a descendent of the wealthy DuPont family, visited and took us out to din-ner, I hoped I could despise him. But he was kind and attentive, and I was ashamed of myself.

I tried to protest, to find a voice to tell my own story in other ways. In my creative writing class, I wrote a tale about a man who could barely read, a character who I can now admit was a melodramatic exaggeration of my father. (Although I never saw my father read a book or write a letter and al-though my mother euphemistically described his literacy skills as "limited," my dad obsessively read the tabloid newspapers his entire life.) Painfully aware of the presence of one of the Getty boys in my class, I had written this story in a spirit of defiance, hoping to comfort myself by drawing attention to and surreptitiously pricking at his privilege. (He appeared unperturbed.) As a scholarship student, I was asked to speak to alumni and wrote out on 3 × 5 cards a speech that I considered a manifesto. I wrote about Southeast Chicago and stated that the people I grew up with were no less intelligent or worthy than those who went to schools like Exeter. In my mind, it seemed a bold attack, although reading it back years later it now seems overly timid and polite. On the day I gave the speech, I cried and couldn't get through it. Afterward, instead of responding to it as the attack I intended, several alumni came up and told me what a good speech I had written and that they were proud of me. Ashamed that I was grateful for their praise even when I had been actively courting their anger, I smiled back in confusion. Later, I came to realize that they could not hear the story of class I wanted to tell—a story of injustice and anger at class inequalities in the United States couched in the self-righteousness of a sixteen-year-old—because it was too readily subsumed by the broader narrative of America as a land of opportunity. For the assembled alumni, my own presence at Exeter merely confirmed this; even more for the liberal minded, since my speech acknowledged those left behind. I felt trapped by my inability to find an object upon which to vent my rage, trapped by my inability to find my own voice, trapped by an inability to be heard.

As difficult as it was during those two years at Exeter, it was even more difficult to come home. I recall a day in the early 1980s when I was on summer vacation in Southeast Chicago. During the summers, I worked multiple jobs, once again including a stint on the government-sponsored CETA jobs program for poor youth. Along with many other teenagers, I was assigned to work as a tutor for elementary school children. The tutoring program was located in the local grammar school on the East Side that I had attended, yet most of the other tutors were African-Americans bused in from the poorer parts of the South Side that lay beyond the steel mill neighborhoods. Although the school's Italian-American vice-principal was friendly to me (he himself was from a poor immigrant background and, as a child, had slept with four siblings to a bed), he was clearly afraid of my black teenaged co-workers. In the long downtime in the periods before and after our students arrived, he would force us to sit in silence with our heads on the desk so we wouldn't cause trouble. I didn't know how the African-American teenagers—who were regularly accorded such treatment—could stand it. I remember sitting there, my head lying on the same wooden desks with holes for inkwells that my parents, grandparents, and great-grandparents had used. I thought about how, only a few weeks earlier, I had been in the marbled and red-carpeted assembly hall at Exeter being told that I was one of the future leaders of America. Now I was sitting with my head on a desk, an object of distrust, someone to be controlled.

Here were all the paradoxes. I now realized that the white working class, including my own family, as well as the vice-principal, were victims of class in a way I had never imagined before I left Southeast Chicago. Yet, as one of them, I couldn't comfort myself with romanticized ideas of the moral righteousness of the working class. The respectability, as it were, of the steel mill neighborhoods was built upon a hatred of those on the rung below: those living in deeper poverty in other parts of the South Side, many of whom were African-Americans. I was forced to admit that all victims could, in other contexts, be abusers. It reminded me of going out to dinner with my Exeter housemate's father and being flummoxed because I couldn't bring myself to hate him. What does one do with the recognition that there are rarely simple villains or heroes in the world and no single vantage point from which to make sense of its all too real cruelty and oppression? The only way I could find to withstand this tension was by an act of dissociation. I came to believe that one had to hate the thing—class injustice or racism—without hating the people who embodied it. Otherwise, one could find reasons to hate all of humanity. While some people address such conundrums through religion, I chose the kind of social scientific thinking fostered by anthropology as my chosen route to try to achieve this sort of dissociation. It provided a way to challenge such hateful social realities while also leaving space to understand how such realities had come about. And it did so, while implicitly recognizing the common humanity of both victims and abusers in a highly unequal world.

## Between Two Worlds

For two years, I shuttled between Exeter and Southeast Chicago, two seemingly separate worlds that refused to recognize each other. On vacations, my parents never asked me about life at school and pretended as if it didn't exist. Like a chameleon, I tried to assimilate into the neighborhood again. When my father angrily told me to stop using such big words, I let my sentences drift back into ungrammatical form, afraid that speaking differently would confirm his fears that I now looked down on him. I worked multiple jobs, both because I needed the money and in order to keep myself out of the house. My mom needed emotional support in dealing with the traumas that had befallen our family, but the weight—like my father's depression—seemed too heavy to bear. In the rare hours when I wasn't working, I hung out with my old friends. We spent a lot of time drinking, driving around the neighborhood, and hanging out in parking lots. At such moments, I enjoyed being back in the neighborhood and told myself (borrowing from middle-class literature that romanticized the working class) that it was somehow more "real" than Exeter. But the fact that I was becoming increasingly different was impossible to escape. Despite my efforts to reshape myself as I moved back and forth between Exeter and home, who I was and even the way I spoke and handled myself were changing. Once at a neighborhood yard party, the cousin of a friend brought his Catholic high school buddies over to listen to me "talk." "See, what did I tell you?" he told them in a voice laced with both mockery and admiration. I wasn't like the other girls they knew; I was an "intellectual" oddity you could be friends with but couldn't quite date.

In later years, my need to make sense of the two worlds into which my life had been split led me to be fascinated by the stories of others who had experienced unusual class journeys. I devoured academic and journalistic accounts as well as novels—at least on the rare occasions I could find them—that spoke from places I could recognize. During college, it was the story of the educated son of the British coal miner in D. H. Lawrence's *Sons and Lovers*. As an adult, it was books like Carolyn Steedman's *Landscape for a*

*Good Woman*, Richard Rodriquez's controversial *Hunger of Memory*, or a series of edited volumes that contained the life histories of middle-class professionals from working-class backgrounds that Lubrano called "straddlers."[6] Of course, not all upwardly mobile individuals are traumatized by the social transitions they have made in life. I recall visiting a childhood friend of my mother's during a vacation from Exeter. She and her husband, a man who had become a high-ranking military officer, now lived an upper-middle-class lifestyle on the East Coast. She was excited that I was going to Exeter and generously invited me to visit their vacation beach house since I didn't have the money to go home. I was taken aback, however, by her lack of sympathy for the working-class Southeast Chicago of her youth. For her, it was simply a place from which to mark distance. Clearly, for some, American ideals of meritocracy reinforced the idea that they deserved to get ahead while others were left behind. Yet the written accounts of many straddlers suggest more complex reactions. Many describe a sense of living between two worlds and a range of emotions similar to my own: a desire for a different way of life, a profound ambivalence about upward mobility, and a fear of competing loyalties and of betraying one's family and friends.

The stories recounted by straddlers in Lubrano's book *Limbo: Blue-Collar Roots, White-Collar Dreams* suggest that upward mobility may be difficult not only for the young people on such journeys, but for their parents and loved ones as well. In the United States, there is a widespread assumption that upward social mobility is what all parents desire for their kids—again, it is part of our national story of how the American dream works. Yet real-life dynamics are more complicated. These accounts confirmed what I had experienced in my own life: that while many parents do want their children to do well, many also hope their children will stay close to home, remain part of their family's social world, and continue to value what they value. Modest success within known social worlds may seem more attractive to some parents than outside success as defined by elite educational institutions. (When educated elites shake their heads at the "ignorance" of such parents, they fail to recognize that there may be love and the fear of losing one's children embedded in such sentiments.) Finally, the life stories collected by Lubrano led me to acknowledge that darker emotions are also commonplace. In many accounts, family members felt jealous or resented an upwardly mobile member for "putting on airs" and actively tried to bring him or her down a peg. And straddlers could feel less than generous feelings towards their families and old friends. Many resented or were embarrassed by working-class habits, values, or tastes, from which they sought to distance themselves. These accounts, in short, confirmed for me that class mobility is as much a subject of strain, friction, and bitterness as one of celebration.

It is education, the standard gatekeeper between these two worlds, that is often symbolically positioned at the core of such tensions. While education promises and offers much, it also requires painful choices while forging constraints of its own. In his autobiographical account of growing up as the son of working-class Mexican immigrants, Richard Rodriguez describes the ruptures created for working-class and non-Anglo children by formal (and particularly elite) education.[7] Education, he argues, teaches working-class children to aspire to be more than their parents. In doing so, it directly or indirectly insults the parents by depicting them not as models for behavior, but as models of the kind of life one shouldn't want to lead. While middle-class and upper-class kids find continuities of expectations, norms, and values between school and their home lives, working-class kids experience competing viewpoints and values that starkly separate the world of school and family life. In the end, Rodriguez depicts this difficult experience as having been worth it, since it allowed him to change classes and gain access to a public world in which he hadn't been fully able to participate before. However, he fails to address the larger question of why such radical class differences existed in the first place, in part by naturalizing such differences as being primarily ethnic ones.

Given the American propensity to emphasize race and ethnicity but downplay class, my own journey offers a twist upon such experiences. Rather than differences in skin color (and, in Rodriguez's case, language) being used to symbolize the division between the world of home and school, the fact that I was white like most of my Exeter classmates was often assumed to erase the depth of the divide. Although being white or "unmarked" in racial terms is a privilege that minority individuals can never experience, there can be, nonetheless, for upwardly mobile whites, a kind of unacknowledged discomfort associated with being unmarked. For those of us who "pass," there may be a failure to recognize other forms of difference integral to one's identity. In my own experience of attending Exeter, it often seemed as if I were the only one who wanted to acknowledge that I was living in two radically different worlds. To call attention to it was either perceived to be insulting (at home) or bad manners (at Exeter).

My own experience of education has left me feeling profoundly ambivalent. On the one hand, the act of becoming educated—a process that kicked into high gear at Exeter—was an extraordinarily rich and exciting one of gaining knowledge about the world and of exploring diverse ideas. Yet, at the same time, it was impossible to escape the less high-minded ways in which education was bound up with the transmission of social class. The middle-class parents of many prep school and college friends often uncritically presented education as an unalloyed good or as simply a source of credentials that held the key to maintaining or, better yet, improving upon one's position in the world. Sociologists might add that education provides the institutional space where individuals learn to remake themselves in class terms and where they acquire the social markers by which other people come to "read" their class position. Schools are, after all, places where one learns how to speak, think, and act in the world as one of the "educated" (read: middle class or above). I have been struck by the argument of the influential French social scientist Pierre Bourdieu (not coincidentally, himself the son of a rural French postman) that the impact of formal education primarily consists not of the content officially taught at universities, but of what is informally assimilated as tastes, values, and a particular orientation to the world that marks one as being of a certain class. Through informal channels, students learn from peers and professors what books or films to admire, what ideas to value, what jokes to laugh at, what food to eat, how to dress, and even (I would add) how to rebel in class-appropriate ways.[8]

In my own journeys through elite educational institutions, I have experienced the need to *perform* both class and intelligence as a constant weight. I have been discomforted by pressures to act "smart" in ways that accord with the middle- and upper-middle-class norms embedded in academia. After all, it doesn't take long to discover that the use of long words, the referencing of authors, books, or periodicals well known to intellectual elites, and the reliance upon abstracted styles of argumentation are considered to be not only a class-based performance of being "smart," but actually being smart. In this sense, formal education can be destructive. This is not only because education channels some people into particular life courses while sharply curtailing the options of others, but also because education promotes the widespread idea that those who pass through its institutions or adopt its values are actually brighter. This is one reason why people I knew growing up in Southeast Chicago referred to themselves as "middle class" rather than "working class" (and why my father and other steelworkers so thoroughly resented the college-educated young engineers who periodically showed up in the mills to tell them what to do). Being labeled or thought of as working class smacked of being called stupid. I was reminded of this after my mother read an early version of the family history found in chapter 1 and surprised me by pointedly remarking, "Not all the Walleys were stupid." Her comments stemmed from the idea that my drawing attention to my father's family background as being long-term poor white stock might inadvertently imply the insult that they were dumb or lazy. In a country taken to be a meritocracy, such feelings are part of what Richard Sennett and Jonathan Cobb refer to as the "hidden injuries" of class in the United States. It is for such reasons that many working-class people may feel that class is better left undiscussed. Claiming middle-class-ness, instead, becomes a way to reference a shared humanity with those from other class backgrounds.

From the time I was a child, my own ideas about education, knowledge, and smartness were hopelessly conflicted and tangled. First of all, I wasn't so sure I was smart. Later, I would realize that this was in part due to the cultural tendencies of both Scandinavian immigrants like my mother's family and poor native whites like my father's. For both groups, it wasn't considered good parenting to make too much of your kids, causing them to "get a big head" or think they were better than others. This contrasted strongly with the cultural tendencies of some of my Italian-American friends' parents and, later in life, my Jewish friends' families which were expected to brag about their kids. There is a phrase used to describe this phenomenon in Appalachia, I later learned, called not "getting above one's raisin.'"[9] In retrospect, there is something inherently democratizing in this attitude that I find appealing; nevertheless, there is also something about it that can be destructive.

When I was in the third grade, I experienced this destructive edge in a visceral way. I scored unusually well on the first standardized national test I had taken. My teacher made a great fuss over my score, which both pleased and embarrassed me. My mother, however, came to school and insisted that I retake the test because I couldn't possibly have scored that high.[10] The Italian-American vice-principal was incredulous that she thought the school had *over*estimated her daughter's abilities. I retook the test in a lonely room by myself, puzzled by a sense that I had somehow done something wrong. Once again, I received the same score. Only later as an adult would I understand what was at the heart of my mother's reaction: if you are not raised to have confidence in your own intellectual abilities, why have confidence in your children, with whom you closely identify? My mother would also ponder this moment in future years. When I was in my early twenties, I was moved when she wrote a note apologizing for this incident even through we had never spoken of it in the intervening years. My ability to analyze such "class" moments as an adult, however, cannot assuage my own deep-seated suspicion that I am not so smart, a feeling that has plagued me my entire life, even as a tenured professor at an elite university. Throughout my life, such doubts led me—and presumably many other working-class kids—to constantly underestimate my abilities in relation to others from more privileged backgrounds. If I have had relative success in my life, ironically, it has stemmed from the profound need to overcompensate in "proving myself" in order to dispel such insecurities.

My ambivalence about education reached a peak during my senior year at Exeter. For the second time in my life, I felt an overwhelming desire to run away. Committing what was considered to be heresy in a striving prep school environment, I decided to go to a small liberal arts school that I picked with indifference out of my roommate's guide to colleges. Despite its good reputation, my fellow classmates dismissed it as a "backup" school, and I didn't bother to explain that at my old high school in Southeast Chicago, the vast majority of students never even went to college. My major criterion was that my future college be as far away as possible from both New England and Chicago, or, more accurately, from the class conflicts both places represented. I preferred to think of my choice not as a form of escape, but, more bravely, as a conscious choice. This would be my own (in retrospect, ludicrously minor) rebellion against a system of elite status whose existence had been painfully thrust into my consciousness. My dormmates, however, prodded me to apply to at least one of the top Ivies. Everyone at Exeter did, they argued; what could it hurt? While home on vacation in Southeast Chicago, I composed an application to Harvard on the typewriter in the church basement where my mom, as church secretary, prepared the Sunday bulletins. I recall my admissions essay as being a class diatribe, a more pointed version of my speech to the Exeter alumni. In my mind, I characterized the essay as politely flipping off Harvard. (Since I kept no copy of the application, it is hard to judge it in hindsight.) On what was called "Black Friday" at Exeter, the day when students received their college acceptance notices, I was warned to be wary of a skinny rather than a fat envelope. When I discovered a fat one from Harvard offering full financial aid in my post office box, I felt a rush of conflicting emotions. A part of me longed for the validation the acceptance implied, yet a larger part was skeptical. I found it hard to believe that my grades and scores were better than many of my Exeter classmates. I cynically imagined that for a university where everyone was dying to get in, it was too intriguing a novelty to pass up someone who was openly disdainful. Or, perhaps, more likely, I was simply a diversity token once again?[11]

I told my housemates about my acceptance to Harvard. They were perplexed when I informed them that I still wasn't going. At least you have to tell your parents, they insisted. I called home from the tiny phone booth in the dorm common room. Although a small piece of me hoped for praise, the reaction was what I had anticipated. My father expressed the fact that he missed and loved me by asking shyly whether I didn't want to come home instead and go to secretarial school downtown like my high school girlfriends from Southeast Chicago. My mother complained that she had already informed her friends that I was going to Pomona College, the liberal arts school in California that I had said was my first choice. My grandmother simply wondered what Harvard was. It was not a reaction I could explain to my friends at Exeter and reinforced the impenetrable rift between my two worlds. Instead, I made a show of rejecting Harvard and ritually burned my acceptance letter with my dormmates sitting around offering support, or perhaps simply being intrigued by the transgressive nature of it all.

A few days later, I was called into the Exeter college placement office to explain my decision. The top Ivies had an unofficial quota of students they took from prep schools like Exeter. Why, they asked, did I take one of the coveted spots for an Exeter student when I had no intention of going? I was taken aback, since this thought had never occurred to me. I had assumed this was simply a personal decision, my own minor rebellion. Did they really care *that* much? At Exeter, school officials had always been careful to insist that it was possible to get an excellent education at a wide variety of colleges. Their annoyance, however, made clear that this was a calculated attempt to soothe young psyches frayed by prep school competitiveness and underscored my own naïveté about the stakes of reproducing class through such elite institutions. In private, I spelled out my reasons for not going to myself. First, I didn't want people to treat me differently based on what university I had gone to and not because of who I was. Second, I feared a sense of rupture with people who were not in this elite world. To carry the label "Harvard," I decided, is to ask for a lifetime of people either treating you better than you deserve or resenting your presumed smartness and trying to take you down a peg. I didn't want either. But what I didn't tell myself was that I was also scared: I did not have the confidence to see if I could try. And I didn't know if I had the internal resources to keep living with the striking dissonance between my worlds.

Upon leaving Exeter, I dealt with this dissonance by deciding that formal education was, as my father might have said, bullshit. I spent my years at Pomona College drinking at parties and having intellectual conversations outside of, rather than inside, the classes that I irregularly attended. I did only enough work to keep up appearances. After all, if I lost my financial aid package, what would I have done? I had exaggerated fears of ending up cutting ham at the deli counter at the local grocery store on the East Side, and despite all my ambivalence, such prospects sent me into a cold sweat. While rich kids, like those who dominated at Exeter, might playact at dropping out, they had the means to get back in if they chose. Rebellion for someone with such a precarious life course as myself carried far more serious penalties. Indeed, for years I lived with exaggerated feelings of living at the edge of a precipice; I worried that at anytime that the life I was building outside Southeast Chicago might be ripped out from under me and that I would end up in a devastated world of nothingness, as my father had. The experience of having watched my father's fall gave me almost literal vertigo. If anything, I had even farther to fall. One day, I wandered into the counselor's office at my college and said that I had "issues" that I needed to talk about. I sat down and explained about my dad and the mills going down. After half an hour, the counselor told me that it seemed like I had it all thought out and he didn't think he could help me. While I didn't have much of a language to talk about social class, he clearly didn't either. How does one officially ask for help for a "problem" that counters all our national narratives of what upward mobility is supposed to feel like?

## Becoming a Sociocultural Anthropologist

My need to make sense of the ruptures in my world led me to graduate school in sociocultural anthropology, a discipline whose practitioners have long made a habit of crossing social boundaries. This life path, however, was not an immediately obvious one. I also conjured up other vague dreams. In one, I would become a nursery school teacher in New Mexico, wear a lot of denim, and learn to ride horses. In another fantasy scenario, I would spend my life back-packing around the world, working odd jobs, sleeping on beaches, and living in the moment. Such paths seemed to pleasantly skirt many of the class issues in my life. In the meantime, I spent time waiting tables with a friend in New Orleans before deciding to apply to a program that sent college graduates to teach high school in rural Kenya. While my experience in East Africa would be profoundly different from others in my life, it was a relief to discover that this kind of "culture shock" was explainable to others, since cultural and ethnic differences were recognized to exist and were accorded a legitimacy and weight not always afforded to class differences. As a result, it was a far easier journey than the one from Southeast Chicago to Exeter that had proven to be the most deeply dislocating of my life and the one most difficult to articulate to others.

Upon returning from Kenya, I began anthropology graduate school in New York City. I am now aware that this was an unusual and esoteric choice for an upwardly mobile working-class kid from the Midwest. Many young people who leave behind working-class backgrounds choose "practical" professions like business or engineering that offer the material rewards that make sense to their families. I understood the logic: my Little Grandpa used to mock me for wasting time and money in school when others, like my cousin who was a mechanic, were already making a good salary and had a house, car, and family. My grandfather's attitude was not simply an anti-intellectual one (although it certainly was that), but rather part of a generational conviction that the American dream was meant for more than just the highly educated. Yet it never occurred to me to work for a corporation. After having watched the way my father and his coworkers had been treated during Wisconsin Steel's demise, I didn't want anything to do with the corporate world. I feared it would make me a traitor to my father. In fact, my ambivalence about class meant that I found it difficult to acknowledge that I might become a middle-class professional of *any* sort one day. I even managed to detach the decision to attend graduate school from any aspiration toward a professional future by insisting it was simply another way to defer a growing mountain of student loan debt.

Once in graduate school, however, I found myself enthralled with anthropology. Its efforts not only to understand human differences and diverse cultural worlds, but also to examine the inequalities of daily life lifted me out of the malaise of my undergraduate years. It was during graduate school that "class" as a concept fully began to enter my consciousness. Nevertheless, there were points of friction along the way. As mentioned in the introduction, I worried for a while that only by mastering the arcane discussions of class found in social theory texts would I really begin to understand "class" and be able to make sense of my own life. It took me longer to realize the classism implicit in feeling unable to speak about one's experience without filtering it through the validating lens of academic study. Despite the fact that my and my family's experiences seemed distant from the accounts offered in the more abstracted social scientific books I read, I was, nonetheless, emboldened by the fact that social class was considered a worthy topic of research and thought.

I decided to write my master's thesis on deindustrialization in Southeast Chicago before returning to East Africa for Ph.D. research. Although the long period of apprenticeship, debt, and employment insecurity involved in becoming an academic made this choice a daunting prospect for someone without family resources, a part of me relished the financial insecurity. Living as a financially strapped graduate student meant not having to fully acknowledge that my class position had irrevocably changed. I managed to ignore the fact that *studying* class could lead me to become a professional, which would in turn irrevocably *change* my class. I also failed to anticipate the ways in which my own class trajectory would shape the experience of becoming an academic. Perhaps I assumed (or hoped) that the issues I had struggled with in the past had been safely left behind in Southeast Chicago or at Exeter.

In the end, I discovered that my class background was in some ways unexpectedly helpful in becoming a professional anthropologist, even as it served as a source of tension in others. As someone who had regularly moved back and forth between worlds in which I felt myself to be a partial outsider, I had learned to be intensely watchful. In middle- and upper-middle-class contexts, I was watchful because, at least initially, I often felt ill at ease and did not always understand the rules by which others were conducting their lives. While middle-class and upper-middle-class friends might take certain social norms for granted, I was careful to observe before I acted to avoid mistakes that might reveal my "outsider" status. In Southeast Chicago, I was watchful as well. Seeing my home through the lens of the other places I had lived made it strange and distant in its own way. I was also conscious of the many ways I had changed and was sometimes reluctant to show such changes in case they caused offense or were perceived as putting on airs. Consequently, I often hid my old self in my new world, and hid my new self while in Southeast Chicago. In the end, this self-consciousness born of living in ruptured worlds helped me to develop the watchful gaze that is a tool of the trade for an anthropologist.[12]

My class background also provided an odd sense of comfort as I conducted Ph.D. research in a tiny island village in Tanzania (a feeling that contrasted strongly with the unease I often felt in professional academic settings).[13] On the surface, this might seem surprising. Ostensibly, the rural African village where I lived was as different a setting from Southeast Chicago as could be imagined. Travel writers describing coastal East Africa might focus on the long robes and colorful head cloths of some Muslim residents, the mud- or coral-walled coastal houses, or the fact that village ancestors once took part in the ancient Indian Ocean trading world. Yet, underneath this seemingly "exotic" surface, there were unexpected social similarities between this Tanzanian village and Southeast Chicago. In both places, an ethnically diverse population had assimilated into a kind of "melting pot" culture, and residents were bound by a dense web of social and familial ties rooted in place and built up over generations. In both areas, the emphasis upon attending weddings, funerals, and other social events (as well as the use of guilt to shame me when I let work interfere with social obligations) suggested both the importance that residents placed upon these social networks and their dependence upon them when times were rough. In each place, it was through such social networks, rather than through the professional credentials or educational degrees that were so important to the better off, that people defined themselves. I also recognized the cynicism that men and women in this Tanzanian village, like those in Southeast Chicago, displayed in casual conversation toward those in power—a cynicism that spoke volumes about how they felt themselves to be positioned outside such structures. In both regions, residents with limited education also shared a similar experience of being looked down upon by educated elites and being forced to rely upon local power brokers to make connections with seemingly impenetrable government bureaucracies. In other words, the social dynamics of this marginal, yet stable, community seemed oddly familiar.

My class background also shaped the kinds of questions I asked in East Africa in ways I didn't fully recognize at the time. For example, I found myself trying to make sense of how class and other inequalities played out among both Africans and Euro-Americans living or working in the region where I conducted research. I wanted to understand how the language of being a "developed" or "developing" country served as a kind of international marker of class status, and why the knowledge of villagers was so often denigrated by formally educated "development" experts. I also wanted to comprehend the different ways in which race and ethnicity were conceived in coastal East Africa, a reality that seemed so different from the essentializing discourses of race so often used by both whites and blacks in Southeast Chicago as well as in many other parts of the United States.[14]

When I began doing research in Southeast Chicago, this academic training was both helpful and an emotional crutch. It was almost too easy to experience Southeast Chicago and the world of my family through the distance-creating practices of writing fieldnotes (or, later, looking through a video camera lens). Social science jargon and presumptions sometimes opened up chasms that brought conversations to a crashing halt. I recall a conversation with my best friend from Southeast Chicago during a time when I was still in graduate school and home visiting on vacation. Although I usually hesitated to "share" in this way, I offered an analysis of some social dynamic in Southeast Chicago (I no longer remember what) and recall being proud of my analytical abilities to figure out what was "really" going on. My friend countered with disdain, "You make us sound like bugs under a microscope." I was cut to the quick and feared that she might be right. Yet what I learned doing field research in Tanzania would also in the end transform my experience of Southeast Chicago. Doing ethnographic fieldwork encourages a radically heightened sensitivity to the minutiae of daily life and can help one to look at the world—even those places with which one is already deeply familiar—in a new way. As anthropologists know, doing ethnography means not observing from a distance, but engaging in a dialogue, an intense form of interaction, a relationship. It is about learning to draw close—and be close—to others while simultaneously being able to stand back and analyze with a critical eye. When done correctly, analysis with this critical eye encourages understanding, rather than simply marks differences. When I brought this lesson home and learned to apply it to myself and my family, it helped transform the sense of estrangement I felt moving between class worlds and turned it into a quest to comprehend that served as a form of rapprochement. In short, fieldwork offered a chance to gain distance on what I was too close to in Southeast Chicago, and a space to draw closer to that which I found too painful to approach otherwise.

Although I traveled long geographic distances as an anthropologist, again it was the social distances at home that often seemed greatest. Academic settings in the United States constituted another place beyond Southeast Chicago where the hidden tensions generated by moving between classes continued to reemerge for me in sometimes unanticipated ways. The primary symptom was a nagging sense of being ill at ease. Although I developed a certain level of comfort as a teacher (one could nurture tiny classroom communities with their own social norms over the course of a semester), I never got over a sense of awkwardness in the class-saturated contexts of public lectures, academic conferences, or university-wide faculty meetings. I even consciously avoided such activities whenever I could. It was in such venues that I felt the strain of having to prove my "smartness" in terms that never seemed natural. I was intensely aware, for example, that the standard English and the long words expected in academic settings were not my first language. Such language, when I used it, felt put on, like donning a mask. The strain of having to daily perform smartness often left me exhausted. In my early years as an assistant professor, I would sometimes come home and curl up on the bed in a fetal ball. At other times, to release the strain of engaging in such "class" performances by day, I would feel compelled to compensate at night by littering my speech with the nongrammatical English and casual swear words that I associated with my father.

When I did speak in academic settings, I was generally plainspoken. I liked to think that this was a principled stance; however, in large part it was simply because I had never learned to speak "high academese" fluently (although I certainly tried during graduate school). Practitioners of the humanities and some social sciences in elite US educational institutions generally value European scholarly styles that valorize rhetorical skill. It took years for me to realize that the points made in academic venues (sometimes relatively straightforward points couched in complex syntax) were not always the sole purpose of what was being said. Academic speaking styles were not simply about conveying ideas, but about a competitive form of verbal performance in which the ability to weave together words in a erudite, even opaque style, is admired. Speaking in this kind of esoteric manner contrasts strongly with the straightforward directness of the American working-class style in which I was raised. Like an immigrant who can never fully rid him- or herself of a linguistic accent, I came to "high academese" too late in life to ever fully lose my own "accent." Just as linguistic accents are often perceived by others in stereotypical ways, these other kind of class "accents" also provoke stereotypical responses, even if the reasons for such responses are not fully recognized. Some theoretically minded academics, for example, seem to read this kind of direct speaking style as suggesting the overliteralness of an unsophisticated mind.

I wonder whether in my old age I will revert to my first language (just as my husband's grandfather reverted to the forgotten German of his childhood as he approached death). Will I be able to dredge up the nonstandard English littered with swear words, nonstandard pronunciations, and colorful, yet grammatically imprecise, phrases that I associate with my father and that was the language he bequeathed to me? Will I ever have the confidence to be both "smart" and fluent in this first language that was once my own?

While the face-to-face encounters that speaking in professional contexts demands have long been a fraught class activity for me, writing has represented something of a refuge. On the surface this makes no sense, given that writing is a highly classed activity in its own right. Growing up, however, I found that writing (like reading) offered a space to construct a private world outside the bonds of neighborhood and family. In this space, I could write what it never occurred to me to say. Even though I might model my writing on the styles of authors from different class backgrounds than my own, I interacted with them on the familiar turf of my imagination. In the bedroom I shared with my sister and, later, in dorm rooms at prep school and college, I would sit hunched over sheets of paper, frustrated that I couldn't make the words that I was writing mean what I wanted. I felt self-conscious, and this lack of self-confidence at times led to avoidance. But over years of writing, I gradually learned to pummel the words into some semblance of the shape and feelings I wanted—or at least to have the confidence that I could get closer if I tried long enough. Writing, I discovered, offered a way to communicate my observations (and at times alienation) from the worlds in which I was living in a way nothing else could. It is not surprising that I write rather than tell this account, since it is only through the intermediary of the printed word that I feel fluent.

My sense of unease in middle-class professional contexts extends not only to verbal communication but also to emotional style. In the years immediately after leaving Southeast Chicago, I found myself dealing with a minefield of class tensions whenever I became angry without having mastered the appropriate norms for expressing the emotion. The personal accounts of other straddlers often remark upon the chasm between middle-class and working-class emotional styles, particularly in situations of tension. As Alfred Lubrano laconically notes, "working class people yell."[15] He and others describe how working-class emotional styles tend to emphasize a direct form of "telling it like it is" and challenging authority when one feels wronged. Like Lubrano, I had grown up in a place where yelling was the norm. In Southeast Chicago, yelling signified many things. Sometimes, it was simply an emotional style and nothing more. In other instances, it was a way to vent frustrations or to demand respect when none was offered by others. At home, it might emerge in a bossy style of parenting in which power and control are exercised, not in the work space, but among one's relations.

I remember my dad telling stories of incidents in the steel mills that captured how yelling and confrontation were embedded in its masculinized workplace culture.[16] In his stories, foremen and union reps investigating grievances might make a public display of yelling at each other and almost coming to blows in front of coworkers. According to my dad, however, they could amicably settle a dispute ten minutes later once they moved out of the line of sight of others. "It was all a show," my dad would note with bemusement.[17] In such instances, yelling symbolized workers' public demands— not simply for wages, but for respect—a dynamic forged from long histories of industrial grievances and union struggle. Such emotional styles formed a stark contrast with those that C. Wright Mills noted for middle-class employees of large bureaucracies.[18] While yelling might be seen by elites as an affront to refinement and good manners, it might, for a middle-class bureaucrat, actually jeopardize one's job. This lack of directness and the avoidance of conflict (and the greater identification with the status quo and willingness to settle conflicts through back-door channels that it signifies) would have struck my father and his coworkers, however, as cowardly or even immoral.

Particularly when I was younger, I was perplexed that stating opinions too bluntly, forcefully, or emotionally (in other words, in classic working-class style) could cause unease in middle-class settings. At the time, I was puzzled that this emotional style of arguing was taken seriously and not recognized as simply a style. Since then, I have myself become ambivalent about such styles and the way they can escalate conflict. In my own life, I have also had to reconsider my unconscious tendency to assume that all tensions between those of different classes are David-versus-Goliath battles where it's justifiable to attack the more powerful, since, well, they are more powerful.[19] Living a middle-class existence, I have learned to rework my own ways of interacting. Now, if anything, I overcompensate and completely avoid conflict, since I'm never sure what will be considered an appropriate response or simply overreacting. I regularly conscript my diplomatic husband into reading e-mails I write to others in order to check for signs of being overly direct. (Sometimes, I still can't tell.) My husband teases me that I've now become a complete pushover. Of course, on rare occasions, I can still flash the "dagger eyes" I inherited from my father. However, at this point in my life, I find the working-class emotional styles I grew up with to be just as alien as I initially found middle-class ones. Like so many caught between social worlds of various kinds, it is easy to become stranded betwixt and between.

My feelings of unease in middle-class settings have also extended to matters of politics. I sometimes find my perspectives out of sync with middle-class commentators, even with those with whom I otherwise agree. As anthropologists might say, we are socially "positioned" in different ways, and I find myself troubled at times by how "working-class" people are depicted. I had my first inkling of this as a child in Southeast Chicago. In the late 1970s, my older sister had a friend whom I'll call Barbara. In my ten-year-old imagination, I was fascinated by the fact that her fingers were double-jointed and would bend backward whenever she tried to catch a ball (with the unfortunate consequence that she was generally picked last when we broke up into kickball teams for gym class). Slightly less fascinating to me, but still of interest, was the reason why her family had moved to the East Side. Rumor had it that her father was a radical political activist from an upper-middle-class background who was heavily influenced by the 1960s counterculture (it was said that Barbara's godfather was Tom Hayden, Jane Fonda's former husband, although at the time I had no idea who this was). Even though I had no idea what any of this was about, I remember being troubled and offended that Barbara's parents presumably thought that residents of Southeast Chicago needed to be "converted" to a more revolutionary brand of politics. Why, I wondered, should people who didn't even know us think we should be different? It was the same feeling I had when evangelical Christians went door to door in our neighborhood and annoyed people by trying to change their ideas about religion. Didn't it imply that such individuals thought there was something wrong with you to begin with?

As a graduate student in New York, I would myself come to romanticize a certain brand of left-leaning politics that mirrored my post-Exeter anger and that I valued for the paths it provided to talk openly about class in the United States. I also deeply admired the political conviction of some activists and intellectuals that I met around the city and their commitment to forging a more just world. At the same time, I became increasingly uneasy that although "Class" (with a capital C) was spoken about overtly, there was often little self-reflexive attention to other class dynamics: why, for example, were so many of the "radicals" I knew in New York individuals from middle-class or upper-middle-class backgrounds, many of whom were deeply concerned with differentiating themselves from their own suburban upbringings? Why was there such a distressing lack of knowledge of actual working-class people? When many such activists did know working-class people, I discovered, it tended to be individuals who shared their own political viewpoints, confirming their own view of working-class perspectives, rather than acknowledging such perspectives might be part of a kaleidoscope of opinions, or perhaps even a minority one, within working-class neighborhoods. The core question that troubled me was why was there such a strong desire to get "the working class" to conform to a preexisting set of political beliefs?

Such observations, ultimately, led me to the conclusion that many political debates in the United States were really a kind of gladiatorial battle between differing factions of the middle and upper middle classes, with conservatives and liberals (and a much smaller group of radicals on both sides) all battling for their vision of what society should be. Even the terms "liberal" and "conservative" seemed to me to divide the world into right and wrong from a largely middle- or upper-middle-class point of view. In contrast, the working-class people I knew rarely fitted the neat political categories outlined in news media and some scholarly accounts. Like my Big and Little Grandpas, their politics ricocheted around the entire spectrum, following far more complex logics and histories than pundits and even many academics acknowledged. In these gladiatorial battles, the working class and poor often seemed to be reduced to rhetorical pawns. While conservatives espoused programs that benefited elites and hurt the poor and working class (and then, later, in a remarkable sleight of hand, tried to simultaneously pass themselves off as the salt of the earth in contrast to "liberal elites"), liberals from middle- and upper-middle-class backgrounds often valorized the "disadvantaged" but seemed to harbor their own ambivalence, particularly about the white working class.

This ambivalence consisted, on the one hand, of a tendency to romanticize the "working class" and see workers as more "real" or "authentic" or even deserving. On the other hand, there was also a tendency to find fault with working-class people. For many liberals, working-class whites were sexist and racist.[20] For many radicals, the American working class failed to understand the nature of capitalism and the true workings of power. After all, why did the American working class lack revolutionary consciousness compared to those in other countries? Was the working class deluded by a false consciousness that could be corrected with political education (i.e., one directed by sympathetic members of higher classes)? While critiques of working-class people from the vantage point of those from higher class positions might hold an element of truth, these caricatures usually failed to ask the questions that are bread and butter to anthropologists: How do those from working-class backgrounds understand their own actions? What social and historical dynamics feed into whatever beliefs might be at work? Might working-class individuals, in fact, have something worthwhile and even unexpected to say? How are working people, like the "poor," complex human beings who equally defy both romanticization and unsympathetic critique? In the end, I find myself still struggling to forge a political perspective that would be true to the trajectory of the life I have led and that would resist entrenched political narratives of either variety about "the working class."

Finally, I now also recognize that, beneath my bouts of unease and my awkward class moments, there lies a longing that will never be satisfied. I crave the self-assurance that I saw in many of my Exeter classmates, who casually took for granted that their norms of behavior or understandings reflected what was appropriate in the larger world (or, at least so it seemed to me as I looked in from the outside). Perhaps it is partly the desire to avoid the unease and discomfort that comes from moving beyond one's class comfort zone that causes some working-class individuals to sabotage themselves once they've embarked upon a path to upward mobility. Perhaps the desire to avoid feeling like a fish out of water leads some from the working class to set their sights lower than their middle-class counterparts as a way to sidestep such awkward moments. I suspect that some of the most conventionally successful people from working-class backgrounds are attracted to professions like business where (for men) a certain kind of working-class directness can become part of a respected persona. Or perhaps such individuals simply reject their pasts entirely and spend their energies trying to differentiate themselves from where they came from. Perhaps those most successful with these transitions have families that are less ambivalent about upward mobility: perhaps some have downwardly mobile parents who conveyed their aspirations to their children or parents who once nursed dreams that were painfully thwarted. Certainly, my own experience of moving between Southeast Chicago and Exeter came out of particular social circumstances. Crucially, it happened at the pivotal age of sixteen—a point when an individual is neither a fully formed adult nor a malleable child. It also happened at a time when my own family was actively downwardly mobile and where there was little support for a trajectory of upward mobility. Although my unease may have been heightened by such factors, I strongly suspect that feelings of existential angst and unease also haunt others in their more private moments, however such feelings might be interpreted. After all, is it so easy to split a life in two?

As I have become older, the class questions that now preoccupy me are less about the need to negotiate the conflicting worlds that I experienced while attending Exeter, and more about how to forge a coherent life and a sense of identity from the disparate pieces of my class experiences. Can one ever fully surmount the resulting sense of rupture? For much of my life after leaving Southeast Chicago, I have dreamt about home. In one dream, I struggle to walk to my grandparents' house on Avenue G through the snow and have to cross narrow but infinitely deep crevices in the sidewalks that threaten to swallow me in their claustrophobic depths. More often, however, my dreams have been hodgepodge affairs that I have always interpreted as attempts to bring the different pieces of my life into alignment, to create a coherent sense of self. Some are so embarrassingly self-evident that they require no interpretation. I have dreamt of my graduate school dissertation committee living across the street from a church on the East Side. As I talk to them about my anthropological ideas, they warn me to lower my voice: the churchgoers across the street might hear me and take my words as a critique of them. I dream that I see the back of a woman from East Africa. She is wearing a colorful *kanga* cloth wrapped under her armpits and cooks over three rocks in a thatched hut. I recognize her to be Bi Sharifa, the kindly yet feisty Tanzanian woman who had served as a sort of surrogate parent during my field research. I go up to her and greet her and see that she is, in fact, my grandmother Ethel. She is wearing cat's eye glasses perched on her pale face and gives me the puzzling smile I remember from childhood.

I pore over the accounts of Lubrano's straddlers and others who worry about their class identity: are we working class, middle class, or some mixture of the two? In Richard Rodriguez's view, the radical disjunctures between the different class worlds created by education are inevitable: he is both grateful for leaving behind the class world of his childhood and mourns it with nostalgia. The radical economists J. K. Gibson-Graham[21] instead argue that individuals may be simultaneously from more than one class. In their view, each of us may hold multiple class positionings at a single time. They offer the example of an Australian man who is a laborer and union supporter but also owns a rental building that generates income, has a small business on the side, and relies upon the unpaid labor of a spouse. His wife is the daughter of a successful Filipino businessman, a former nurse, and a stay-at-home mom whose work is "expropriated" by her family. All these instances suggest different sorts of class positioning.

In my own view, our identities are like patchwork quilts forged of many pieces; even if we are forced to choose from the scraps made available to us, we choose how to arrange them and create a larger pattern and meaning. In class terms, this means that I am working class in my memories, in parts of how I relate to the world, and, even as I describe in the next chapter, in the chemical composition of my body. Yet I am middle class in education, profession, residence, and those tastes and habits that I have acquired as an adult. I am inextricably connected to and shaped by people in both worlds. When I travel to East Africa, I am an elite who has the ability to leave and get medical care, to access money, to have linguistic and social connections with a part of the world that makes powerful decisions over its poorer regions. I am made up of many pieces, the meanings of which shift in relation to those around me. Given that writing this book has been about generating a way of speaking about class that feels true to my own upbringing, this language must necessarily be a hybrid one.

---

Deindustrialization has given rise to countless stories about the changing class landscape of the United States, including those in this book. Telling stories through the prism of upward mobility exposes still other dimensions of class. The counternarrative of upward mobility offered here, like that of deindustrialization in the previous chapter, concentrates on moments of rupture. In doing so, it exposes the profound linkages between class and identity that are revealed when those links are challenged. Like the class stories told in the next chapter, this account of upward mobility also underscores how our experiences of class are always, as anthropologists might say, "embodied" ones. Although the tensions generated by moving between class worlds may be most apparent for straddlers, I suspect that such stories are intensified versions of what most people deal with, perhaps in unconscious ways, as part of their everyday lives. After all, regardless of our class backgrounds, we are all "many." We have the positions into which we are born and those into which we shift over the course of our life cycles, sometimes by choice, sometimes not, sometimes in sync and sometimes in opposition to our friends, families, neighborhoods, and nations. We are all constantly in motion, the product of the subtleties of our souls as well as the material realities of our jobs and social positions, constantly defining ourselves in relation to each other as well as our own pasts.

Recognizing that we all have stories that emerge from our particular class positioning is not to imply a cultural relativism of the "we all have 'problems' whether we're rich or poor" variety.[22] Ultimately, the stories we tell and our class-based hopes and fears for the future are potent precisely because of how they span relations of inequality. This is what makes them matter so deeply to most of us. Because class is ultimately about inequality, it also means that certain people have a far greater ability to have their perspectives heard, to mold what narratives will become dominant ones, and to have their experiences taken as a standard by which to judge others. But paying attention to how we experience the minutiae of class in our daily life—a recognition that can be heightened by moving between different class terrains—can help us better understand how these inequalities manifest themselves in the world. My own experience has forced me to question conventional accounts of upward mobility that some might apply to my own life (and that I might be tempted to use in my less reflective moments). It forces me to consider how questions of inequality are bound up with experiences of "upward mobility"—those moments when we have supposedly broken free from economic constraints—but which may create ruptures that we ourselves didn't anticipate.

Finally, and most crucially, I must ask, why are the stories of upward mobility currently valorized in the United States the kind of individual success stories that played so well to Exeter's alumni, rather than the collective accounts of upward mobility that once made the American dream a reality for countless communities like Southeast Chicago? Individual success stories operate, much as they did in the nineteenth century, to undermine those who are poorer or working class by suggesting that if they hadn't "made it," they have only themselves to blame. In such a context, it is not surprising that my father and many others would prove deeply ambivalent about "success," even for the children they loved.

## CHAPTER FOUR

# The Ties That Bind

Despite having lived for many years in other places, I always return to South-east Chicago. Members of my family still live there, and these are ties that bind. However, when I go back home now, the area where I grew up is very different. It is strange to think that, in only a few generations, my family witnessed the rise and fall of the steel industry in the Calumet region. From my immigrant great-grandfather's first venture into the mills during their rapid expansion in the early twentieth century, to my grandfather's struggles in a unionizing era, to the deindustrialization suffered by my parents' generation, their lives were inextricably intertwined with that of an industry. This industrial way of life, once considered the bedrock of the US economy, has proven far more ephemeral than any of us could have imagined.

On these return visits home, I am struck, however, by the way the old steel mills continue to assert their presence, despite their physical disappearance. Immediately after the shutdown of Wisconsin Steel in the early 1980s, I would sometimes drive past 106th Street and Torrence Avenue with my dad. As we passed the abandoned buildings of the mill where he had spent so many years of his life, he would mutter bitterly about how he'd like to blow the place up. The empty buildings, overgrown with weeds, seemed to mock him. But it wasn't until 2000, twenty years after the mill shut down, that the last of the buildings that had so offended my father were finally torn down. Even today, the enormous lot—like those of Republic and US Steel–South Works—remains largely vacant. Although there have been various plans for these spaces over the years, so far these vast brownfields have proved too polluted or too costly to convert to new uses.[1] Through such open, gaping wounds on the landscape—and through their more invisible toxic legacy—the steel mills still manage to dominate Southeast Chicago.

When I go back to visit Southeast Chicago now and ask my mother for stories about the closing of Wisconsin Steel, she gently chides me: "That was a long time ago. Things have changed. You can't keep hanging onto the past." Despite the fact that I left long ago, I realize that for me it's impossible to move on without a full reckoning with that past. For the country, I believe, it is the same. There is an unacknowledged national need to look back, to reevaluate how and why certain choices were made, and to consider the causes and consequences of deindustrialization and how it has transformed the class landscape of the United States. Without such a reckoning, the social dislocations and resentments set in motion by deindustrialization will continue take their human toll and will haunt the political culture of the United States in destructive ways.

Although I tend to think of my ties to Southeast Chicago as primarily familial or psychological, I've been forced to acknowledge, as an adult, another kind of tie that binds, one rooted in biology. Social theorists generally consider the "materiality" of class to be expressed in things like bank account balances or how one's job fits into an overall field of social relations or economic production. But there is another kind of materiality to class that is less often talked about and that environmental justice advocates gesture toward.[2] Although I may have traveled far away from Southeast Chicago during the course of my life, I am forced to acknowledge that, along with many other current and former residents, I carry the legacy of time spent there in the chemical composition of my body. Just as the industry of Southeast Chicago remains, even after it has left, so too the land, water, and air of the area have become a part of me, even though I no longer live there. My surgical scars are a reminder of this and of the fact that moving on requires yet another kind of reckoning—an environmental one.

Up until now, I have told the life stories of particular individuals: my great-grandfather, my grandmother, my father, or myself. The stories told in this chapter, however, are about a place. Rather than serving as backdrop, Southeast Chicago and the Calumet region as a whole now shift to center stage. The need to focus on this area as a place should not be surprising. After all, it is the places where we live or have grown up that shape much of the class experiences of our lives, help determine the backgrounds of our neighbors as well as the habits of our daily lives, and provide the setting for memories that offer a sense of stability and continuity to who we are. Scholars of working-class studies argue that this is particularly the case for historically industrial areas like Southeast Chicago, where the jobs in which people worked and the social networks they built over generations were tightly linked to particular geographic locations. However, in this account, I focus on place in another way. I see the landscape of Southeast Chicago as a physical and environmental space that has come to be thoroughly bound up with the bodies that have lived there. Telling stories about the region in this way requires acknowledging that our bodies, and not just our psyches, have histories. It requires tracing the links between land and industry and between pollutants and disease. And, it requires considering how divisions of class as well as race and gender have been bound up with both.

In this chapter, I also explore the postindustrial visions deemed possible for Southeast Chicago. In recent decades, the ideas of the free market advocates who have dominated public discussions in the United States have presumed that a seemingly outmoded and collapsing industrial economy would "naturally" be replaced by a dynamic new economy based on services, information, or other so-called sunrise ventures. In such accounts, "the economy" comes to be depicted as akin to a force of nature, one that, if left unfettered, moves forward of its own internal volition in an evolutionary fashion. Only the foolhardy would challenge its preferred and natural path. However, the profound gaps that exist between the rallying cries of new-economy boosters and the contemporary reality of places like Southeast Chicago demand explanation. In the Calumet and in many other formerly industrial regions, no new-economy future has appeared. The closest thing has been the floating lakefront gambling boats that were constructed along the Indiana side of the state border in the 1990s, bringing limited and debatable benefits in their wake. Clearly, those who have suffered the impact of deindustrialization have not been the ones to benefit from these new-economy visions of the future. In fact, working-class people are almost entirely absent from such visions at all.

In recent decades, many have wondered what would become of Southeast Chicago's vast postindustrial wastelands. By the time the steel industry began to falter in the late 1970s, a rapid expansion of landfills and waste disposal sites in the area had already begun. As a result, some residents feared that the Calumet region's future would be as an enormous toxic waste pit. At one point, the city's mayor, as described below, suggested physically wiping out much of this deindustrialized region entirely. In more recent years, city officials have taken a different tack and joined with community activists and environmentalists to offer a new vision for the Calumet region. This new vision has redefined the area's remaining wetlands and toxic brownfields as valuable "open space" for parks and for redevelopment for present and future generations of urban dwellers. Although city officials and community activists have been adopting the language of "sustainable development" for very different reasons, they agree on the goal of simultaneously revitalizing the wetlands and the industrial lakefront both to create recreational spaces and as part of the uphill struggle to attract "clean" industry and new jobs. Despite the shifting nature of these competing visions for Southeast Chicago's future, there has been a common thread: the need to revisit the environmental legacy of this once heavily industrialized place.

In the previous chapters of this book, I have offered alternatives to various hegemonic accounts about immigration, labor, deindustrialization, or social mobility in the United States. I have argued that these more dominant perspectives have too often silenced aspects of the stories that some in Southeast Chicago—including myself and various family members—might wish to tell. This chapter does something different. Here, I use my training as a researcher to explore a variety of angles on Southeast Chicago's environment and future. This chapter considers the toxic substances interwoven with bodies and landscapes, the community struggles as well as the racial and ethnic divisions and alliances found around environmental issues, and the brownfield-influenced visions of the region's future that have ranged from gambling casinos to parks and "open spaces." Rather than providing a counternarrative to more hegemonic accounts of what a postindustrial era is supposed to be, this chapter, in the end, emphasizes what is missing: the fact that working-class lives have been largely erased from public visions of the future in the United States. Standing back and taking stock of Southeast Chicago and other postindustrial landscapes, I argue, also means considering what the unevenly dying pasts and uncertain futures of such regions are likely to offer—and not offer—both residents and the nation as a whole.

## Making Bodies

My original interest in what might amorphously be referred to as Southeast Chicago's "environment" was literally academic. During the early 1990s, as I was writing my master's thesis about the collapse of the region's steel industry, I began paying more attention to the battles over pollution occurring in Southeast Chicago. Industrial pollution in the area, of course, has a long history. It has also been a touchy subject in the Calumet region. Like many other Southeast Siders, I grew up hearing stories about the red iron oxide dust that used to spew from the steel mills in the old days, settling on porches and dirtying clothing left to dry outside on clotheslines. Many steelworkers, particularly those who worked in the most hazardous jobs like those in the coke ovens, found it impossible to ignore the health impacts of the work. Nevertheless, most residents took it as axiomatic that pollution was the price that people in the area had to pay for stable, well-paid jobs. My father used to approvingly quote older area residents who lived through the Depression and who used to say, "The more smoke the better—it means there's food on the table and the kids are eating!" Historians working in the region, as well as those in other old US industrial sites, have documented this widespread, long-standing symbolic association between pollution and prosperity.[3]

By the 1970s, however, there were growing concerns about industrial pollution in the Calumet as elsewhere.[4] However, the largely middle-class environmentalist movement of the time often ended up angering Southeast Chicago residents as much as inspiring them. Steel companies offered dire warnings that the air pollution controls and other environmental measures with which they were being forced to comply would put them out of business.[5] As a consequence, many in Southeast Chicago feared for their jobs, a fear that the later closing of the steel mills seemed to confirm for some. I also suspect that some people, like my dad, resented what they perceived as middle- and upper-middle-class environmentalists failing to show proper concern for how working-class people earned a livelihood or fed their children.

However, not all of the area's pollution came solely from the steel mills when I was a kid. After tightened environmental regulations limited the kinds of waste that could be disposed of in water, more and more waste was deposited on land. This meant that growing amounts of it were brought into Southeast Chicago from other regions of the city and country. Although this started happening before the steel mills began closing, deindustrialization sped the process, and landfills would become one of the few "growth" industries in the region during the 1970s and 1980s. I first recall hearing about such issues as a teenager, when a high school friend's sister began climbing over chain-link fences at night to try to document illegal dumping. Even my own family had a passing connection with the dumps. In the aftermath of Wisconsin Steel's shutdown, my mother worked temporarily as an office worker at one of the growing number of landfills encircling the Calumet region. At the time, my parents appreciated the job because the location was close to home and easy to reach with a broken-down car. The landfill site, however, made even my environmentally skeptical father nervous. My mother wore street clothes while she worked in the on-site trailer that served as an office, but the men who worked just outside wore protective suits and masks. Although my father didn't know what exactly was being disposed of, decades later he was still voicing his concerns.

Historically, Southeast Chicago residents have long lived close to waste, ranging from the industrial waste dating back to the beginnings of the steel mill neighborhoods to the city-owned municipal garbage dump that between the 1940s and the 1980s filled in more than a quarter of Lake Calumet. In the wake of deindustrialization, however, the region seemed to be increasingly viewed as simply a site for waste disposal. In 1989, even the old Wisconsin Steel site was (unsuccessfully) promoted as a site for a new garbage incinerator. With prospective landowners reluctant to take on the legal liabilities of converting potentially hazardous former industrial sites to other uses, already polluted communities like Southeast Chicago often ended up being environmentally punished a second time.

It was during the 1980s, in the wake of the expanding waste problem in Southeast Chicago and the toxic scandals at Love Canal and elsewhere, that environmental protests finally reached the region in major.[6] The activists included area homemakers, schoolteachers, religious leaders, and others—many of them women. It is not surprising that, when environmentalism gained traction in Southeast Chicago, it was in relation to a waste industry that brought few jobs and decreased home real estate values, severing the long-standing equation between pollution and prosperity.

Despite my growing awareness of these environmental realities, I was totally unprepared when my world turned upside down a third time. By 1993, I was living in New York City, preparing for my Ph.D. exams and future fieldwork in East Africa. Emboldened by a graduate class I had taken on feminism and biological reproduction,[7] I had resolved to "take charge" of my health. Although I had long complained to doctors of intense pain during my monthly menstrual cycle, excessive bleeding, and a sense that something was amiss, doctors had always been dismissive of my worries. One even advised me to see a psychotherapist. Finally, a doctor skeptically agreed to perform an exploratory procedure if it would help make me "feel better" (psychologically, that is). Clearly believing that nothing out of the ordinary would turn up, she appeared almost as shaken as I was when she called me into her office and offered the diagnosis of uterine cancer. Her medical colleagues were equally taken aback. Women with this type of cancer tend to be postmenopausal; obesity is also a major risk factor. I was twenty-seven and weighed 110 pounds.

When I went to meet with the anesthesiologist before my hysterectomy, he stuck his head in the room, took one look at me, and went out again assuming he must have made a mistake and entered the wrong room. Nurses reading my charts did a double take thinking they had picked up the wrong file. They were also uncommonly gentle as they took blood and put in IVs, an unspoken sympathy for an unexpectedly bad turn on life's roulette wheel. As the doctors puzzled over my cancer, they asked whether my mother had taken DES, a synthetic estrogen used to prevent miscarriages that instead turned out to cause cancer in their children. She hadn't. They puzzled over the other ways my cancer didn't fit the usual profile. Instead of the common pattern of a thin layer of cancer cells along the uterine lining (a pattern that responds well to treatment), my tumor was thicker and concentrated in one area. A specialist in New York informed me that, although extremely unusual, he had seen a few similarly puzzling cases in younger women in recent years. Although too rare to generate a statistical profile, the disease appeared to be much more aggressive in these instances.

In the end, I was lucky. The cancer, it turned out, was caught just before it would have entered my lymph system. After paying the price of the loss of my reproductive organs, I would recover fully from the ordeal. After two operations at the University of Chicago hospital, I convalesced at home on the Southeast Side. During this period, my mom cooked for me, and my younger sister steadied my arm during walks in the evenings past our grand-parents' house, our old grammar school, and other sites of our childhood. My mom's friends, many of whom, as older women, had also had hyster-ectomies, brought casseroles and gave me tips about avoiding stairs. My father even agreed to smoke his cigarettes on the front porch. During these months of treatment and convalescence, I also recognized that I was lucky in another way. Despite the fact that my family had gone for long stretches without health insurance after Wisconsin Steel's demise, the student insur-ance from my university paid for most of my bills. To cover the remaining bills, I maximized my student loans. I was touched when friends offered to help me write letters pleading for debt forgiveness from doctors and hospi-tals, a moment in time when such things were still possible.

As I imagine is the case for many others, I went through various stages in my experience of cancer. Before I knew much about the type of cancer I had or even the degree to which it was treatable, my initial response, not surprisingly, was fear and the rebellious and restless reaction of someone in her twenties who didn't want to imagine what the end of life might be like. Later, there were sensations so well described by Anatole Broyard in his book *Intoxicated by My Illness*, when the background specter of the possibility of death brings on feelings of exhilaration, of life taking on a heightened sensual quality in which every moment is lived fully and none taken for granted. The fact that my cancer turned out to be treatable, despite the fact that it perplexed my doctors, meant that I had the opportunity to experience such sensations without having to pay the ultimate price, as Broyard had. Later, there came a sense of strength from "managing" my disease, reading and learning about it, making decisions, exercising and caring for my body with heightened attention, and, ultimately, gaining a sense of clarity about what was—and was not—important in life.

On occasion, this newfound calm would be punctured. I developed, for example, a (temporary) fear of riding in planes and cars. (I now recognize those moments as ones in which a sense of the precariousness of life would resurface and break through a reemerging taken-for-granted assumption that life would keep on going.) In general, however, I made it through what I thought of as "the cancer ordeal" with an enhanced feeling of strength. In this sense, my cancer experience contrasted strongly with that of the earlier collective trauma of deindustrialization that had haunted me for more than a decade. Although I felt the experience of illness to be one I had squarely dealt with and could leave behind, what *did* remain was the desire to explore the possible causes of a disease that had so puzzled my doctors. It was then that my training as a researcher would kick in; in later years it would underwrite a search to make sense of the socioeconomic, political, chemical, and ecological forces that had come together to generate the industrial landscape of Southeast Chicago and the bodies of those of us who had lived there.

When I had described the pollution found in Southeast Chicago to my doctors and asked whether my own illness might have an environmental link, they had smiled dismissively, asserted that there was no evidence for such a link, and changed the subject. My father also pooh-poohed the idea (much as he dismissed the links between cigarettes and lung cancer). To him, entertaining the possibility would have meant blaming his former livelihood, the steel mills. He instead postulated wildly that I had gotten cancer because I had been hit in the stomach during a softball game when I was twelve.[8] My mother, however, sat at the kitchen table and pondered all the people she knew who had cancer—young and old. Her group of women friends that met at the local diner for breakfast almost all had experiences with cancer—some several varieties. Somehow, she sighed, it just didn't seem like something was right. In the months and years ahead, I found myself reading whatever I could find about pollution in Southeast Chicago as well as the general relationship between toxic pollutants and cancer. In the basement of my home in Cambridge today, I still have a dusty cardboard box of reports and articles that I collected on the topic during the mid-1990s. More than a decade later, I would find myself reading over a new and far larger pile of articles and reports that weren't available when I was diagnosed. There was an odd bittersweet satisfaction to watching the pieces of this old puzzle begin to fall together.

The abstract scholarly reports and articles that my search dug up brought back to life stories from childhood—stories which pointed to the incredible transformations that the landscape of Southeast Chicago had undergone and the amount of industrial and other waste that circulated through, or underlay, the region. I remember the tales my grandfather recounted of an elderly neighbor who described how, in the "old days" in Southeast Chicago, he used to tie a rowboat to his back porch on the East Side and paddle it to work at Republic Steel. This story had an air of mystery, given that the neighbor's porch was nearly a half-mile away from water when I was a child and I hadn't yet learned to envision Southeast Chicago's past as a watery world of wetlands. I also remember my parents reminiscing about such incidents as the time manhole covers came flying up off the streets of the East Side and Hegewisch after mysterious sewer explosions that were later linked to chemical dumping at Republic Steel. I recall friends telling stories of older brothers and uncles who worked construction and saw fellow workers pass out from the fumes when they dug the cellars of the new ranch-style houses on the fringe of our neighborhood, an area some suspected had been built on old industrial dumps.

Through such accounts, I have learned to see the landscape of the Calumet region in new ways. What I grew up thinking of as "swamps" in Southeast Chicago are now transformed in my mind into what used to be the largest wetland complex in the Midwest, and what continues to be a notable stopover area for the migrating birds that hug the Lake Michigan shoreline rather than fly across its wide expanses.[9] Prior to the arrival of the steel mills in the late nineteenth century, the area was primarily known as a hunting and fishing paradise, attracting less-well-off subsistence hunters and fishers as well as wealthy visitors from the city of Chicago to the north.[10] George Pullman, whose model industrial town lay on the other side of Lake Calumet, sponsored sailing regattas on its waters. The famous architect Frank Lloyd Wright even designed an "amusement resort" for Wolf Lake in 1898, to be located between the East Side, Hegewisch, and Whiting, Indiana. Although never built, the resort was to include a bandstand, track and field area, boat houses, bathing pavilions, gardens, and a pergola for watching boat races.[11] In the ensuing years, many of the existing wetlands and bodies of water in Southeast Chicago would partially or completely disappear. This picture from 1915 (fig. 18) shows track being laid across Hyde Lake, a small body of water that no longer exists but once separated the East Side and Hegewisch. It is strange to think that much of what I had grown up thinking of as land was in fact composed of fill. This fill included toxic sludge dredged from the bottom of the already industrial Calumet River, as well as slag, a relatively stable waste product from steelmaking that, nevertheless, can be

18. Laying streetcar track across Hyde Lake in 1915. Courtesy of the Southeast Chicago Historical Museum.

laced with toxic heavy metals that can stunt vegetation and affect human health.[12]

I have learned to see the landscape of the Calumet region through the pollutants generated, or disposed of, there. I have learned about the enormous amounts of smoky particulate matter given off by the steel mills' coke ovens, which provoked "antismoke" drives even in the early twentieth century[13] and substances like cyanides, phenols, naphthalene (a component in coal tar), and sulfuric acid (a "pickling liquor" used to remove rust from steel) that were all part of the steelmaking process.[14] I have learned of the enormous amounts of solid and liquid waste that the steel mills historically deposited on land surrounding the mill sites or dumped untreated into the Calumet, the river that snaked past the area's mills and the site of tugboat rides with church groups during my youth.[15] I have learned about industrial chemicals used after World War II, including PCBs, that contributed to the heavy load of toxic industrial pollutants already generated by the steel mills. In 1991, my father's mill, Wisconsin Steel, was declared a CERCLA, or Comprehensive Environmental Response, Compensation, and Liability Act, site under superfund legislation. Since then it has undergone an intensive PCB cleanup in addition to the remediation of other hazardous substances, including PAHs (polynuclear aromatic hydrocarbons generated during the coke-burning process) as well as lead, arsenic, chromium, zinc, and asbestos.[16] I have learned of the pollutants associated with the other car, railroad, and chemical manufacturing plants in Southeast Chicago that arose as satellites of the steel industry, including a paint factory that produced lead paint as well as arsenic-based pesticides, and later DDT, as a sideline.[17]

I have also learned that 90 percent of all landfills in the city of Chicago, including approximately 51 landfills and 423 hazardous waste sites, exist in Southeast Chicago, making it one of the largest concentrations of waste disposal sites on the North American continent.[18] I have learned that experts fear that compounds from the eighty-seven-acre superfund site known as the Calumet Cluster, an area just past Wisconsin Steel and the old Interlake site where my uncle Don worked, has been leaking high concentrations of PAHs, benzene, toluene, ethylbenzene, xylene, chlorobenzene, and vinyl chloride through Lake Calumet into the Calumet River and, on occasion, into Lake Michigan, the city's water supply.[19] I have learned that the "cluster" includes a defunct incinerator that illegally burned PCBs during the 1970s and 1980s, a time when my sisters and I were in grammar or high school.[20] I have learned that the poorly constructed Paxton landfill once owned by the Mafia nearly collapsed onto Stony Island Avenue in 1999 and threatened what the media dubbed a toxic "garbalanche" that would have called for large-scale evacuations.[21] I have learned that during the 1990s the US Environmental Protection Agency was regulating the cleanup of twenty-five superfund sites in the Calumet area and monitoring toxic releases at ninety more on both sides of the state border.[22] I have learned that the Whiting, Indiana, oil refinery where my mother worked allowed 16 million gallons of oil to seep underground over the years.[23] In short, I have learned many things that my father did not want to hear.

For many years, the primary fears associated with toxic pollutants were that such substances caused cancer. In fact, many of the pollutants found in the air, water, and soil of Southeast Chicago are known or suspected carcinogens, including PCBs, DDT, PAHs, arsenic, chromium, naphthalene, benzene, and vinyl chloride. Toxic substances, however, can transform the body in multiple ways. Some substances are also endocrine disruptors, a group of chemicals that mimic hormones in the body and produce a range of developmental and reproductive problems for animals and humans, particularly for fetuses and the young in vulnerable stages of the life cycle.[24] In contrast to classical toxicology models, which posit that the higher the dose of a poison the greater its damage, experts in endocrine disruption argue that even tiny amounts of hormone-influencing substances can have profound impacts if exposures happen at crucial points in the developmental cycle. Known and suspected endocrine disruptors like PCBs, DDT, arsenic, PAHs, naphthalene, and vinyl chloride, for example, have been variously linked in studies to thyroid disruption, miscarriages, chromosomal instability, decreased sperm counts, premature births, and birth defects. In addition, some of the toxic pollutants found in the area, including the lead and cyanide associated with steel production, as well as benzene, toluene, and DDT, generate neurotoxicological effects. Some of these substances, like PCBs and benzene, also affect the immune system.[25] In sum, understanding how the bodies of those of us who were raised in Southeast Chicago were "made" means looking at how this industrial landscape came into being, the substances that became part of the air, land, and water, the poorly understood ways these toxic substances worked both alone and in interaction with others, and the equally poorly understood ways such substances influenced the diverse but interacting biological systems within our own bodies.

Because toxic substances have to make their way into bodies to have their effects, I have pondered the routes by which I—or others linked to Southeast Chicago—might have come into contact with substances capable of causing illness. I wonder, for example, whether my father brought home the residues of PCBs or other contaminants on his clothing when he returned from his shifts at Wisconsin Steel? Or had I breathed these substances in the air as they were illegally burned in nearby waste incinerators? Did I drink them in water tainted by runoff from the Calumet River when it reversed course after storms and flowed into Lake Michigan? Had I ingested them as we enjoyed crunchy fried lake perch or absorbed them through my skin as we swam in industrially polluted waters during hot summer months? Had I been exposed to DDT that moved "off-site" from the local paint factory or when it was sprayed to control mosquitoes in the area? Or had my parents been exposed to any or all of these things before I was conceived or when I was a fetus in the womb? Like so many others, I was a fetus, baby, and toddler during the mid-1960s and early 1970s, a period when agents like PCBs and DDT were still in free use. Even today, however, there are just as many question marks. The chemical legacy of these older toxic substances remains in Southeast Chicago, even as little-understood newer chemicals have rapidly entered the picture.[26]

In *Inescapable Ecologies*, a historical account of agricultural chemical exposures, Linda Nash stresses that our bodies are permeable and have individual histories. We do not all react in the same way. Our responses vary with our biological histories, the particular toxic exposures we have experienced at different points in the life cycle, sometimes with past "hits" priming us for heightened responses when exposed to other substances later in life. For such reasons, putting a finger on the exact trigger for my illness, or on the illnesses of many neighbors and relatives, necessarily remains elusive. There are too many possible culprits, too many potential hits, too much lag time between exposure and subsequent illness to pinpoint the exact causes and mechanisms of our diseases.[27] Nevertheless, just as throughout our lives we drag our class experiences and the related aspects of who we are with us, our bodies also carry this legacy of chemical exposures as we move into the future.

## Devalued Landscapes: The Airport Struggle

The toxic pollution and industrial brownfield sites found throughout Southeast Chicago have limited the kinds of futures possible for the region.[28] Few have wanted to pay the costs of cleaning up these sites or to take on the liability for their health risks. During the 1980s, as much of the steel industry in Southeast Chicago was disappearing and as activists were drawing attention to the widespread pollution in the area, there was a growing attitude within Chicago that the Calumet was now a worthless landscape. Once celebrated as the source of the city's industrial strength, a region that had built skyscrapers and won world wars, the area was now viewed by many downtown as a nonproductive and illness-causing eyesore. It is both intriguing and disturbing to me as an anthropologist how the degradation of a landscape can so easily be transferred symbolically to the people who live there, devaluing and potentially erasing them in the process.

During a visit home from graduate school in 1990, I found that many residents of Southeast Chicago were up in arms. Then newly elected mayor, Richard M. Daley, was proposing building a third airport for the city of Chicago literally on top of the old steel mill neighborhoods. The city claimed that environmental problems in the region were so extreme that the best solution was to move residents, cover the area with concrete, and give Daley and the city a longed-for third airport in the process. According to newspaper accounts, the proposed Calumet airport, at a projected cost of $10.8 billion and sprawling over 8,200 acres, would have been the largest public works project in Illinois state history. The plan called for eradicating the entire neighborhood of Hegewisch, as well as parts of the East Side, South Deering, and the surrounding working-class suburbs of Burnham, Calumet City, and Hammond. It would have wiped out 8,350 or more single-family and multi-family homes in the process and would have displaced up to forty thousand residents.[29] My family's home would have been at the end of a runway.

In retrospect, I think of the airport proposal as the nadir of Southeast Chicago's postindustrial existence, a moment when the region was deemed as so lacking in value that the only possibilities it offered were in creating work for people to wipe it out. Yet it was striking how the proposal generated a fighting spirit among many residents, particularly those in the old, tight-knit, largely Polish-American neighborhood of Hegewisch, which was slated for total destruction. Those opposed to the airport argued that the city itself had provided the permits to locate the dumps in the Calumet region (in a process that many argued represented a corrupt and cozy relationship between politicians and waste companies).[30] They muttered in disbelief that, after locating the dumps in the region (an act a Hegewisch former steelworker commented bitterly implied that Southeast Chicago residents were as worthless as garbage), the city was now proposing a cleanup "solution" of wiping their homes out entirely. While some families we knew sighed and said that they would use the relocation money to get out of what they saw as a dying area and start someplace new, others were furious. Many, especially elderly residents who had spent their entire lives in these communities and who worried that they could not afford to live elsewhere, were bitterly angry. This picture (fig. 19) depicts some of those who picketed, protested, and fought.

For a region that had an ambivalent relationship at best to mainstream environmentalism, it was striking how some residents began using arguments forwarded by middle-class environmentalists as their best bet to stop the airport proposal.[31] Grassroots groups handed out flyers that argued that the airport shouldn't be built in Southeast Chicago because it would destroy much of the remaining wetlands in the region. Such groups charged that the toxic waste from the existing dumps would be capped and covered with concrete rather than cleaned up, raising the possibility of poisoning underground aquifers. Some residents even went out hunting for endangered species in the "swamps" to help throw up legal challenges to the proposal (it turns out there are several endangered species in the region, including the Franklin ground squirrel, the Blandings turtle, and several species of waterfowl). I found it poignant that area residents had to reckon with the fact that the plight of ground squirrels was legally given more weight than their own homes and lives.

I have often wondered why the airport proposal generated more public protest than the demise of the steel mills. Perhaps that struggle seemed beyond residents? After all, with the steel mills, whom could one fight? Steel companies merged, moved away, declared bankruptcy, and reopened with new businesses under new names. Politicians appeared stymied. Newspapers argued that the collapse of the steel mills was simply a product of unstoppable globalization. "What could the little guy do?" as my father

19. Protesting the proposed airport in Hegewisch. Courtesy of the Southeast Chicago Historical Museum.

used to say. The airport proposal, however, offered a clear target and the old-fashioned kind of battle that residents could rally around: here was city hall spitting on them. When the airport proposal died in 1992, some commentators attributed it to political factors unrelated to the protests. In the eyes of many Southeast Chicago residents, however, they had won. This outcome would also have broader consequences for environmental activism in Hegewisch and surrounding areas. A number of veterans of the airport struggle were already antilandfill activists. Others, as I describe later, would be galvanized by the environmental arguments used against the airport to fight for yet another vision of Southeast Chicago's future.

## Devalued Landscapes: Two Sides of a Landfill

Although I had begun collecting materials on pollution and environmental activism in Southeast Chicago around the time of the airport struggle, it was only after my own experience with cancer that I began paying closer attention to these issues. In subsequent years, I found myself collecting materials on the histories of environmental activism in the region. I did so mainly because of my personal health stakes in such efforts. However, over time, I became absorbed by the question of how environmental activism in the region could both underscore and help bridge the social and racial divisions that had so long divided it.

In 2005, I helped my husband shoot a short video documentary for a Southeast Chicago environmental group based in Hegewisch. The job offered a chance to explore the region's environmental questions close-up and to shoot video in the midst of industrial marshes and lakes and (from a helicopter) over the Calumet's industrial brownfields. One day in 2004, my husband and I set up our tripod on the top of the enormous Paxton II landfill. The landfills provide the highest elevations in the region (some having been filled far beyond legal limits), and they rise like a small mountain range over the flat landscape of Southeast Chicago. The Paxton II landfill, located a short distance from the landfill where my mother had worked, was locally known as Mt. Trashmore. As we drove up the steep side of the landfill in the jeep of a former Illinois EPA employee, red-tailed hawks glided in the updrafts as they hunted for mice on the giant mounds.

The view from the top of the landfill offered a graphic illustration of the cleavages—both environmental and social—that divided Southeast Chicago from the rest of Chicago as well as internally. In a landscape checkerboarded by industry, water, and distinct ethnic and racial enclaves, the landfills, for example, divide the largely white neighborhood of Hegewisch from the African-American community of Altgeld Gardens. Although Altgeld Gardens has gained fame in recent years as the site of President Barack Obama's youthful community organizing, I barely knew that it existed when I was growing up, even though it was only a short distance from Hegewisch, which was a central part of our social world. Unlike the older neighborhoods of Southeast Chicago that historically arose in response to the steel industry, Altgeld Gardens had been built in 1945 as a Chicago public housing facility for returning black World War II veterans.[32] From the top of the landfills, one could see that Altgeld Gardens was geographically cut off from the rest of Southeast Chicago by the physical barriers of Lake Calumet, the Bishop Ford Expressway, industry, landfills, and wetlands. However, as someone raised in the area, I also knew that the most intractable barriers to interaction were the less visible ones of racial antipathy and related class fears that "middle-class" steelworking families had long associated with low-income housing. Not surprisingly, many residents in Altgeld Gardens would identify with the largely African-American Southwest Side rather than the Southeast Side.

Yet the toxic pollution that physically divided these two neighborhoods also linked them together through its shared effects. A few years ago, I sought out Altgeld Garden activist Cheryl Johnson, the adult daughter of Hazel Johnson, whom some have referred to as the "mother of the environmental justice movement." Emerging in the late 1980s, the environmental justice movement bridged concerns about toxic pollution, environmental racism, and, in some cases, occupational health.[33] It also offered two profound challenges to middle-class environmentalism. First, it shifted attention away from a simple focus on "nature" to the relationship between toxic pollutants and health, and, second, it underscored the unequal exposures to environmental hazards faced by minorities and low-income groups. The groups most commonly associated with environmental justice movements have been African-Americans, although others have also been involved, most from poor, working-class, and lower-middle-class backgrounds. A striking proportion of environmental justice activists have been women, particularly mothers concerned about the health of their children.[34]

When I visited Altgeld Gardens in 2009, Hazel Johnson, who had been Altgeld Garden's leading environmental justice activist, was elderly and no longer gave interviews. However, her daughter Cheryl described how her mother had been a civil rights organizer and community activist. Galvanized by the untimely death of her husband from cancer, Johnson began documenting, during the 1970s, high rates of death and disease in the area, including cancer, reproductive problems, asthma, skin diseases, and other ailments. It turned out that the Altgeld Gardens public housing project had been built upon the turn-of-the-century sewage "sludge farm" of the Pullman railroad car company. To an even greater degree than other neighborhoods, the area was surrounded on all sides by waste sites and former industry. In 1979, Hazel Johnson founded People for Community Recovery (PCR), for many years the only primarily African-American environmental group in Chicago.[35] Over the course of the 1990s, Johnson became increasingly well known beyond Chicago. When visiting the PCR office in 2009, with its peeling paint and dilapidated feel, I was struck by the proud row of pictures on the back wall depicting Hazel Johnson shaking hands with various US presidents. Famed for her speaking abilities and for bringing tears to the eyes of audiences, Johnson was first brought to the White House by George H. W. Bush and then, in 1994, stood next to President Bill Clinton when he signed executive order 128898, popularly known as the "environmental justice" legislation, which prohibited discrimination in the siting of environmental hazards based on race or income.

When I interviewed Cheryl Johnson in 2009, she told stories of how, when she was growing up, black kids from Altgeld Gardens like herself would get bottles thrown at them if they ventured over into all-white Hegewisch. To her consternation, her mom, nevertheless, insisted on bringing her as a kid to environmental activist meetings there. Cheryl described her nervousness at being forced to go and her surprise at how nice everyone was to them at the Hegewisch meetings. Her comments simultaneously underscored the history of virulent racism in the region, the bravery of leaders like her mother, and the conscious attempts of environmental activists to bridge these divides.

In 1985, Johnson and PCR had joined with other Southeast Chicago activists, white, black, and Latino, as part of a coalition of community environmental organizations that included groups from neighboring Hegewisch.[36] The coalition fought against the landfills, an improperly operated incinerator (one of only three in the country then licensed to burn PCBs), and other pollution problems. In 1989, Southeast Chicago coalition activists, with environmentalists from Greenpeace by their side, were arrested for civil disobedience for blocking trucks entering the widely contested waste incinerator. They also managed to have the permit of one landfill revoked and blocked the creation of a new landfill on a local wetland near Acme/Interlake Steel. Ultimately, the coalition succeeded in pressuring the city to impose a moratorium on future dumping. (Given the well-funded nature of the waste companies, it is a battle that is repeatedly fought when the moratorium periodically comes up for renewal). In the end, however, the bridges that this environmental coalition built across the divided landscape of Southeast Chicago were difficult to sustain. The coalition petered out and observers made vague references to tensions among the various Southeast Chicago groups, some linked to competing goals, others perhaps linked to jealousy and competition among groups and communities.[37]

In the months after my visit with Cheryl Johnson, I made plans to meet with another prominent Southeast Chicago activist with a long history of environmental organizing. Marian Byrnes cut an unusual figure in Southeast Chicago. A well-educated white schoolteacher and former civil rights activist herself, Byrnes had once worked for politician Clem Balanoff, a state senator from Southeast Chicago who had offered a progressive challenge to the Chicago Democratic machine. Byrnes was known for her ubiquitous presence in area environmental struggles. In 1985, she organized the Southeast Chicago umbrella environmental organization CURE (Citizens United to Reclaim

20. Protesting the dumps—again

the Environment) and had reportedly offered assistance in forming PCR.[38] Like Johnson, she had been arrested for civil disobedience at the 1989 incinerator protest. She would also head the coalition-based Southeast Environmental Taskforce.

Anthropologists might call Marian Byrnes—like Hazel Johnson—a "culture broker." In Byrnes's case, she was involved in environmental struggles that spanned the nature preservation efforts of middle-class suburbanites and the landfill struggles and health concerns that galvanized working-class and poor residents. She was someone who served as a bridge among racial and ethnic groups within working-class and poorer parts of Southeast Chicago and, later, between working-class or lower-middle-class activists in Hegewisch and middle-class environmentalists in the south suburbs. I had interviewed Byrnes before, but these were formal video interviews in coalition offices on the East Side and Hegewisch. I hadn't known at the time that the question I really wanted to ask, not for the cameras, but for myself, concerned how she, Hazel Johnson, and other activists had managed, if fleetingly, to bridge the ferocious racial and ethnic divides of Southeast Chicago. Could the environmental effects of a common landscape, in the end, help trump the divisions that have been such a distressing part of Southeast Chicago's history?

I arranged to meet Marian in the area where she had lived for most of her life, the enclave of Jeffrey Manor within South Deering not far from Wisconsin Steel. Built in the 1930s, Jeffrey Manor, like Altgeld Gardens, was another city-built housing development largely cut off from the surrounding mill neighborhoods. The enclave had originally been a largely middle-class Jewish neighborhood that became a largely middle-class African-American one in the 1960s. (Like nearly all later housing developments built in Southeast Chicago, this one was also built upon a waste dump.) Although Byrnes was living in senior citizen housing in Hegewisch by the time we arranged the interview, we met at the Catholic church she still attended in Jeffrey Manor. Other than the priest, she was the only white congregant. Elderly and frail, she steadied herself by clutching the arms of her former African-American neighbors, while a musical mixture of traditional Catholic liturgy and music that I associated with African-American evangelical traditions soared through the building. The bridging of racial divides that this music symbolized, and that I had so rarely witnessed growing up in Southeast Chicago, took me pleasantly by surprise. When I reached out to shake her hand, however, Marian looked at me both apologetically and blankly: she had forgotten our appointment and, I suspect, much of the history that I had hoped to hear from her. In a few failing words, she suggested that she was preparing for the next life and was unable to talk about the past. Less than a year later, Marian Byrnes would pass away. In another year, Hazel Johnson would also pass away.

Since the early neighborhood-bridging efforts of the 1980s and early 1990s, the environmental struggles in Altgeld Gardens and Hegewisch have taken different paths. PCR activists have formed ties with middle-class environmentalists and academics interested in issues of environmental racism as well as questions of public health, social justice, and public housing policy.

They have sought to expand the concept of the environment to include all that makes a community healthy, safe, and economically and socially vibrant, using it as a bridge to the civil rights concerns of previous generations. Activists in Hegewisch, instead galvanized by the airport struggle of the early 1990s, have attempted to stop landfills and other "unwanted uses" in the area in another way. Working with Marian Byrnes, among others, they formed coalitions with middle-class nature conservationists and joined with city planners. As described in greater detail later, their goal was to preserve the Calumet's remaining wetlands and dunes as parks. While their middle-class coalition partners have focused primarily on conservation and recreation issues, Southeast Chicago activists have also insisted on the need to create new clean jobs and to celebrate the cultural and historical heritage of the old steel mill neighborhoods along with their natural heritage.

The divergent activist paths of Hegewisch and Altgeld Gardens are related to how, as anthropologists might say, their residents are differently "positioned" both socially and economically and to the kinds of legal and moral arguments they can consequently make.[39] There is a world of difference between Hegewisch, in which white and increasingly Latino working-class residents are fighting to hold onto "middle-class" respectability, and Altgeld Gardens, in which African-American residents have long struggled to find any work at all. The strategies and discourses to which minority public housing residents can appeal are also different from those of white working-class homeowners who want to emphasize environmental narratives that increase rather than decrease the values of what is often their only important economic asset—their homes. Although it is difficult for Southeast Chicago residents from a variety of backgrounds to find affordable housing or the means to create new lives elsewhere, it is significantly harder for African-Americans, who face far greater housing and job discrimination. Even back in the heyday of the steel industry, environmental hazards did not affect all Southeast Chicago steelworkers equally: African-Americans were disproportionately placed in jobs like the ones in the coking ovens that had carried heightened health risks.[40]

Yet, I remain struck by the vision from the top of the Paxton II landfill and the recognition that these different environmental struggles exist on two sides of a common mountain of waste, even as they are often depicted as distinct by journalists, academics, and residents themselves. The academic environmental justice literature on the region, for example, almost entirely erases working-class whites from the picture, perhaps because the legal, moral, and political claims being made on the basis of race are deemed most salient.[41] Conversely, the "open spaces and wetlands" strategy of predominantly white activists that piggybacks on the conservationist concerns of middle-class environmentalists directs attention away from the common ground of health concerns in this historically industrial region that link predominantly white activist groups with those in Altgeld Gardens. Yet it is equally important to recognize what unites these groups. Both want to stop toxic pollution, protect their own and their children's health, and create a more economically and environmentally vibrant and vital place to call home. Both do so in a deindustrialized context that has, on the one hand, severed the positive associations residents once made between jobs and pollution and, on the other, created a downward economic spiral that has devalued neighborhoods in ways that make it more likely that others would pollute there.

When the Hegewisch environmental group had trouble identifying African-American or Latino leaders to interview for the short environmental video I was helping my husband make during 2005, it became clear that the earlier coalition links built among Southeast environmental groups had faded. Nevertheless, the potential for overlapping concerns among diverse residents remained, even as the strategies for addressing their concerns diverged. While conducting impromptu video interviews with park users at Wolf Lake and the Powderhorn wetlands bordering Hegewisch, we spoke with an African-American fisherman who recounted how, growing up in the rural South, he had been raised to believe that when worries about bills or other life problems were mounting, you could always "take your troubles to the water" and find a sense of peace outdoors. He had brought his neighbors' teenage sons fishing with him and talked about the importance of outside recreational activities to help keep kids "out of trouble." Just as his statements underscored that "nature recreation" was not simply a white middle-class concern, health issues remained a central subtext for working-class whites even as local activist strategies shifted toward issues of open space and conservation.

The African-American fisherman and his wife came to a screening of the finished environmental video in a union hall near the Memorial Day Massacre site, a spot located between largely white Hegewisch and the mixed Latino and white neighborhood of the East Side. However, they found themselves to be the only African-Americans in the room, an ongoing legacy of the social barriers that have long divided this region. At the time, I was frustrated that these divisions seemed, once again, insurmountable. Yet as this book goes to press, I read in the news that a new meeting has just taken place at that very same union hall, bringing together residents and activists from Hegewisch, Altgeld Gardens, the East Side, and elsewhere to create an Environmental Justice Alliance of Greater Southeast Chicago.[42] Their goal is to protest a newly approved coal gasification plant to be installed on a portion of the old Republic Steel site across the street, a few blocks from the high school my sisters and I attended. While supporters argue it will provide new clean energy technology, activists and residents in the area argue that, like the waste incinerators before it, it will bring new environmental health concerns to an area that already has high rates of cancer, lung disease, and other ailments relating to industrial pollution.[43]

It is exciting to hear about the renewal of these environmental alliances, despite the depressing sense of déjà vu that such alliances are needed yet again. Given the fraught relations found among Southeast Chicago residents, I continue to ponder the obstacles to thinking of such activism in multiethnic terms. The historic tendency in Southeast Chicago for neighborhoods, blocks, and parks to be perceived as "owned" by particular ethnic groups remains strong, even as troubled economic realities as well as prejudice and fear continue to create tensions among those groups perceived as entering or being "pushed out" of the area.

In order to think clearly about the divisions that separate Southeast Chicago as well as what brings various groups together, we need to simultaneously acknowledge and differentiate both race and class—where their effects run parallel and intensify each other and where they operate along separate tracks, bumping up against each other and creating divergent crosscutting forms of inequality. As noted earlier, racial difference is often used as a substitute means for talking about class in the United States, through the symbolic equation of black skin with lower economic status, and white skin with middle-class status or higher. However, the conflation of race and class makes it difficult to understand either, as sociologist Julie Bettie has argued in *Women without Class*. Certainly, it makes it difficult to understand the complex patchworked realities of places like Southeast Chicago that have been characterized by multiple historic forms of overlapping inequality. The symbolic conflation of race and class also erases both middle-class blacks and poor and working-class whites from view. After all, given that when race and class are so tightly linked together conceptually, those who fall outside such conjoined categories easily become invisible.[44] As Julie Bettie has noted, academics regularly argue for the need to consider how race, class, and gender intersect, even though such categories are rarely given equal weight in practice. Instead, there is a tendency to emphasize one category or another, or to meld the categories into each other without considering when they might work differently.[45] In contrast, Bettie argues for the need to consider how race, class and gender come to be "coconstituted" in relation to the other. In other words, how is each formed in dynamic interaction with the other?

The view from the top of the Paxton II landfill underscores those cleavages that divide Southeast Chicago, yet it also makes clear how residents are bound together. While the landfills and industrial barriers heighten the social divides among neighborhoods, waste and pollution also unite the region in a common landscape that affects the bodies of all who lived there, even if in unequal ways.

## Gambling on a "New Economy"

Although the dominant free market narratives of recent decades suggest that the economy is best left to its own devices, there are no market solutions to the problem of vast toxic industrial brownfields in places like Southeast Chicago. The legal frameworks that regulate how environmentally contaminated land can be used as well as future liability, the costs of cleanup and health care for those whose health has been impacted, and political choices about how to tax businesses, individuals, and land all determine what happens or not to such spaces. The future does not unfold in an evolutionary fashion: it is inextricably linked to public decision making, whether or not its outcomes are always intended.

Although the future has been slow in arriving in Southeast Chicago, a few visions of what its postindustrial landscape might look like surfaced after the airport struggle of the early 1990s. My first glimpse of one such vision appeared on a visit to see my parents in Southeast Chicago in the mid-1990s. I was surprised to find an enormous, blinking neon sign rooted along Indianapolis Boulevard, the dividing line between Southeast Chicago and northwest Indiana that runs a few blocks away from my parent's house. The neon sign shouted the arrival of one of the few new industries to appear in the Calumet region since the demise of the steel industry: floating gambling casinos. Although approved by the Indiana state legislature and located on the Indiana side of the state line, the casinos have been directed toward Chicago residents, who, in large numbers, come speeding down the Skyway from the north. Casinos, a growing phenomenon in the United States in recent decades, have appeared in some old industrial areas and may be an option for land limited by toxicity concerns to restricted uses. Casinos are found not only along the lakefront in Indiana's former steeltowns of East Chicago and Gary, but also in places like the former site of Bethlehem Steel in Pennsylvania.

When my husband and I started working on our documentary about Southeast Chicago, we dubbed the film *Exit Zero* after the number for the exit ramp from the Chicago Skyway to Indianapolis Boulevard and to the steel mill neighborhoods below. It seemed like an appropriate commentary on the sense of being overlooked and forgotten that permeated the region in the wake of the collapse of the steel industry. Now Exit 0 also serves as the entrance to the Hammond casino and an adjoining lakefront marina built for suburbanites' pleasure boats. The exit ramp has now been widened and landscaped in a way that matches the glitz of the neon signs.

Although I was initially taken aback by the rapidity of changes along Indianapolis Boulevard, those of my parents' and grandparents' generations seemed less surprised. They had already witnessed large-scale changes there. When my parents were young, "the Boulevard" was lined with gas stations that catered to passengers fueling up before they crossed the state line, including the one where my father had a job at age sixteen. It was also known as an exciting place for entertainment. As kids, my parents and their friends would walk or take the bus to the Boulevard. They waxed nostalgic about the go-kart rides, donkey baseball games, women's softball leagues, and an ice cream parlor that lined the border in an effort to attract interstate traffic. "There was always something to do over there," my father wistfully recalled. The photograph in figure 21 shows the Chicago Skyway being built in 1956 during the period of urban renewal. It would bisect Southeast Chicago, ensuring that car traffic would pass high above the steel mill neighborhoods. The businesses below withered, except for a few local gas stations and cigarette stands geared to Chicago residents eager for Indiana's cheaper taxes.

Hammond's casino now dominates the Boulevard. Although the gambling boats are designed to be stationary and rarely leave the dock, the Hammond boat, in order to demonstrate conformity with Indiana law, must scuttle sideways out into Lake Michigan once a year to prove that it is seaworthy. When gamblers enter, the staff pretends it is for a "cruise." The "gangplank" is raised and customers are forbidden from exiting for a specified period of time. Despite the Hollywood images of gambling as suave high rollers out for enjoyment, the reality, of course, is very different. When I've been to the gambling boats in northwest Indiana, the slot machines have been packed with the elderly and poor of all races, including obese men and women in wheelchairs who are hooked to oxygen tanks. With slot players holding drinks in hand and haloed by cigarette smoke, the place gives off an air of multiple addictions. Most distressingly, it reeks to me of a desperate need for hope, for belief in the possibility that one's luck might change in a traumatic postindustrial economy or, at least, for a bit of excitement to offset a disappointing world. For me, visiting the boats brought back sad

21. Constructing the Skyway in 1958. Courtesy of the Southeast Chicago Historical Museum.

memories of a close relative of my father's who had spent time in prison and used to send us kids lottery tickets as Christmas presents from jail. Here, it seemed, was a similarly desperate need to dream. While the casinos promise an escape from the outside world in their glowing, neon-lit interior, somehow they manage only to intensify what it is so many people seem to be trying to escape from.

The outward flash of the casinos belies the risks and instabilities of what, during the 1990s, was touted as the new economy. In fact, residents of the Calumet region have had reason to debate whether the casinos have been a portent of new life or of further decay. Some, like the managers of the casino that we spoke with, emphasized the benefits that the casinos have brought to northwest Indiana in jobs and tax revenues to help compensate for the declining taxes paid by the remnants of Indiana's steel industry. Some of my extended family members and neighbors also like the casinos. A few enjoy playing the slots; others, particularly the elderly on fixed incomes, frequent the boats for the free breakfasts and subsidized food. Some have noted that the streets in Hammond don't have potholes for the first time in living memory because of taxes from the casinos. Others, however, are not so sure, noting that since the arrival of the casinos, many of the restaurants that had existed for generations in Whiting and Hammond have closed.

When I talked to my father about it, he signaled his skepticism with a story. While he was bullshitting with the owner of a hardware store in Whiting, the owner had told him about the problems he was having with long-term customers. Although many were living on fixed incomes, they were, according to him, gambling away their checks and no longer able to pay their bills. The owner worried about his store's ability to survive. Other neighbors muttered about whether it was right for priests to take busloads of the elderly from their churches to the gambling boats. One neighbor speculated conspiratorially that the priests were being paid off to do so. Others simply noted that the jobs from the casino "weren't doing anything for the people around here." These jobs were relatively few compared to the old steel industry and didn't offer anything like the pay, benefits, or way of life. The so-called new economy was no replacement for what had gone before.

The debates over the pros and cons of casinos in the Calumet region have not been limited to the Indiana side of the border. Since the demise of Southeast Chicago's steel mills, there have been suggestions at various times to turn Chicago's brownfields into gambling establishments. At one point, a casino was proposed for the old US Steel–South Works site, and more recently for the former Wisconsin Steel site where my father worked. During 2006, I followed the debates over the proposed Wisconsin Steel casino in the local newspaper. One woman stated that a casino was a great idea since the boats are "where half of South Deering goes anyway" and that a Chicago casino would bring people into the area. Instead of sending all the Chicago money over to Indiana, she argued, the money should be kept on this side of the state line. Another resident countered that "a casino probably hurts a community as much as it helps it because people gamble away their rent money" and argued for the industrial development of the site instead.[46] Although it seems increasingly likely that a Chicago-based casino would be located downtown rather than on the steel mill brownfields of Southeast Chicago, the mere possibility offers a graphic symbol of a changed economy. Like a Freudian dream in which the underlying message surfaces through economic rather than sexual symbolism, it suggests the extent to which the new-economy vision of the 1990s and beyond has been built on risk that cannibalizes rather than sustains communities. Although the high wages and good benefits historically associated with the steel industry were the product of protracted struggle, the end result was stable, even middle-class communities. The best new-economy future for this deindustrialized, working-class landscape has so far been skimming money from low-income people at slot machines to fix the potholes in northwest Indiana's streets.

## A New Environmentalism: From Brownfields to "Open Spaces"

The alternative, if as yet largely unrealized, public vision for this region is the one that environmentalist activists in Hegewisch and some of the surrounding areas have advocated for more than twenty years. In the 1990s, Chicago's mayor, Richard M. Daley, who once wanted to eradicate large sections of Southeast Chicago for a new airport, underwent a change of heart. As he settled into the role of long-serving mayor once held by his father, Daley developed a broad vision of making Chicago one of the "greenest" cities in America. His economic goals became linked to transforming this raw historically industrial city into an attractive, "livable," environmentally friendly, and gentrifying place desirable to middle-class professionals, both residents and visitors alike. That goal included opening up greater public space along the lakefront for both recreational and aesthetic purposes.[47] Visiting downtown Chicago now, I too am captivated by the stunning beauty of its revitalized lakefront, with its necklace of parks, museums, and public spaces.

Yet what is the place of old industrial areas of the city and their residents, within such a vision? Although city officials emphasized gentrification of the city during the booming real estate markets of the 1990s and first few years of the new century, there were also some efforts to attempt to attract new industry, a recognition of jobs lost and communities displaced by deindustrialization. At the same time, city officials sought to maintain the city's futuristic self-presentation by publicly advocating new environmentally clean industries, despite the uphill nature of such efforts.

The future of the city's brownfields, including Southeast Chicago's massive steel mill sites, have been tied to the legal strictures of superfund legislation. Passed in 1980, CERCLA, or the "Superfund" Act, offered landmark environmental legislation in the United States that rightly placed the costs of environmental cleanup on industrial polluters. However, it also inadvertently led many formerly industrial sites to fall into disuse, since companies were reluctant to pay these high costs and because purchasers were wary of incurring future legal liabilities. City officials and residents associated these empty, toxic spaces with urban blight and lost tax revenue and saw them as contributing to the downward economic spiral of old industrial neighborhoods. In response, Chicago initiated a Brownfield Initiative program in 1993, becoming an urban leader in rehabilitating old brownfield sites.[48] In the mid-1990s, President Bill Clinton also instituted a federal Brownfields Initiative that similarly lowered environmental cleanup standards, offered reduced legal liability, provided tax incentives to companies that would come in and reuse such sites, and distributed seed money to local and state governments for rehabilitation.

Most of these remediation efforts have happened in sites more centrally located within the city. Southeast Chicago's massive brownfields and interspersed wetlands have posed particular challenges as well as opportunities for planners. The new public vision for Southeast Chicago actually began with the same Calumet environmental activists who were once Mayor Daley's foes. In 1993, the year after the airport proposal was shelved, activists from Hegewisch and others parts of Southeast Chicago joined middle-class activists from the Calumet suburbs to propose turning parts of Southeast Chicago and northwest Indiana into what they called a Calumet "ecological park." One Hegewisch activist, the daughter of a steelworker who had worked in the offices of Republic Steel as a young woman, told me how her own views had been transformed during the course of the airport struggle. After becoming familiar with the environmentalist arguments being made against the airport, she came to realize the extent and richness of the wetlands left amid Southeast Chicago's industries—places she used to go fishing with her father and uncles as a child. For other working-class residents as well, the industrial wetlands were familiar places through long-term relationships based on hunting and fishing (see fig. 22).[49]

However, just as Hegewisch residents had earlier searched for endangered species to throw up legal roadblocks to save their homes, these newer efforts would similarly rework more mainstream environmentalist narratives for homegrown ends. Galvanized by the airport struggle, these Southeast Chicago activists pressed the city for a positive regional vision to offset the need to endlessly react against city proposals for uses like landfills that many residents opposed. Fighting for a "park" offered many lines of argument. It offered a way to contest the waste industry's desire to expand dumps and other noxious facilities by allowing residents to contend that such plans represented an "incompatible usage" with nature areas. And it offered a way to argue for cleaning up the old steel mill and waste sites in the hopes that new businesses, previously leery of legal environmental liabilities, might move into the region, creating jobs that would allow young people to stay in their communities rather than force them to move away in search of work and a better life. Although the activists' ambitious petition to designate the area a national park was denied by Congress, they succeeded in 1998 in having the Calumet region declared a "national heritage site."

The idea of extending parks throughout the Calumet has fit in with the concerns of middle-class conservationists as well as the vision of Mayor Daley and other city environmentalists who hoped to create a contiguous green

22. Fishing in Whiting's wetlands

space around the southern tip of Lake Michigan. It was envisioned that this green space would follow the perimeter of Chicago from the north, through the downtown parks, to the Southeast Side and finally extend through northwest Indiana to the Indiana Dunes just east of Gary. In 2000, a new land use plan devised by the city of Chicago for the Calumet region was unveiled. In response to the city's interests as well as pressure from local activists, it operated on two fronts. It called for turning three thousand acres of the Southeast Side into nature-protected areas (crucially helping residents argue against future dumping) as part of a Chicago Open Space Reserve.[50] And it also called for converting three thousand acres of brownfields to new industrial use, creating an industrial economic district with tax incentives in order to encourage new and cleaner industrial development in the region. Although how much of this vision would be translated into reality was unclear, for the first time since the loss of the mills, the city government had a positive vision for Southeast Chicago.

My husband and I came to know these community activist efforts well as we worked on the short video documentary for the Hegewisch environmental group. The video focused both on the history of the Calumet River and on the proposed ecological park. While middle-class suburban environmentalists that partnered with Southeast Chicago residents emphasized wetland preservation, local activists also maintained the need to focus on people and jobs and to underscore the rich historical as well as natural heritage of the old steel mill communities. Along with the Southeast Chicago Historical Society, they worked tirelessly to save the last standing large-scale steel industry structures in Southeast Chicago, located at the old Acme (formerly Interlake) steel mill site, before they were torn down or stolen by metal scavengers. Their goal was to create a steel heritage museum within the ecological park. At the 2006 screening of the video we made for the Hegewisch environmental group, a crowd of about a hundred community residents, including former steelworkers and their families, gathered at the old union hall near the Republic Steel site. They were visibly moved when the steel heritage museum idea was discussed. Nodding their heads, they murmured in agreement when well-known area labor leader Ed Sadlowski explained on screen that "[the museum] isn't about the steel industry, but about the people who built the steel. [Building a museum] is not too much to ask." With support from an area labor union, the activists successfully raised money to buy part of the property. However, they weren't able to secure funding to continue the payments, and the steel heritage museum idea died a few years later. Selling conservation goals to a middle-class public in other parts of the city was one thing, selling an interest in documenting working-class industrial history proved to be something else.

Although the desire to encourage new, cleaner industry in the region remains a heavily uphill battle, small steps have been taken. Given that cities are now regularly forced to lure industry with incentives, the city of Chicago had to compete fiercely to get the Ford company to build a new environmentally clean supplier park on a portion of the old Republic Steel site. Ford had long had a plant on Torrence between Hegewisch and South Deering. The new supplier park, completed nearby in 2004, created one thousand jobs, raising the credibility of activists among those Southeast Chicago residents still skeptical of environmental concerns. Ford also agreed to fund the restoration of wetlands around the supplier park as well as a Ford Environmental Center, designed by award-winning architects to celebrate the natural and cultural heritage of the area. Although such victories may seem small given the massive industrial scale of Southeast Chicago's history, they have been significant and hard won.

Nonetheless, it is necessary to stand back and consider whether such visions will have a lasting impact. Given the global pressures to search for cheaper wages elsewhere, will industry—and, particularly, cleaner industry—return to Southeast Chicago? And, if it does, will it be industry that pays decent wages and allows for a middle-class standard of living, as the steel industry had? Or will it be work that is so mechanized, like northwest Indiana's remaining steel industry or Southeast Chicago's own recently expanding container transport trade, that it is nearly devoid of workers? Will there be the kind of ties that bind that once linked industries and workers in ongoing relationships that were commonly depicted—whether cynically or hopefully—as familial ones? Or will such ties remain unraveled? And, if Southeast Chicago's environment is "remediated," who will ultimately benefit? Will it be local residents or, as some worry, more prosperous city residents looking for recreational opportunities and new lakefront properties? And what will be the effect of the recent economic downturn? Already construction of the Ford Environmental Center has been slowed to the point that it is unclear whether it will be built. Given that the real estate boom that helped revalue the industrial brownfields of Southeast Chicago as open spaces is over and that mayors have changed, will Chicago's city government remain committed to its new vision for Southeast Chicago? And, most crucially, if it does go forward, will local activists continue to have a voice in shaping the future that unfolds, or will the definition of this once industrial landscape be co-opted, as it often has in the past, by more powerful players?

As I put the finishing touches on this book, new plans are afoot for the brownfields of Southeast Chicago (even though it is still unclear whether they will materialize or disappear like so many previous plans). These plans illustrate two competing visions of what the future of Southeast Chicago might be. One is the aforementioned coal gasification plant approved for part of the former Republic Steel site and that continues the decades-long trend of seeing Southeast Chicago as an environmental dumping ground and one that carries the potential to damage residents' health. Although boosters call such developments "green" (in this case because the coal will be turned into cleaner-burning natural gas for use elsewhere), resident activists worry about the potential deceptive doublespeak implicit in such language. The other far more positive vision, and the one with community activist backing, is the vision of open space and environmental and economic rehabilitation in the Calumet, one that attempts to revitalize the area in a far more fundamental way.

Yet, the potential for the agendas of those other than residents to dominate even this more positive vision is, of course, always present. This is evi-

dent, for example, in both the hopes and worries for the slag-built promontory of the old US Steel–South Works. Because it did not have coking
operations, the six-hundred-acre US Steel–South Works site is less toxic
than Wisconsin Steel and other former steel brownfields in Southeast Chicago. At various points over the last twenty years, there has been speculation that the vacant South Works brownfield would become a casino, a
cup factory, a school, and a children's museum, among other ideas. The
site is now being envisioned as part of a "mixed-income" housing development complex complete with malls and a boat marina that developers call
"Lakeside."[51] Plans for Lakeside have perhaps gone further than the others.
Developers sought to raise the profile of the site in the summer of 2011 by
busing middle-class concertgoers onto a South Works site hastily cleared
of rubble for a concert by the Dave Matthews Band, introducing those who
may have never set foot in this part of the South Side to the stunning vistas of
downtown Chicago from this slag-built promontory.[52] Although many are
happy to hear of anything at all being built on the site, critics worry that the
Lakeside project may serve as a form of gentrification that will force out existing residents. On one visit home, I noticed hand-painted signs protesting
the real estate development near the South Works site. Others are skeptical
that anything will be built, pointing to Southeast Chicago's distance from
downtown and South Works' location next to the blown-out buildings and
poverty of South Chicago that must give even seasoned gentrifiers pause. I
myself wonder whether the attempts of brownfield programs to lessen environmental cleanup standards more generally will result in long-term environmental health impacts—ironically, increasingly a risk for better-off gentrifiers who inhabit old industrial loft spaces and converted industrial sites.[53]

Driving around Southeast Chicago as a child listening to my father's stories about the place that generations of my family called home, I would
never have envisioned the current barrenness of South Works, the mill that
had so frightened my Big Grandpa as a seventeen-year-old greenhorn immigrant. Nor, however, would I have envisioned the possibility of middle-class
professionals eager for breathtaking vistas of downtown Chicago buying
homes on a site where steel had been made for a century. What the Lakeside development vision shares, however, with the coal gasification plant
proposed for the old Republic Steel site is that both visions—one that continues to treat the region as a dump, the other that reenvisions it as an environmentally appealing space ripe for gentrification—is that both visions
place working-class people on the margins. In all the visions for the future
deemed possible for old industrial regions like Southeast Chicago, it is this
lack of space for working-class people that is perhaps the most telling.

## Other Ties That Bind

It was while standing on top of the Paxton II landfill with my husband in 2005 that I viewed the waters of Lake Calumet with the naked eye for the first time. Although only a short distance from my family's home and a defining geographic feature of the region, this fenced-off body of water is without public access and entirely hidden from view for those on the ground. From our vantage point on top of the landfill that day, I could see the large section of Lake Calumet that had been filled in with municipal garbage by the city and then turned into a golf course during the 1980s largely for the use of well-off tourists.[54] I could see the Calumet River to the east, coiling past the remains of industry strewn along both its banks. I could look out over the barren stretches of what had been Republic, Wisconsin, Interlake, Iroquois, and US Steel in the spaces between the old mill neighborhoods of South Chicago, the East Side, Hegewisch, and South Deering as well as Altgeld Gardens. I could see the dusky red of the coal-burning State Line Power Plant lining the hazy blue waters of Lake Michigan as well as the now empty site of the old Falstaff brewery towers, where my mother used to bring her grandfather, Hans Hansen, his lunch in a bucket. Standing there, I took in visually for the first time the full expanse of the land of my childhood—both beautiful and deadly, breathtaking in both its industrial and natural scope, linked and deeply divided.

Today, many area residents ruefully note that Southeast Chicago is "cleaner than it's ever been." Despite the ongoing pollution risks posed by the remaining waste and industry and by the now capped landfills, the loss of the steel mills has meant cleaner air and water than those of us who grew up in the area ever knew. The ruefulness stems from the fact that this cleaner environment has come at the price of so many jobs, hopes, and lives. Not only has the devaluation of the landscape at times been symbolically transferred to those who live there, but residents have also sometimes been held personally accountable. At a family party a few years before my father died, my cousin's school-age son asked my father whether he had worked in the steel mills. When my father answered, yes, the boy began lecturing my father on how dirty the steel mills had been, an environmental lesson presumably learned at school. The thrust of his critique, however, was directed against my father, who was somehow held to blame for the pollution of an industry. Even adults from other parts of the city who are pleased to see a cleaner environment in the Calumet region similarly fail to acknowledge what the steel mills offered apart from the pollution. I remember the hurt look on my father's face that the industrial way of life that had defined his and his parents' generations could be so easily dismissed, not only as obsolete, but as something destructive rather than generative of a valued social world. On that occasion, my father, once again, retreated into the silence that ensued whenever it became too difficult to counter the more dominant narratives that swirled so tightly around us.

Despite the cleaner environment, I strongly suspect that many Southeast Chicago residents, like my father, would never have wanted to pay the price exacted by the loss of the steel mills. Yet, if those of us who lived there when I was growing up had been aware of the health costs of living in the midst of so many pollutants, would we have wanted to pay that price either? The key question, of course, is why this dilemma is still often viewed as a choice: that working-class people can either have jobs that harm their health and that of their families or a healthier environment without jobs. Making it seem like a choice makes it appear to be a pitched battle between those who suffer from job losses and those who have been sickened, when in fact, as my own family is intimately aware, we are often the same people. Although some of my academic colleagues might argue that the concept of "sustainable de-velopment" has been so co-opted by powerful interests as to become devoid of meaning, I would argue that it *can* retain a critical edge, even if only as a reminder that people like those who live in Southeast Chicago should not have to choose between healthy environments and their jobs.

My mother tells me that, in the end, we must all move on. The plans to obliterate large sections of Southeast Chicago for an airport have long ago been shelved, and the area itself has been trying to move on in its own un-certain fashion. Yet the environmental questions at the core of the airport and landfill debates remain and underscore the fact that moving on requires a reckoning with this past and with the ongoing linkages among industry, landfills, and bodies found across this landscape. The toxic realities etched in the landscape of this place are eloquent, not only about individual bod-ies, but about the divisions of inequality that have disproportionately af-fected Southeast Chicago's residents. Such divisions appear in the industrial histories of how toxic pollution came to be located in this area, the kinds of jobs people depended upon that disproportionately exposed them and their families, and the economic constraints (as well as positive pull of family and neighborhood) that has kept them living in heavily polluted regions. Just as exposure to pollutants both divides and connects area residents, so too the industrial pollution that exists in the air and water of Southeast Chicago both differentiates this region and links it to places beyond. Acknowledging these kinds of ties that bind means directing our gaze not only within, but also beyond Southeast Chicago.

Looking out beyond Southeast Chicago means recognizing the role that social class has played in these kinds of environmental debates: whether in the ways that contemporary brownfield landscapes and their residents have been dismissed as evolutionary throwbacks to an earlier industrial era or in the bitter dilemma of positing false choices between jobs and health.[55] It means acknowledging how the devaluation of such landscapes has blended together with the devaluation of working-class lives implicit in how de-industrialization was allowed to play out. And it means recognizing the lack of a place for working-class Americans in new-economy visions of a future. Although the positive and appealing environmentally green open-spaces vision being developed for Southeast Chicago is crucial in helping move beyond this kind of jobs-versus-environment debate and in seeing such postindustrial landscapes as part of a future, even here the attempts to improve working-class lives are forced to do so indirectly, via a city-wide orientation toward the recreational interests and economic clout of better-off downtown residents or middle-class suburbanites. In the end, area activists are left to keep pushing forward, negotiating such pressures as best they may. Standing back and taking stock, I would argue, means reckoning with such realities and how working-class communities are being forced to try to move forward in a national context in which their lives are now rarely depicted as part of the larger picture.

Although I have for the time being safely weathered my own health concerns, the history of toxic pollution in this region remains not only part of the landscape, but also part of my body. The permeability of our bodies underscores that there is a kind of materiality to class that is rarely fully acknowledged and that remains with us, just as our class backgrounds remain part of who we are even when our lives appear to move in different directions. Just as the toxic legacy of the former steel mills continues to shape the future of the Calumet region, the bodily legacy of my class background has continued to shape my own. When I was growing up in Southeast Chicago, family ties were always considered to be the most important kind of ties that bind. Yet the way in which my own body came to be bound up with the landscape of Southeast Chicago also meant its biological inability to produce future generations of our family. As I pondered the lives of my grandparents and great-grandparents in the years after my experience with cancer, I was left to wonder to whom I would bequeath my own family stories. It is to these other kinds of generational ties that bind that I must return to in the end.

# From the Grave to the Cradle

Although a large part of my father died with the steel mills, his physical death came in 2005, twenty-five years after Wisconsin Steel abruptly expelled its workers. His death not only marked a passage of generations within my own family—my son would have no firsthand experience of his grandfather—it also marked a change of generations in societal terms. Those like my father, who had come to adulthood anticipating the promises of an expanding middle class rather than the expanding social inequalities of the late twentieth and early twenty-first centuries, seemed increasingly like dinosaurs on the verge of disappearing.

The neighborhoods through which my father and I took leisurely drives when I was a child became very different in the years preceding and following my father's death. Amid the toxic brownfields where the old steel mills once stood remain the increasingly run-down wooden clapboard houses and brick bungalows of former steelworking families. In an analysis of novels examining the lives of the "next generation" of those born into already deindustrialized landscapes, Sherry Lee Linkon has asked: what is the half-life of deindustrialization?[1] It is a question worth asking of Southeast Chicago as well.

In the 1980s, after the closure of most of Southeast Chicago's mills, the impact of deindustrialization took a particular form in the region. The stories of friends' parents and neighbors all seemed to be variations on a collective theme. Such stories were about the loss of jobs, cars, homes, and dreams and, perhaps most insidiously, an intangible but deeply felt loss of a sense of what could be counted upon in the world. In these early years, some people moved away in search of work; many others, like my own family, stayed. Just as for previous generations, long-standing social ties among family and friends were what people continued to depend upon in times of hardship. This was not something easily given up, even though the stresses of unemployment and bitterness often tested such relationships.[2]

In the decades since then, the longer-term impacts of deindustrialization have become more discernable. I see it in the way that the lives of those I have known since childhood have increasingly split apart. Such changes are also apparent within my own family. Some of my cousins on my father's side have been thrown back into hard-core poverty, living in trailers, trying to make do while limited to minimum wage jobs or the informal economy. In contrast, some of my cousins on my mother's side have managed to move away to the nearby suburbs. A few have used positions as skilled laborers to move up to jobs increasingly dependent on computer technology; another went back to college and is now a businessman. On both sides of the family, single and divorced women raising kids remain the most vulnerable. For all of them, however, there is a greater sense of precariousness than my parents' generation experienced. Jobs in the new economy are no longer for life, and the health care and housing costs that skyrocketed with the start of a new millennium put pressure on middle class, working class, and poor alike. Indeed, heightened risk has underlain both the expanding dreams of some and the diminishing expectations of others.[3]

Such trends extend far beyond my own family. In a context in which education is now the only clear route to upward mobility in the United States, some on the Southeast Side who might have entered the mills out of high school or become homemakers in years past have decided to continue their education. Those individuals who benefited from attending Catholic schools rather than the troubled local public ones have had an extra boost in this direction. Others have managed to find working-class jobs—albeit often at lower pay and with fewer benefits and less security—in other regions. Those with the ability to make such choices—many of them white—have often moved away from Chicago's old mill neighborhoods, contributing to a process often glossed as "white flight," a phrase that downplays the economic factors interwoven with racial ones. Many, like some of my cousins, have moved to the working- and lower-middle-class suburbs outside Chicago or across the state line in Indiana and have constituted new communities built upon the social networks forged in the old steel mill neighborhoods.[4]

During visits over the years to the East Side, where my mother and sister still live, I see that those who remain include both the most economically vulnerable and some of the more stable and middle class. Among the more stable have been elderly pensioners who remain tied to the mill neighborhoods through the homes they own, the lives they have built, and the memories that they are loath to leave behind. Despite the pressures of contracting retiree benefits and high health care costs, they—and often their families—continue to be sustained, at least in part, by the pensions earned from the steel mills. They are, however, a dying breed, even more than when I started writing this book. The most middle class are the cops and firefighters who form the old elite of the mill neighborhoods. Unionized, paid by the city, and possessing stable benefits, they hold jobs that tie them to city boundaries. For many women, it is jobs in the health care sector that have been the most stable.[5]

Many of the younger generation who remain in Southeast Chicago, however, are in much more vulnerable positions. In some ways, they are lucky compared to those living in other parts of the so-called rust belt—the small industrial towns in places like Pennsylvania, Ohio, and Michigan or cities like Detroit and Cleveland. As a formerly industrial region, Southeast Chicago has weathered these economic changes better than many places. The fact that Southeast Chicago is within the limits of a still dynamic city has prevented the collapse of school districts or municipal services, as has happened in some small formerly industrial towns. Some Southeast Side residents, like my younger sister, have managed to find commuter jobs in downtown Chicago, and a few more prosperous parts of the old mill neighborhoods now serve as bedroom communities for individuals working in the Loop. Nevertheless, most Southeast Chicago residents have been relegated to the few, increasingly unstable, industrial jobs that remain, the local service economy, the informal economy, and, in some parts of Southeast Chicago, the drug economy. Except for the latter, all options (including the office jobs downtown) are more poorly paid and more uncertain than the unionized steel mill jobs that were lost. In such a context, people make do with whatever work is to be had and depend heavily upon families. In a throwback to an earlier period, women find themselves having to work for wages whether they wish to or not and shouldering more of the burden of providing for families. Multiple wage earners, extended family support, and grandparents with pensions and time to care for kids have all become crucial, not only for aspirations for a middle-class life, but for day-to-day survival.

The loss of the steel industry has also meant a fundamental shift in what it means to be an immigrant in Southeast Chicago. Newer immigrants, most with origins in Mexico, have arrived in large numbers in the area in recent decades. Many have settled on the East Side, the largest community in Southeast Chicago and once a dominantly white ethnic neighborhood. This has been the first wave of immigration not drawn by work in the steel mills. The United States that these immigrants find is one deeply shaped by the loss of heavy-industry jobs, including jobs that have left for lower-wage parts of the world (including, ironically, Mexico).[6] While ethnic tensions have a long history in Southeast Chicago, those between long-term residents today and newer Mexican immigrants carry a profound irony. After all, it is the same forces shorthanded as globalization that have led many in these groups to become neighbors in the first place. The free market trends of the 1980s and 1990s, including trade agreements like NAFTA, contributed to the economic dislocations in rural areas of Mexico that pushed many into immigration.[7] The US corporate shift away from production and heavy industry to more lucrative ways of making profits in the worlds of high finance or sunrise enterprises has simply been another side of these same forces.

In other ways, however, contemporary dynamics carry strong parallels with those of the past. Just as the early steel industry pitted groups of workers against each other, so too the "race to the bottom" for those holding the lower-end jobs of contemporary capitalism continues to create competition among ethnic groups. Now, however, it happens through the expansion of the informal economy as well as low-wage work that targets new immigrants and that further destabilizes the shifting sands under the remaining working class.[8] The main difference is that now there are fewer routes for one group to be converted into the other and for both to be transformed into America's middle class.

In short, the old patterns of urban ethnic tension and "succession" identified long ago by University of Chicago sociologists continue. However, such trends carry a new poignancy. Perhaps it is the sense of quiet desperation at work, as some cling to the middle-class status that continues to slip away while others try to gain access to it. Although some new brick bungalows came to fringe parts of the East Side during the 1990s, such limited pockets of ongoing middle-class prosperity have failed to counteract the overall economic decline. At the same time, there are fewer countervailing forces or experiences to bind these disparate groups of residents together. Although the steel industry of the past exploited and exacerbated divisions among ethnic groups, it also forced them to work together and "get along in the mills," as some people I knew put it, "whether they liked it or not." Now, few common experiences create a sense of mutual recognition across the divides. There is a fragmentation of experience and also, for those who remember the old neighborhoods, a disconcerting fragmentation of community. While ethnic tensions reveal these economic and social fault lines, they fail to explicate the processes that got us, as a country, into such a position.

Among those affected by deindustrialization in Chicago, African-Americans have been hardest hit. Some African-American women (like their white counterparts) have found employment possibilities in professions such as health care even as others have been relegated to poorly paid service or clerical jobs. For men and boys the loss of employment in heavy industry has meant that even the hope of finding rungs up the economic ladder in a society long riven by racism has too often been dashed.[9] During the 1990s, such realities contributed to the appeal of gang-organized drug economies that ripped apart portions of the old mill neighborhoods once known to sociologists for their safety and stability.[10] In some places, such transformations have simply left voids in their wake. A drive through the largely African-American parts of South Chicago that border the old US Steel–South Works site reveals only a few lonely dilapidated frame houses and brick bungalows left in a sea of vacant lots where houses once stood. With the loss of jobs and housing stock, there is an odd sense of depopulation in the midst of a city—a phenomenon found even more intensely in Detroit and some other deindustrialized regions. In the latest census, Chicago reported a declining African-American population, as blacks, like whites, followed jobs to the working-class suburbs ringing Chicago, while others headed south in search of jobs, a reversal of the Great Migration that brought an earlier generation of African-Americans north to work in industry.[11]

As deindustrialization expanded across the country in the 1980s and 1990s, some observers dismissively depicted the loss of heavy-industry jobs as primarily a problem for white men. Such views, however, ignored the sizable number of women who worked in auto and other industries as well as how the loss of industrial jobs for male family members placed additional, often unwelcome, pressures and responsibilities on women relegated to lower-paying jobs. These ideas also ignored the fact that more than half of urban blue-collar African-Americans in the late 1960s *were* employed in manufacturing.[12] Although blacks were discriminated against for the better steel mill jobs until the 1970s, such jobs, nonetheless, provided a strong economic anchor for many African-Americans.[13] A recent survey article notes that deindustrialization in Chicago has encouraged an overall shift toward nonunionized and informal labor as well as an increase in the outsourcing of manufacturing jobs to "temporary" workers, trends that have undermined wages for all laborers. Once again, they note that African-Americans have suffered the largest overall loss of income as a result.[14]

Although the mills of Southeast Chicago could be a harsh working world, there remains much to be mourned in their loss. In the past, after all, the mills and mill neighborhoods served as a crucible that brought together individuals and families of diverse backgrounds and, over time, collectively pointed them in a direction of greater economic prosperity. In the end, however, the belief that the future would necessarily be one of progress and increasingly common prosperity—an assumption taken as gospel by my parents' generation—has proven as transitory as the steel mills that we once thought were permanent. The loss of heavy industry has become a powerful contributor to the expanding social divides that increasingly rend US society as a whole. Given that higher levels of formal education will remain an unattainable or distant possibility for many (how could it be otherwise, given the troubled school systems in so many poor and working-class areas and rising college tuition costs?), the path of upward mobility has now been shut off for many Americans. The fallout of losing a central rung of the ladder of the American dream will be one that continues to haunt the United States for years to come. The half-life of deindustrialization in Southeast Chicago and beyond is yet to be determined.

## Coming Full Circle

My father's death in 2005 was a hard one. It was hard for him and hard for those who loved him. In the same hospital where I had undergone treatment a decade earlier, he was diagnosed with lung cancer. His illness was the product of years of smoking, compounded, I suspect, by years of breathing carcinogenic steel mill emissions.[15] Wasted by the spreading cancer in his body, he would eventually be reduced to skin and bones. There were some better days in those final months in 2004, when under a pain-medication-induced haze of good cheer he talked and even joked with an ease that he hadn't shown in years. These are memories I will cherish: my father laughing and telling the familiar stories of getting into the fight in the German bar or getting his tattoo in downtown Chicago with his buddy. Sometimes, in moments when he was more lucid, he spoke about class inequalities (although he wouldn't have called them that) and did so in ways that extended beyond the racial cleavages of Southeast Chicago that so dominated his thinking at other times. In particular, he obsessed about an African-American couple from the South Side whom he had witnessed in the hospital. The wife had been forced to leave because she couldn't afford the medical care. How could it be, he demanded of anyone willing to listen—his doctors, nurses, and the friends and relatives who came to visit in his last days—that something like this could happen in a country so rich? This incident seemed to crystallize for him all the larger forces he railed against yet could not articulate, and, in his final weeks, our conversations kept returning to this unjust paradox.

Although I prefer to linger on memories of his better days, there were also excruciating moments when the paroxysms of pain hit. These moments would be followed by the frantic efforts of myself, my sisters, and my mother to beg, cajole, or bully him into taking pain medication, which, in his increasing confusion, he came to believe caused rather than alleviated his pain. In his final weeks, his death began to merge in his mind with that of his mother, who had died when he was barely more than a teenager. It wasn't simply that he recalled the nurses who, more than fifty years prior, had come to drain saliva from her mouth as she lay in a coma after a cerebral hemorrhage—an event he had never before talked about. Instead, he appeared to be reliving that time, unclear about which body—his or his mother's—he was experiencing. In these surreal moments, time collapsed and his final days merged with hers.

During his last weeks, I left Chicago for a few days to visit my husband in New York. When I returned to my family's house in Southeast Chicago, my father, now under hospice care, appeared palpably relieved that I had returned, although he could no longer speak. My older sister expressed it well: "He can rest now, knowing that we're all safe at home." The worries of a father, battling to care for those he loved in a world over which he felt little control, remained foremost in his mind until the end. My younger sister and I were taking our turns keeping watch by his bedside when the death rattle began in his throat. When he expelled his final breath, I was holding his gaunt, gray hand tightly in my own. Death, it turned out, was nothing like Hollywood movies. I was suddenly grateful for having read nineteenth-century novels, written in a time when Europeans had a more intimate experience of death and which spoke of the spirit leaving the body in an enormous sigh. Recalling such words offered an odd sense of comfort and a feeling of connection to people in very different times and places. Although the buildup toward death may be heavily marked by class, in its last moments, it is, after all, one experience that transcends it.

In the few years that have passed since my father's death, I have become middle class in another way. Long ago, through the education I had acquired, I had become middle class in social and cultural terms—a painful transition, yet one I had (mostly) assimilated. However, in financial terms, I had continued to live on familiar terrain as a graduate teaching assistant and young assistant professor. In fact, my relatives found it hard to fathom why someone with so much education should live without a car or in such tiny apartments. When I earned tenure at my university the year after my father died, I was sorry I couldn't share the news with him. He wouldn't have cared that it was at a good school—such status seeking was part of a world of middle-class competition that he neither cared for nor understood the rules of. Nevertheless, knowing that I had a secure job would have comforted a piece of his soul. In the ensuing years, my husband found work in Boston, and we stopped long years of commuting between there and New York City. With university housing benefits, we bought a middle-class home in Cambridge. It was part of an old Victorian house with just enough scruffiness to give it character. We loved our half of the house and painted, cleaned, and began fixing things up bit by bit. But I was glad my father never saw it. A short distance away from the well-tended colonial homes and Victorian mansions of Cambridge's elite, the house would have made him uncomfortable. He would not have known why it was "necessary" to have a dangerous fireplace, strange folk art on the walls, or so much space. What really would have bothered him was my having a home in which he felt he didn't belong: a physical reminder of the rupture and the distance that had accumulated between my life and his.

In my first year in our new home—and for the first time in my life—I would periodically awake with panic attacks in the night or lie awake unable to calm an indescribable sinking feeling. There was a profound feeling of being unsettled, as if I had lost my moorings. My self-identity as someone who was working class—with the attendant resentments that entailed—was part of my being. I still felt bitter toward those faceless people who had sent my father's mill into foreclosure, who made economic decisions so callously, and who had taught me to distrust money, capitalism, and the powerful. But now I wondered whether in becoming middle class I had become part of what I had resented. Beneath the indescribable sinking feeling was a profound sense of guilt. Had I finally left my father behind? Now that he was dead and now that I could no longer deny my middle-class existence, was the world in which I was raised—a world I kept a piece of in my heart, cherishing it even when I fought against it—finally lost to me? The old ethical questions I had struggled with in previous years returned: By what right did some live better-off lives than others? By what right should I? The middle-class mantra that such differences were deserved and based on hard work I knew to be, as my father might have said, bullshit. Hard labor, as any working person knows, does not mean equal rewards in this world. My husband gently and justly chided me: But why should you live as if you don't deserve anything? Are you going to deliberately refuse to have a middle-class life just to spite yourself? The underlying fears that I had been suppressing eventually surfaced in my consciousness: But what if I started to believe that I *deserved* this? Would I then become someone else? Would this be the final betrayal of my father—the one he had feared when I left for Exeter? Would I rupture our lives in such a way that I would come to judge his life as a poorer one, not in money, but in spirit?

In thinking back over my father's life, it is clear that not all his troubles stemmed from the closing of the steel mills. Some of the scars he carried came from family; others were class-related scars that preceded the shutdowns. Even when I was a young child, his anxieties were often projected onto our family home. When things broke around the house, he flew into rages, terrified that his world was spinning out of control. Yet he felt too incapable to try to fix them, a damning indictment in a working-class world in which a man's ability to care for a home was often read as a proxy for his ability to care for a family. When the plumbing in our upstairs tub broke, my father perceived asking someone else to repair it as an insult to his manhood. The tub remained unused for a decade, even as other parts of the house crumbled around us. It was the shutdown of the mills, however, that split open the cracks in his defenses and exposed his vulnerabilities. When I was young (I cannot remember whether it was before or after Wisconsin Steel shut down), I had a dream in which I was attacked by wolves that I desperately tried to fight off with a stick. I saw my dad behind me and called to him for help. I turned to see that my father, after offering a sad and sheepish smile, had disappeared. It was not because he didn't want to help, but because he didn't have the strength or self-possession to do so. I continued to battle the wolves on my own and managed to beat them off. However, my satisfaction was overwhelmed by a sinking feeling of being left utterly on my own. Despite the fact that this dream haunted me for years afterward, I avoided its all-too-clear meaning. Although my father loved me, I didn't want to acknowledge that I felt betrayed that he hadn't been able to be the protective father figure our society expects. One of the injustices of class is how hard it is for those with limited resources and scarred by difficult lives to be the kinds of parents others (and they themselves and their kids) desire them to be.

In the inner places of my psyche, I also wondered whether somehow I had betrayed him by choosing to lead a life he could not follow. Had *I* abandoned *him*? I recall a mundane but telling incident in the months before he died. In order to help out while he was undergoing chemotherapy, my husband and I periodically stayed on the East Side a few blocks from my parents in an empty upstairs apartment over the house of one of my mom's friends. One afternoon, on a rare occasion when my father was feeling well enough, he visited us in the upstairs apartment instead of waiting for us to come to him. There was an air of peaceful contentedness about him as he sat drinking tea, eating sugar cookies, and bullshitting about the state of the world. Although he would never have said so, I know that, ultimately, this was all that he had really wanted from me in life: for me to lead an existence of which he could be a part, perhaps to offer a welcoming home nearby that could offer a peaceful respite from the squabbles at his own, and to sit quietly together and enjoy each other's company as father and daughter. I sympathize with both our plights: my father, haunted by his own demons, had not been able to give me what I needed as child, nor could I, compelled to run away in what felt like an effort to save myself, give him what he most wished for from me. The hollow narratives told about upward mobility in the United States speak nothing of the pain of such dilemmas. It was only when I began searching out the accounts of other working-class people who had "moved up" that I discovered similar kinds of stories told by individuals with the same need to salve souls rubbed raw by such experiences.

In the months of finishing an early draft of this book, I again began pondering the scars on my abdomen and the missing reproductive organs that marked my body with its origins in Southeast Chicago and the toxic legacy it encompassed. My husband and I would shortly fly to Vietnam to adopt and to bring home a child. My father's grandchild will never know him although he carries his name "Charles" as a middle name (a name shared by both my father and my husband's father). Just as I imagine my son will ponder the lives and struggles of unknown relatives in a distant country, he may also wonder about a grandfather in the United States he never knew. At least in this case, however, he will have stories and video clips to reflect upon, much as I have had my great-grandfather's memoir, "The Strugle for Existence from the Cradle to the Grave." What, I wonder, will be the narratives—and counternarratives—that my son will draw upon and tell as he ages? Although my husband and I have created a new home for him and for ourselves in New England, what expanded meanings might "home" take on for our child? Will he feel compelled to follow the strands that link him both through people and his own dreams to the rice fields and bustling towns of the Mekong Delta, to my husband's family farm in Wisconsin, or to the dead steel mills of Southeast Chicago? Are these places even as far apart as we imagine? Sitting in a hotel room in Ho Chi Minh City (once Saigon), I read in the business newspapers left at our hotel door about Vietnam's own rapidly expanding steel industry—a product of the economic currents at work in Asia and the shift in steel production to the "developing" world. When we go back to visit Vietnam with our son in future years, will these new mills have created communities like those found in Southeast Chicago or will they have already moved on to other locations with even lower wages, leaving similar spirals of destruction in their wake?

The web of ties that bind me to Southeast Chicago also expand outward, linking me to different times and places: to the relatives in Sweden from which my great-grandfather emigrated and with whom my grandmother corresponded her entire life, to the farms and coal mines in southern Illinois where my Little Grandpa was raised, and to the factories of Bohemia in Central Europe from which my father's mother's family hailed. Similarly, through Southeast Chicago, I am linked to the distant offices of those steel magnates and corporate leaders who made decisions that so affected our lives, to the tractors and buildings worldwide forged from steel made with the labor of family members, and to the waste generated around the city of Chicago that seeped through the landscape of the Southeast Side and into my own body.

My son will be similarly bound by a web of connections that lead outward across time and place. I was struck by this the first time my husband and I brought him home to my mother's house in Chicago. As an energetic and rakishly charming little boy of eighteen months, he claimed the house I grew up in as if he had also lived there forever. Squealing with delight, he played with the carved wooden cars and planes that my dad once collected beneath an announcement proudly pinned to a bulletin board which declared him to be the youngest member of my mother's Swedish Lodge. When I introduced our child to a friend of our next-door neighbor Ruben, more troubling links between seemingly distant peoples and places quickly surfaced. As we spoke across the chain-link fences that separated our backyards, Ruben's friend was unable to disguise a momentary look of pain when we described our son's origins. From the worn, scruffy military fatigues that he wore in countercultural sixties style on a hot summer day, my husband and I had already guessed that he was a Vietnam vet. Despite his look of pain, however, he gently touched our son's hand through the chain link fence. Then he started to talk about the war and how he and his other teenage friends in South Chicago had unsuccessfully tried to beat the draft by rubbing lead on their chests (acting upon false rumors that it would cause mass-like markings on lung x-rays). In the end, he had wound up a marine commando in Danang and Cambodia. He told us how terrible the war was and how he had been wounded three times. He said he knew thirty-six young guys, fellow Mexican-Americans from South Chicago, who had died in Vietnam. In a war fought on the American side largely through the bodies of the working class, Southeast Chicago had suffered in disproportionate numbers; the Mexican-American community even more so. Although we do not know on which side of the war my son's relatives fought or sympathized, our familial and neighborly bonds tie us to the suffering of all those "in-laws," both known and imagined, across a distant ocean as well as across the chain-link fences of Southeast Chicago.

23. A Vietnam War memorial mural in South Chicago. Courtesy of the Southeast Chicago Historical Museum.

I also contemplate the kind of toxic environmental legacies that shaped my own experience and wonder about the possibility of far more dramatic experiences among my son's relatives and compatriots. I do not only mean the impact of dioxin-releasing Agent Orange that was sprayed across the Mekong Delta, affecting both residents and soldiers and depicted visually in the Vietnam War memorial mural near South Chicago's Our Lady of Guadalupe Church and shown in figure 23. I also mean the subtler effects of pollution resulting from the unfolding industrial capitalism now found in Vietnam, just as once occurred in a dynamic early Southeast Chicago. Just as health came to be subordinated to the rhythms of economic expansion in the old steel neighborhoods, so too the exploding economic production in Vietnam in recent years has created waves of pollution in Vietnam's cities and countryside, as largely unregulated agricultural and industrial chemicals seep into the land, water, and food supply. Does my son carry a toxic load in his tissues much as I carry one in mine? Is his body also linked in this unacknowledged way to the place that birthed him, a product of class differentiation on an international scale and a state-socialist version of the kind of unfettered capitalist expansion that marked the history of Southeast Chicago? Just as my great-grandfather's life and those of many other immigrants to these steel mill communities had generated stories that linked far-flung geographic regions, so too will the stories of our family's subsequent generations.

As I ponder these links across space and time, I am brought back to my connection with my Big Grandpa and his memoir, "The Strugle for Existence from the Cradle to the Grave," which he so painstakingly typed at the end of his life. Like him, I too have felt compelled to write this account of my life in Southeast Chicago. Many of the reasons are personal. Southeast Chicago remains a place to which I am tied. It is a place that I both loved and hated growing up, that I identified with and was estranged from, that I felt trapped by but also valued for the dense network of social relationships that bound together those I knew and that gave meaning to our lives. Just as I imagine my great-grandfather seeking to make sense of the disjunctures of an immigrant's life, I too have experienced writing this account as an attempt to make sense of, and come to peace with, the disjunctures that my own life trajectory has created with family, friends, and former neighbors, and even within myself. Writing this book has allowed a conversation between the two sides of me, the daughter of a steelworking family and the middle-class academic, in a way intended to heal the ruptures between them by valuing the perspectives of each.

Yet, as I argued at the beginning of this book, such personal desires cannot be separated from the broader social dynamics of which they are a part. Writing this "autoethnography" has allowed me more than a chance to combine what I have learned as a social scientist with what I remember, thought, and felt as a working-class kid growing up on the Southeast Side of Chicago. It has encouraged me to ponder how experiences of social class are embodied as I have dragged my own class experiences with me, in my psyche, my habits, and in the molecules of my body, as my life has moved across different social and economic terrains. It has provided a chance to consider how the stories of those I grew up among failed to fit with hegemonic accounts of immigration, labor, deindustrialization, and upward mobility, suggesting alternative understandings in the process. It has allowed me a chance to express stories that have demanded love, anger, and analysis in the telling.

This book is not simply a personal account, but one that asks larger questions that force a confrontation with an issue—class—that has alternately troubled and been avoided by observers in the United States for many years. As described in this book, references to class both permeated and were regularly evaded in the world of Southeast Chicago in which I grew up. The language of the "little guy" versus the management "big shots" (already oversimplified) that dominated the masculinized and unionized workplace of the steel mills did not necessarily carry over to the rest of our lives, particularly at a time when many residents desired to move to the center of American life rather than struggle eternally from the outside. It was this lack of a language of class that made it difficult for me to convey things that I desperately wanted to communicate as I came to move between seemingly disparate class worlds.

In the early years of a new millennium, it is hard to avoid the conclusion that we are long overdue for a national reckoning with ideas of class in the United States. Since the time when Wisconsin Steel shut down more than thirty years ago, the country has undergone a profound transformation in which once contracting levels of inequality have undergone a striking expansion as a more aggressive style of capitalism has come to the fore. During this period, the goal of security that was so important to the post–World War II generation was reenvisioned as a drag on innovation, and the massive loss of jobs and the dislocations found in places like Southeast Chicago no longer raised eyebrows but have come to be taken as the norm.

Over these decades, speaking about social class in the United States has been made more difficult by a conservative reworking of populism that has claimed to valorize "working Americans" while simultaneously denying the socioeconomic realities of class and the costs of this newly aggressive capitalism.[16] In the hands of conservatives, this brand of populism has used class resentments not to draw attention to but to distract attention away from class. Over the ensuing years, the amorphous rage linked to the loss of an economic rung of the social ladder has been cynically deflected onto other topics, including race and "family values," in a way that has evaded asking ethical and moral questions about who has benefited and who has been hurt by the new economy. This short-circuiting of public debate has made it difficult both to understand and to remedy the root causes of growing class inequality. Without a concept of class capable of making sense of such economic realities, understandable resentments have fostered a rage bereft of analysis and one that is unable to change the world it rails against because it cannot speak about itself.

Examining the causes and impacts of deindustrialization requires an understanding of class that addresses such inequalities rather than serves as a smokescreen that distracts attention from them. Deindustrialization has been allowed to undermine the American dream in a way that is not easily repaired and that has contributed in profound ways to the spiraling inequality in which the country has found itself. The stories of what happened in places like Southeast Chicago and to people like my father have been at the center

24. My father, Charles Walley, on the Chicago lakefront

of this national transformation. Although the social and economic fallout of the changing class landscape of the United States has become even more apparent in the ongoing aftermath of the 2008 financial crisis, and despite a rising tide of popular discontent and a flood of books attempting to redefine what the United States has lost over the past decades,[17] it is unclear how deep such a revaluation will be. It is evident, however, that powerful interests would prefer to avoid such rethinking. This is apparent in how the new nemesis of free market conservatives has become public unions—teachers and public workers—one of the few holdout spaces where working people can continue to find stability and a bulwark against the growing tides of insecurity.

In this sense, the need for a language of class that "fits" is a societal one. Yet what kind of concept of class would this be? Historically, social classes have often been viewed as collectivities determined in economic terms. Yet class defined in this way too often overlooks the other forms of individual and collective identity, like race and gender, that powerfully shape who we are and that affect in powerful ways how class comes to be lived in our daily lives. It also downplays the cultural worlds through which give our lives meaning. Yet a concept of class that focuses too exclusively on how we distinguish among ourselves based on culture, ethnicity, and identity—without sufficient grounding within those economic relations of inequality that shape our life trajectories—causes the concept of class to lose the critical edge that makes it a potent tool for social analysis. The goal must be to join the two in a way that allows the concept of class to be both a critical analytical tool for understanding the world and a frame of action necessary for changing it. In the end, a revitalization of the concept of class is necessary not only to replace self-destructive with constructive anger among some groups within the United States, while challenging disengagement or self-interestedness among others, but also simply to find any way forward at all.

Finding a way forward means recognizing that even in the face of global economic pressures (pressures that we as Americans have helped to create), we have choices about what future we want to bring into being. Although as this book goes to press, there is a resurgence of discussion about a potential revitalization of manufacturing, it is unclear whether this emphasis is upon attracting decent paying jobs or whether reindustrialization simply seems more viable now because industry and policy leaders increasingly envision the United States as another "low wage" destination given its disenfranchised working class.[18] Again, what is at stake is not simply particular kinds of jobs—industrial work is not something to romanticize—but whether such jobs can foster a society that pays living wages and that supports families and communities.

The stories told in this book about lives linked to Southeast Chicago's steel mills have now come full circle: from my Big Grandpa entering the mills in the early twentieth century to my father and mother struggling to make sense of a deindustrialized world in which the rules had dramatically changed to our now four-year-old son trying to understand how the "mills went down" when he visits his grandma's house. These stories of passing generations have been told with the conviction that telling such stories is necessary to determine what has been lost in the United States and how to move forward. I would argue that, if there has ever been a time to move past our collective difficulties in speaking about class and to assume an ability to speak, that time has come.

INTRODUCTION

1. The steel mill's former owner, International Harvester, had sold Wisconsin Steel to a subsidiary of a company called Envirodyne in 1977. As part of the purchase agreement, Harvester lent $50 million to Envirodyne, retaining rights to Wisconsin Steel's coal and iron ore mines as collateral. It was three years later that International Harvester preemptively enforced its claim to Wisconsin Steel's mines by sending out a Coast Guard boat to call the mill's ore boat back. In response, Wisconsin Steel's other major lender, Chase Manhattan bank, foreclosed on the property, pushing the mill into bankruptcy. In *Rusted Dreams: Hard Times in a Steel Community*, David Bensman and Roberta Lynch suggest that Harvester and Chase acted so abruptly in order to avoid the legal delays in laying claim to mill assets that would have occurred if the mill had been allowed to formally enter bankruptcy court. David Bensman and Roberta Lynch, *Rusted Dreams: Hard Times in a Steel Community* (Berkeley: University of California Press, 1987). See chap. 2 in this book for further discussion of the complex and confusing events surrounding the shutdown of Wisconsin Steel.

2. The cancer was presumably linked to the widespread pollution in the Calumet region, as discussed in chap. 4.

3. There has been a great deal of discussion of expanding levels of socioeconomic inequality in the United States in recent decades. For some media discussions, see "Ever Higher Society, Ever Harder to Ascend," *Economist*, special report, January 1, 2005; David Leonhardt, "What's Really Squeezing the Middle Class?," *New York Times*, April 25, 2007; David Cay Johnston, "Income Gap Is Widening, Data Shows," *New York Times*, March 29, 2007; Chrystia Freeland, "The Rise of the New Ruling Class: How the Global Elite Is Leaving You Behind," *Atlantic*, February 2011, 44–55; and Robert Pear, "Top Earners Doubled Share of Nation's Income, Study Finds," *New York Times*, October 25, 2011. For academic discussions, see Thomas Piketty and Emmanuel Saez, "Income Inequality in the United States, 1913–1998," *Quarterly Journal of Economics* 118 (2003): 1–39; Emmanuel Saez, "Striking It Richer: The Evolution of Top Incomes in the United States," June 17, 2010, http://www.econ.berkeley.edu/~saez/saez-UStopincomes-2008.pdf; Kathryn Neckerman and Forencia Torche, "Inequality: Causes and Consequences," *Annual Review of Sociology* 33 (2007): 335–57; and Hugh Gusterson and Catherine Besteman, *The Insecure American* (Berkeley: University of California Press, 2009). For discussions of the escalation in executive pay,

see Eric Dash, "Executive Pay: A Special Report," *New York Times*, April 9, 2006; and Karen Ho, *Liquidated: An Ethnography of Wall Street* (Durham: Duke University Press, 2009).

4. "Conservative" publications like the *Wall Street Journal* and the *Economist* have also been calling attention to the increasing lack of mobility within the United States. See, for example, "Ever Higher Society, Ever Harder to Ascend"; and David Wessel, "As Rich-Poor Gap Widens in U.S., Class Mobility Stalls," *Wall Street Journal*, May 13, 2005. High rates of mobility in the late nineteenth century appear to have been linked to the ability of the poor to improve their material circumstances through geographic movement from rural to urban areas and through immigration, particularly since advancement through business and industry did not rely upon higher education. Given that upward mobility is now strongly linked to education that requires good school systems and significant amounts of parental cultural capital, there is increasingly less ability to work one's way up from the bottom in the workplace, and social mobility has become more stagnant. While Americans tend to think of US society as more dynamic and Europe as more class bound, upward social mobility is actually now more likely in Europe or the Scandinavian countries than in the United States.

5. From the US Bureau of Labor Statistics. See also Barry Bluestone, "Foreword," in *Beyond the Ruins: The Meanings of Deindustrialization*, ed. Jefferson Cowie and Joseph Heathcott (Ithaca: Cornell University Press 2003), xxi; and Cowie and Heathcott, *Beyond the Ruins*, 14, for similar statistics. Some observers argued that deindustrialization had been exaggerated or was even a "myth." They did so by stressing that the numbers of manufacturing jobs and industrial output had roughly stayed the same in recent decades. However, that scenario ignored the strong decline in the number of manufacturing jobs as a percentage of the overall workforce. Where manufacturing has continued, increased mechanization has resulted in far fewer jobs with lower wages and less unionization while management threats to shut down factories have encouraged workers to give back gains in wages, benefits, and workrules won in previous periods. In short, whether or not the latter constitutes "deindustrialization" from the point of view of manufacturers, it continues to be experienced as deindustrialization from the perspective of workers, their families, and communities.

6. The phrase "half-life" comes from Sherry Lee Linkon, "Navigating Past and Present in the Deindustrial Landscape" (paper presented at the Working Class Studies Conference, University of Illinois at Chicago, June 23, 2011).

7. There is a very large academic literature on storytelling and narratives. Work that has been particularly influential for this account includes Patricia Ewick and Susan Silbey, "Subversive Stories and Hegemonic Tales: Towards a Sociology of Narrative," *Law and Society Review* 29 (1995): 197–226; Mary Jo Maynes, Jennifer L. Pierce, and Barbara Laslett, *Telling Stories: The Use of Personal Narratives in the Social Sciences and History* (Ithaca: Cornell University Press, 2008); Allesandro Portelli, *The Death of Luigi Trastulli and Other Stories: Form and Meaning in Oral History* (Albany: State University of New York Press, 1991); Personal Narratives Group, eds., *Interpreting Women's Lives: Feminist Theory and Personal Narratives* (Bloomington: Indiana University Press, 1989); Elinor Ochs and Lisa Capps, *Living Narrative: Creating Lives in Everyday Storytelling* (Cambridge, Mass.: Harvard University Press, 2001); and Mary Steedly, *Hanging without a Rope: Narrative Experience in Colonial and Post-colonial Karoland* (Princeton: Princeton University Press, 1993). Many scholars offer important cautions about the use of personal narratives, including the tendency to romanticize

them (for example, Judith Stacey, "Can There Be a Feminist Ethnography?," *Women's Studies* 11 (1998): 21–27; Lila Abu-Lughod, "Can There Be a Feminist Ethnography?," *Women and Performance* 5 (1990): 7–27; Ewick and Silbey, "Subversive Stories and Hegemonic Tales"). In addition, personal narratives should not be assumed to be intrinsically subversive of power, a transparent window onto experience or authentic voice of the people, as argued in Ewick and Silbey. Storytelling itself generally follows social conventions, is solicited in particular kinds of social encounters, and may mimic the story lines favored by the powerful.

8. Hegemony is commonly understood among academics as an indirect form of dominance that happens by means other than force. Building upon Antonio Gramsci, poststructrualist theorists Ernesto Laclau and Chantal Mouffe define hegemony as the imposition of an articulating principle upon social relations and practices. They argue that hegemony is not about an external relationship between two preconstituted subjects but about the discursive constitution of those agents in relation to each other. See Ernesto Laclau and Chantal Mouffe, "Recasting Marxism: Hegemony and New Social Movements," *Socialist Review* 12 (1982): 91–113. This work similarly sees hegemony as not about the relationships of rigidly defined groups, but the constitution of those groups through their relationships with others.

9. Carolyn Steedman, *Landscape for a Good Woman: A Story of Two Lives* (New Brunswick: Rutgers University Press, 1986).

10. For the classic discussion of the "hidden injuries" of class, see Richard Sennett and Jonathan Cobb, *The Hidden Injuries of Class* (New York: Knopf, 1972).

11. Sherry Ortner, "Reading America: Preliminary Notes on Class and Culture," in *Recapturing Anthropology: Working in the Present*, ed. Richard G. Fox (Santa Fe, N.M.: School of American Research Press, 1991), 163–90.

12. For other analyses of dynamics around race and ethnicity for working-class whites, see John Hartigan, Jr., *Racial Situations: Class Predicaments of Whiteness in Detroit* (Princeton: Princeton University Press, 1999); Marianna De Marco Torgovnick, *Crossing Ocean Parkway* (Chicago: University of Chicago Press, 1997); and Jonathan Rieder, *Carnasie: The Jews and Italians of Brooklyn against Liberalism* (Cambridge, Mass.: Harvard University Press, 1985).

13. This is not to suggest that Americans do not talk about social class because they have simply been duped by the powers that be into failing to recognize its importance. The perspective offered here is adamantly not a "false consciousness" viewpoint. On the contrary, there are historical reasons why the topic of class has been a difficult one in the United States during certain periods. Nevertheless, the deliberate avoidance of the language of class encourages public debate to move in certain directions and not others, a particularly dangerous tendency in times of growing inequality like the current one.

14. See Karl Marx, *Capital*, ed. David McLellan (Oxford: Oxford University Press, 1995); Marx, *The Marx-Engels Reader*, ed. Robert C. Tucker (New York: W. W. Norton and Company, 1972); Max Weber, *From Max Weber: Essays in Sociology*, ed. H. H. Gerth and C. Wright Mills (New York: Oxford University Press, 1946); and Weber, *The Protestant Ethic and the Spirit of Capitalism* (New York: Charles Scribner's Sons, 1958). Although some sociologists used Weber in a way that evacuated class of its critical content, replacing it with a depoliticized focus on "status," others took the discussion in the more interesting directions referenced in the text. For an overview of debates over Marxist and Weberian perspectives on class, see the introduction in Mark Liechty, *Suitably Modern: Making Middle-Class Culture in a New Consumer Society*

(Princeton: Princeton University Press, 2003); Ortner, "Reading America"; and Julie Bettie, *Women without Class: Girls, Race, and Identity* (Berkeley: University of California Press, 2003).

15. In attempting to combine Marx and Weber, Bourdieu was influential not only for understanding how class inequalities came be reproduced through cultural means such as "taste" and other markers of "distinction," but also for the ways in which our class dispositions come to be embodied through "habitus," or the durable acquired dispositions that we come to possess based on our experiences. See Pierre Bourdieu, *Outline of a Theory of Practice* (Cambridge: Cambridge University Press, 1977); and Bourdieu, *Distinction: A Social Critique of the Judgement of Taste* (Cambridge, Mass.: Harvard University Press, 1984).

16. For the performance of class, see Bettie, *Women without Class;* for generational challenges, see Ortner, "Reading America."

17. For a useful discussion of the differences between anthropological conceptions of culture and "culture of poverty" arguments, see Bettie, *Women without Class;* and M. L. Small, D. J. Harding, and M. Lamont, "Reconsidering Culture and Poverty," *Annals of the American Academy of Political and Social Science* 629 (2010): 6–27.

18. There have also been numerous other attempts to redefine class in addition to those of the theorists already discussed in ways that can contribute to a multifaceted conception. For example, in Britain, efforts to bring cultural content into analyses of capitalism (drawing upon Antonio Gramsci) led to the "cultural" turn in British scholarly work on class, ranging from historian E. P. Thompson to literary critic Raymond Williams to British cultural studies figures like Stuart Hall, Dick Hebdige, and Paul Willis. (For anthropologists, Paul Willis's classic book *Learning to Labor* [Aldershot, UK: Gower, 1977] has been particularly influential). There have also been influential attempts to rethink ideas of social class in light of poststructuralist theory. For example, theorists Ernesto Laclau and Chantal Mouffe have critiqued the "economism" as well the portrayal of the nature of ideology and how we are constituted as class subjects in much of Marxist theory; see Laclau and Mouffe, "Recasting Marxism." In addition, J. K. Gibson-Graham (two economists who wrote as if one person) brought together poststructuralism and feminist theory in an effort to challenge representations of capitalism as a totalizing universal force, to suggest that people may inhabit multiple class positions at the same time, and to allow recognition of economic practice as including capitalist and noncapitalist elements. See J. K. Gibson-Graham, *The End of Capitalism (as We Knew It): A Feminist Critique of Political Economy* (Oxford: Blackwell, 1996). Julie Bettie offers a perceptive ethnographic analysis of the coconstitution of class, gender, and ethnicity in everyday life that is also in dialogue with poststructuralist theory; see Bettie, *Women without Class.* More recently, the paradigm of "new working-class studies" offers a space to focus on the experiential aspects of class and the importance of personal narratives as well as place-based analysis (see, for example, John Russo and Sherry Lee Linkon, eds., *New Working-Class Studies* [Ithaca: Cornell University Press, 2005]). Finally for a Marxist-inspired analysis of the changing nature of capitalism under a regime of "flexible accumulation," a transformation with profound implications for contemporary class relations, see David Harvey, *The Condition of PostModernity* (London: Basil Blackwell, 1989).

19. For an excellent discussion of this, see Bettie, *Women without Class.*

20. Although anthropology has less commonly focused on issues of social class in the United States that have historically been the province of sociology, there is an anthropological literature on class. See, for example, Sherry Ortner, *New Jersey Dreaming:*

*Capital, Culture and the Class of 1958* (Durham: Duke University Press, 2003); Ortner, "Reading America"; Katherine Newman, *Falling from Grace: Downward Mobility in the Age of Affluence* (Berkeley: University of California Press, 1999); and Micaela di Leonardo, *The Varieties of Ethnic Experience: Kinship, Class and Gender among California's Italian-Americans* (Ithaca: Cornell University Press, 1984). For anthropological work on class in relation to deindustrialization, see June Nash, *From Tank Town to High Tech* (Albany: SUNY Press, 1989); Kathryn Dudley, *The End of the Line: Lost Jobs, New Lives in Post-industrial America* (Chicago: University of Chicago Press, 1994); Judith Modell, *A Town without Steel: Envisioning Homestead* (Pittsburgh: University of Pittsburgh Press, 1998); and Gregory Pappas, *The Magic City: Unemployment in a Working-Class Community* (Ithaca: Cornell University Press, 1989). For work done by anthropologists at the intersection of race and class in urban neighborhoods in the United States, see Steven Gregory, *Black Corona: Race and the Politics of Place in an Urban Community* (Princeton: Princeton University Press, 1998); John L. Jackson, *Harlemworld: Doing Race and Class in Contemporary Black America* (Chicago: University of Chicago Press, 2003); and Ida Susser, *Norman Street: Poverty and Politics in an Urban Neighborhood* (Oxford: Oxford University Press, 1982). For personal narratives about living in a contemporary context of expanding inequality, see Kath Weston, *Traveling Light: On the Road with America's Poor* (Boston: Beacon Press, 2009).

21. I would later discover in "new working-class studies" a paradigm that, as previously mentioned, was more attentive to the experiential aspects of class. See John Russo and Sherry Lee Linkon, "What's New about New Working-Class Studies?," in *New Working-Class Studies*, ed. John Russo and Sherry Lee Linkon (Ithaca: Cornell University Press, 2005), 1–15.

22. Although Myerhoff was speaking specifically about old age as a developmental stage, the point, I believe, is more generally applicable. See Barbara Myerhoff, *Number Our Days* (New York: Simon and Schuster, 1972).

23. The classic example of stories being used in this way is the voluminous work of eminent oral historian Studs Terkel; see, for example, *Working* (New York: New Press, 2004).

24. Within anthropology, there has been a strong emphasis on acknowledging "social positioning," or "locatedness," acknowledging that as researchers we come from somewhere and that our perspective and engagement with research subjects is shaped by that positioning. For important theoretical accounts on "positioning" or locatedness, see Donna Haraway, "Situated Knowledges: The Science Question in Feminism and the Privilege of Partial Perspective," *Feminist Studies* 14 (1988): 575–99; and Lila Abu-Lughod, "Writing against Culture," in Fox, *Recapturing Anthropology*, 137–62.

25. Deborah Reed-Danahay, "Introduction," in *Auto/Ethnography: Rewriting the Self and the Social*, ed. Deborah Reed-Danahay (New York: Berg Press, 1997), 9; Alisse Waterston and Barbara Rylko-Bauer, "Out of the Shadows of History and Memory: Personal Family Narratives in Ethnographies of Rediscovery," *American Ethnologist* 330 (2006): 397–412. Other social scientists who engaged in similar projects of exploring and analyzing self and family in broader social terms, although not necessarily using the term "autoethnography," include Carolyn Steedman, *Landscape for a Good Woman*; Neni Panourgia, *Fragments of Death, Fables of Identity: An Athenian Anthropography* (Madison: University of Wisconsin Press, 1995); Kirin Narayan, *My Family and Other Saints* (Chicago: University of Chicago Press, 2007); and Pierre Bourdieu, *Sketch for a Self-Analysis* (Chicago: University of Chicago Press, 2008).

26. Bourdieu in his *Sketch for a Self-Analysis* does not use the term "autoethnography,"

although his work has much in common with some similar projects. He adamantly rejects the idea that this work is "autobiography" and instead emphasizes the need to analyze the self in a social context as part of his long-standing theoretical emphasis upon reflexivity.

27. Waterston and Rylko-Bauer, "Out of the Shadows."

CHAPTER ONE

1. It was renamed South Deering in 1903 in celebration of the arrival of Deering Harvester Company, which later became International Harvester and the long-term owner of Wisconsin Steel; see David Solzman, *The Chicago River: An Illustrated History and Guide to the River and Its Waterways* (Chicago: University of Chicago Press, 2006), 173–74.

2. For overviews of the Haymarket bombing, see Robert Spinney, *City of Big Shoulders: A History of Chicago* (DeKalb: Northern Illinois Press, 2000), 107–13; and Dominic A. Pacyga, *Chicago: A Biography* (Chicago: University of Chicago Press, 2011), 94–99.

3. For discussion of the stockyards, see Pacyga, *Chicago*, 60–62; and Spinney, *City of Big Shoulders*, 56–62.

4. For discussions of Pullman, see Spinney, *City of Big Shoulders*, 93–96; and Pacyga, *Chicago*, 122–24.

5. For discussion of the Trumbull Park riots, see Arnold R. Hirsch, "Massive Resistance in the Urban North: Trumbull Park, Chicago, 1953–1966, *Journal of American History* 82 (1995): 522–50.

6. I put "white ethnic" in quotes here to signal my reservations about this term. In much social science and popular literature, "white ethnic" stands as a code for working-class whites. While it accurately suggests the immigrant background of many residents in Southeast Chicago, its use at times corresponds to the tendency to subsume issues of class within those of race/ethnicity rather than to acknowledge that both may be simultaneously operative in ways that are not reducible to one or the other.

7. This position is one that has been taken by "new working-class studies"; see Russo and Linkon, "What's New about New Working-Class Studies?"

8. Ortner, "Reading America."

9. Erika Johnson, "Scandinavians Preferred: Nordic Ethnic Identity, Gender and Work in Chicago, 1879–1993" (PhD diss., Michigan State University, 2010).

10. Histories of Southeast Chicago are few and far between. I am deeply indebted to local historian Rod Sellers's remarkable knowledge of this understudied region, based on written archival sources, interviews with residents, photo and artifact collections, and other work conducted in conjunction with the Southeast Chicago Historical Museum. As background for this account, I've relied heavily on materials accessed through the museum long before they became available online, including David Brosch, Marcia Kijewski, and Robert Bulanda, *The Historical Development of Three Chicago Millgates* (Chicago: Illinois Labor History Society, 1972); and James R. McIntyre, *The History of Wisconsin Steel Works of the International Harvester Company* ([Chicago?]: Wisconsin Steel Works, International Harvester, 1951), an industry perspective that, nevertheless, includes a considerable amount of oral history. For published accounts of Southeast Chicago history, see Dominic A. Pacyga's *Polish Immigrants and Industrial Chicago* (Chicago: University of Chicago Press, 1991); the photo histories offered in *Chicago's Southeast Side*, by Rod Sellers and Dominic A. Pacyga (Charlestown, S.C.: Arcadia, 1998); and *Chicago's Southeast Side Revisited*, by Rod Sellers (Chicago: Arcadia, 2001). Also the information collected through the Southeast Side history project—

a project with Washington High School students and overseen by Rod Sellers and other teachers—offered helpful information. See http://www.neiu.edu/~reseller/sesidewlcme.html.

A classic sociological account on industrial work, William Kornblum's *Blue Collar Community* (Chicago: University of Chicago Press, 1974), was based on research at my father's mill, Wisconsin Steel, and conducted during the 1970s. For an intriguing environmental history of the region, see Craig E. Colten, *Industrial Wastes in the Calumet Area, 1869–1970: A Historical Geography* (Champaign: Hazardous Waste Research and Information Center, Illinois Department of Energy and Natural Resources, 1985). For histories of the Calumet across the Indiana border, particularly for Gary, see S. Paul O'Hara, "Envisioning the Steel City: The Legend and Legacy of Gary, Indiana," in Cowie and Heathcott, *Beyond the Ruins*; and Andrew Hurley, *Environmental Inequalities: Class, Race and Industrial Pollution in Gary, Indiana, 1945–1980* (Chapel Hill: University of North Carolina Press, 1995). For a brief, general overview of Chicago history, see Spinney, *City of Big Shoulders*. For discussions of other steel mill communities, see, among others, Jack Metzgar, *Striking Steel: Solidarity Remembered* (Philadelphia: Temple University Press, 2000); Robert Bruno, *Steelworker Alley: How Class Works in Youngstown* (Ithaca: Cornell University Press, 1999); Sherry Lee Linkon and John Russo, *Steeltown, U.S.A.: Work and Memory in Youngstown* (Lawrence: University Press of Kansas, 2003); Thomas G. Fuechtmann, *Steeples and Stacks: Religion and Steel Crisis in Youngstown* (Cambridge: Cambridge University Press, 1989); and Judith Modell, *A Town without Steel.*

11.  For example, the curving roads of Brainard Avenue, South Chicago Avenue, and Indianapolis Boulevard were originally Native American paths (interview, Rod Sellers, Southeast Chicago Historical Museum, August 2004).

12.  The North Chicago Rolling Mill Company was a precursor to Illinois Steel and had a mill built in South Chicago in 1880. The mill was called South Works to distinguish it from the company's other operation on the North Side of Chicago. Illinois Steel emerged in 1889 from the merger of several Chicago-area steel mills with the two North Chicago Rolling Mill plants (the one on Chicago's North Side and South Works in South Chicago). South Works was also known as Carnegie Steel before Carnegie's holdings became part of US Steel in 1901. The history of the Acme/Interlake mill in Irondale/South Deering is even more complex. A coke plant on Torrence Avenue was built in 1905 and known as By-Products Coke. During the same year, the Federal Furnace plant was constructed at 107th and Burley. Acme Steel, which had a plant in Riverdale, was a separate operation at that time. In 1915, Federal Furnace and By-Products Coke merged, and, in 1929, they joined with other companies to form Interlake Iron. (Interlake Iron and Acme Steel combined in 1964 to form Interlake Steel.). Iroquois Iron was originally located on the East Side on the Calumet River south of 95th on the east side of the river (between the 95th Street bridge and the multiple railroad bridges across the Calumet River at about 97th Street). Due to the lack of room for expansion, it moved after 1910 to land created at the mouth of the Calumet River across from US Steel's South Works. Iroquois later became the Sheet and Tube Company of America, later Youngstown Sheet and Tube, and eventually Youngstown Steel. Thanks to Rod Sellers of the Southeast Chicago Historical Museum for explaining this complex history.

13.  *Online Encyclopedia of Chicago*, entry for Standard Oil Co. (Whiting), accessed September 21, 2011, http://encyclopedia.chicagohistory.org/pages/2863.html.

14.  George Hammond had founded the town of Hammond around his meatpacking

plant just over the Indiana border from Southeast Chicago in 1869. Although harvesting ice to supply railway food transporters had become a regular winter activity on Wolf Lake and Lake Calumet, Hammond would later help develop the railroad car refrigeration techniques needed to safely transport the meat of Chicago's packing industry back east. See William Cronon, *Nature's Metropolis: Chicago and the Great West* (New York: W. W. Norton and Company, 1991), 233–35; and US Department of the Interior, *Calumet Ecological Park Feasibility Study* (Omaha: Midwest Region National Park Service, 1998), 14.

15. Pacyga, *Polish Immigrants*, 3. For related statistics on numbers of immigrants in Chicago, see Spinney, *City of Big Shoulders*, 124; and Lizabeth Cohen, *Making a New Deal: Industrial Workers in Chicago, 1919–1939* (Cambridge: Cambridge University Press, 1990), 17.

16. For discussion of the remarkable loss of life and limb in South Works, see Pacyga, *Polish Immigrants*, 90–94; and Hard, William. "Making Steel and Killing Men," *Everybody's Magazine* 17, no. 5 (1907): 579–91.

17. For a helpful account that recognizes the often-ignored migration of poor whites from Appalachia to work in the industrial centers of the Midwest, see Hartigan, *Racial Situations*.

18. Mention of skyscrapers built with steel from South Works is found in Solzman, *The Chicago River*, 160.

19. For accounts of the hours worked by steelworkers, see Brosch et al., *The Historical Development of Three Chicago Millgates*.

20. During this period, the massive US Steel conglomerate had agreed to unionization; however, the smaller mills of "little steel," including Republic Steel under the notoriously antiunion Thomas Girdler, held out and sought to break the emerging union movement. See John P. Hoerr, *And the Wolf Finally Came: The Decline and Fall of the American Steel Industry* (Pittsburgh: University of Pittsburgh Press, 1988); and Michael Dennis, *The Memorial Day Massacre and the Movement for Industrial Democracy* (New York: Palgrave Macmillan, 2010).

21. John Hoerr notes that in the steel mill regions of Pennsylvania's Monongahela Valley, the derogatory epithet "hunkies" was used to refer indiscriminately to any Slavs. Hoerr, *And The Wolf Finally Came*. See similar comments in Margaret Byington, *Homestead: Households of a Mill Town* (1910; reprint, New York: Arno Press, 1969).

22. During periods of disruption to European immigration, management used other ethnic and racial groups as sources of labor as well as strikebreakers. For example, management used African-Americans as strikebreakers in the labor-management steel battles of 1919 (Pacyga, *Polish Immigrants*, 237; Spinney, *City of Big Shoulders*, 168). (It should also be noted that African-Americans were largely excluded from early unionizing efforts, which may have limited their sympathy for white workers.) Mexicans were also brought in train cars en masse during this period and used in similar ways. Such dynamics had historical counterparts among immigrant whites. In the early years of the steel industry, Byington noted that Slavs played a similar role and were also heavily racialized and resented by native whites and earlier immigrants in Pennsylvania (see Byington, *Homestead*).

23. Hoerr, *And the Wolf Finally Came*.

24. Byington's turn-of-the-century account of the steel mill region of Homestead, Pennsylvania, as well as the reanalysis of the book in Steven Mintz and Susan Kellogg, *Domestic Revolutions: A Social History of American Life* (New York, Free Press, 1988), as part of a broader discussion of working-class family life, notes that the typical family

of a steel mill worker lived below the poverty line. They state that taking in boarders or washing contributed about a quarter of a family's income, while the wages of older sons constituted about a third of family income; Byington, *Homestead*; and Mintz and Kellogg, *Domestic Revolutions*, 84.

25. Edith Abbott, *Women in Industry: A Study in American Economic History* (New York: D. Appleton and Company, 1910); Joanne Meyerowitz, *Women Adrift: Independent Wage Earners in Chicago, 1880–1930* (Chicago: University of Chicago Press, 1988); Johnson, "Scandinavians Preferred"; Lisa Fine, *The Souls of the Skyscraper: Female Clerical Workers in Chicago, 1870–1930* (Philadelphia: Temple University Press, 1990). Interestingly, Fine notes that women clerical workers in Chicago during this period were more likely to be the children of working-class immigrants than in other cities, where such individuals were more commonly native-born middle-class women.

26. For a discussion of how working-class lives were bound up with family economies, see Mintz and Kellogg, *Domestic Revolutions*. Other scholars have noted the tendency for some women from the end of the nineteenth century to the early twentieth century to seek wages in more independent ways; see Meyerowitz, *Women Adrift*. Johnson discusses the phenomenon of young Swedish women who emigrated to Chicago apart from their families and often ended up working as domestics for wealthy families; see Johnson, "Scandinavians Preferred."

27. For example, see discussion in Mintz and Kellogg, *Domestic Revolutions*, 86.

28. Of course there is a long academic history beginning with Karl Marx that discusses the "alienating" nature of industrial work. More recent ethnographic accounts, however, have challenged the oversights of analyses that fail to adequately consider the ways that industrial workers managed to take pride in their work while also forging meaningful social bonds with coworkers. (For example, see the sensitive discussion in Dudley, *The End of the Line*.) In my own experience, I found family members and neighbors might express both viewpoints simultaneously without acknowledging a contradiction: one could take pride in the work and a job well done (what else could one do in order to make work meaningful?) but also recognize that such work was dangerous, hot, at times soul deadening, and not necessarily something you wanted your children to do.

29. Family life in Southeast Chicago was profoundly heterenormative. Based on the amount of taunting children received for any behaviors deemed acting "gay" in school, it is easy to imagine how constraining the environment might have felt for those who were gay or lesbian. Although I don't have personal or familial stories that would be revealing of such realities, there is a small but enlightening body of work on personal narratives for individuals who identify as both gay and working class or from working-class origins. For example, see the review essay by Christopher Renny, "Shame and the Search for Home," *Feminist Studies* 30, no. 1 (2004): 178–92.

30. Kathryn Kish Sklar, "Hull House in the 1890s: A Community of Women Reformers," in *American Visitas: 1877 to the Present*, ed. Leonard Dinnerstein and Kenneth T. Jackson (New York: Oxford University Press, 1995); Linda Gordon, "Social Insurance and Public Assistance: The Influence of Gender in Welfare Thought in the United States, 1890–1935," *American Historical Review* 97, no.1 (1992): 19–54; Jane Adams, *Twenty Years at Hull House* (1910; reprint, New York: New American Library, 1960).

31. Anthropologist Judith Modell noted a similar phenomenon in her work on Homestead, Pennsylvania, in which women as well as men in their life stories downplayed womens' work for pay. Such work was simultaneously pervasive in women's stories and also dismissed as "exceptions." Modell, *A Town without Steel*.

32. Some have suggested that early German and Swedish immigrants in steel mill communities in Pennsylvania voted Republican to differentiate themselves from the ethnic immigrant groups associated with the New Deal. For example, see Jack Metzgar, *Striking Steel*. Both ethnic and gendered elements may well have been part of this political positioning.

33. For example, Johnson, "Scandinavians Preferred."

34. For a discussion of "hard living" versus "settled living" members of the working class based on the work of Joseph Howell, see Bettie, *Women without Class*, 13.

35. Johnson, "Scandinavians Preferred."

36. Although African-Americans did live in some parts of Southeast Chicago, such as South Chicago's Millgate and Bush areas as well as Jeffrey Manor during the 1960s, African-Americans were most heavily concentrated in neighborhoods further north on the South Side.

CHAPTER TWO

1. The process of what would later be termed "deindustrialization" happened first in the older industries and mills of the East Coast, leading some to suggest that deindustrialization began in the 1960s or earlier. For the major industries of the industrial heartland, the late 1970s and early 1980s were crucial years, in which factory shutdowns became widespread. In the steel industry, the older mills in the Pittsburgh-Ohio area started closing in the late 1970s; in the Calumet region, Wisconsin Steel was the first to close, in 1980. The concept of deindustrialization itself came to the attention of scholars and a broader public largely through the text *The Deindustrialization of America*, by Barry Bluestone and Bennett Harrison (New York: Basic Books, 1982). For some of the academic literature on the demise of the steel industry, see Bensman and Lynch, *Rusted Dreams*; Modell, *A Town without Steel*; Linkon and Russo, *Steeltown, U.S.A.*; and Thomas G. Fuechtmann, *Steeples and Stacks*. For a highly detailed journalistic account of the collapse of the steel industry, see Hoerr, *And the Wolf Finally Came*. For some of the literature on deindustrialization more broadly, see Cowie and Heathcott, *Beyond the Ruins*; Dudley, *The End of the Line*; Steven High, *Industrial Sunset: The Making of the North America's Rustbelt, 1969–1984* (Toronto: University of Toronto Press, 2003); J. Nash, *From Tank Town to High Tech*; and Pappas, *The Magic City*.

2. At the site where Dudley worked in Kenosha, Wisconsin, this was the case both for middle-class businesspeople and for some schoolteachers. The latter resented that those with less education made more money than they did and that the ready availability of well-paid industrial work led their students to devalue education itself. See Dudley, *The End of the Line*.

3. This would have been after Prohibition was ended in 1933. Presumably, the establishment had been a speakeasy in the Prohibition days and had a continued existence afterward.

4. See Richard Taub, *Paths of Neighborhood Change: Race and Crime in Urban America* (Chicago: University of Chicago Press, 1987), for a discussion of the density of social and generational ties in Southeast Chicago.

5. My father's first adult encounter with unionizing came when he was seventeen and pumping gas at a station along Indianapolis Boulevard. Large, intimidating men entered the station, ordered him to stop pumping gas, and then threatened the owner with physical violence if he didn't immediately unionize his workforce. Although my dad laughingly told how they were unionized and he got a raise the next day, he

told this story with deep ambivalence. He and other neighbors sometimes noted disturbing similarities between some CIO affiliates and Mafia thugs during those years. Before working at Wisconsin Steel, my father had worked at Republic Steel on the East Side and was a member of the United Steelworkers of America union. During the 1950s and 1960s, when unions became increasingly mainstream institutions, some members of the rank and file like my father seemed to feel almost as distant from the union's powerful leaders as from management itself. Wisconsin Steel was represented by the Progressive Steelworkers Union (PSWU), a "company" union. The lawyer for PSWU was Edward Vrdolyak, the area's long-standing "ward boss," who has been mired in repeated corruption scandals over the years and served ten months in prison in 2010–2011. As the PSWU's lawyer, Vrdolyak also received a campaign contribution from Envirodyne, the mill's owner. See Bensman and Lynch, *Rusted Dreams*, 55.

6.   The debates about the "high" wages in the steel industry are discussed at length in Hoerr, *And the Wolf Finally Came*. Hoerr quotes thirty dollars an hour as an industry average; however, it is important to note that take-home pay was half that or less. To explain the difference, it must be recognized that about half of the wage figure included benefits that expanded steadily for steelworkers over the 1970s. Many of these benefits were also hypothetical, or forms of insurance that only kicked in if certain conditions came into play (for example, benefits designed to stabilize workers' salaries in the event of cyclical industry layoffs or extended vacation time to workers with high levels of seniority). As a consequence, such benefits might never be claimed or paid and did not represent income for steelworkers. In addition, the pay scale for skilled laborers who worked many hours of overtime considerably skewed the "average" and did not actively reflect the pay of more rank-and-file workers. Finally, in the case of Wisconsin Steel, steelworkers at the mill worked forced overtime in its final years, a union concession to help the industry by increasing flexibility and allowing the company not to have to hire additional workers. Consequently, workers like my father made far more money in the last year or two of their working careers than was customary in an "average" year. As a result, citing average salary at the time of the mill closing is misleading.

7.   The following discussion of the demise of Wisconsin Steel and the complex machinations around its closing draws heavily upon the very helpful overview offered in Bensman and Lynch, *Rusted Dreams*. I also draw upon Gordon L. Clark, "Piercing the Corporate Veil: The Closure of Wisconsin Steel in South Chicago," *Regional Studies* 24 (1990): 405–20; as well as a memoir by a labor lawyer for Wisconsin Steel workers: Thomas Geoghegan, *Which Side Are You On?: Trying to Be for Labor When It's Flat on Its Back* (New York: Farrar, Straus and Giroux, 1991). Numerous newspapers articles documenting the demise and aftermath of the mill in the *Chicago Tribune*, the *Chicago Sun-Times*, and the local paper the *Daily Calumet* provided additional information.

8.   See discussion in Clark, "Piercing the Corporate Veil."

9.   Bensman and Lynch, *Rusted Dreams*, 51.

10.   See Bensman and Lynch, *Rusted Dreams*, 50.

11.   In an interview with the *Chicago Tribune*, Envirodyne CEO Ron Linde noted that their business plan was to do a highly leveraged buyout of a major company that could provide them not only with a manufacturing base, but "cash flow" (the latter presumably for other interests). William Gruber, "Fearless Buying: Tiny Firm Tackles Ailing Steel Outfit," *Chicago Tribune*, August 7, 1977.

12.   For example, see Ho, *Liquidated*.

13. High, *Industrial Sunset*.

14. The following account relies heavily upon the discussion found in Bensman and Lynch, *Rusted Dreams*.

15. Bensman and Lynch note that two paychecks bounced. Other steelworkers including Save Our Jobs activist Frank Lumpkin and my father claimed that considerably more bounced. It may have been that Frank Lumpkin was saving checks, waiting to cash them for use on an extended vacation that he was due; the result was that he had twelve paychecks bounce. According to Bensman and Lynch, Chase Manhattan froze the payroll accounts, making the argument that secured lenders should be reimbursed before employees. When in 1981 Chase tried to remove Wisconsin Steel's inventory for sale, they were prevented from doing so by angry picketers, and they agreed to negotiation. The outcome was that workers were eventually reimbursed three-fourths of what was owed them of the bounced paychecks. Bensman and Lynch, *Rusted Dreams*.

16. For example, in a text produced by the US Steel Corporation on its fiftieth anniversary in 1951, steel company managers stressed the centrality of steel to the national economy and the patriotic role the industry had played. The text emphasized both at a moment when the "United States prepares to defend itself against the present threat of Communist aggression" (i.e., the Korean War, for which US Steel was at that time increasing production for military hardware). The text continued, "In one form or another, that steel has been used by practically every industry in the land. United States Steel has helped substantially to build America and to make it the powerful nation that it is today. . . . We are proud of the fact that United States Steel has served this nation to the best of its ability both in war and in peace." See US Steel, "Steel Serves the Nation" (US Steel Golden Anniversary Publication, 1951).

17. See Brosch et al., *The Historical Development of Three Chicago Millgates*; and McIntyre, *The History of Wisconsin Steel Works*.

18. This topic would become the subject of my master's thesis: Christine J. Walley, "Steeltown Stories: Deindustrialization on Chicago's Southeast Side" (MA thesis, New York University, 1993).

19. For an overview of the roles of various local politicians, see Bensman and Lynch, *Rusted Dreams*. At the national level, the response to plant closings by US president Jimmy Carter was tepid; see High, *Industrial Sunset*, 161.

20. Bensman and Lynch, *Rusted Dreams*, 55.

21. Robert Bergsvik, "Rally Marks 9th Anniversary of Wisconsin Steel's Closing," *Daily Calumet*, March 29, 1989. In the previous year, John F. Wasik put the number at six hundred in "End of the Line at Wisconsin Steel," *Progressive* 52 (1988): 15. See also a report on the psychological fallout of the mill shutdowns by Julie Putterman and the Steelworkers Research Project *Chicago Steelworkers: The Cost of Unemployment* (Chicago: Hull House Association and Local 65 United Steelworkers of America, 1985).

22. "Flexible accumulation" refers in part to corporate strategies to expand profits by making labor more "flexible," that is, through outsourcing, subcontracting, hiring part-time workers, and other measures that would allow companies to decrease wages and benefits and make it easier to shed workers. See Harvey, *The Condition of Postmodernity*.

23. This refinery was initially built under the ownership of Standard Oil and, later, would be sold to British Petroleum (BP).

24. Estimating numbers of jobs lost has been far less straightforward than it might appear. Most mills did not end as abruptly as Wisconsin Steel but shed jobs gradually

before finally closing. The question then is how to choose what historical moment to begin counting the number of jobs lost: at the peak of employment in Southeast Chicago or closer to the point when the mills actually closed? In my estimates, I have used the numbers most widely used in literature and media accounts regarding various mills (although I have seen both higher and lower numbers).

25. In particular, the grassroots Save Our Jobs Committee formed by Wisconsin Steel workers who felt betrayed by their own union was extremely active and was responsible for the class action suit that earned a settlement from International Harvester and some restoration of lost pensions. Leaders of the group included African-American and Latino steelworkers, particularly the highly energetic and respected Frank Lumpkin.

26. For example, see Martha M. Hamilton, "Jobless Benefits," *Washington Post*, February 19, 1981.

27. A pseudonym.

28. According to High, American unions inadvertently contributed to the corporate narrative that deindustrialization was largely an inevitable result of foreign imports and global competition (rather than, say, about the internal transformation of corporations themselves with the financialization of the economy). One of the few ways that US unions could try to help their members in the face of plant shutdowns was to argue that the problem was trade dislocation based on foreign imports and thereby file for enhanced benefits under the Trade Adjustments Act (TAA). Thus, plant shutdowns were often contested by workers and unions through a nationalistic rhetoric against "foreign" imports that alienated liberals and those on the left in the United States who associated such jinogistic language with the presumed conservatism of the working class shown during the Vietnam War. See High, *Industrial Sunset*, 135–37.

29. The "Rowthorn model," which became the dominant viewpoint of deindustrialization in many academic circles, argued that deindustrialization was not primarily a product of globalization (globalization being understood narrowly here as international economic exchange rather than a global division of labor spanning the production processes of multinational companies). According to the Rowthorn model, deindustrialization stems from rising economic productivity (i.e., replacement of workers by technology) as well as rising levels of "economic development." In this developmentalist account, a country is seen as reaching a point of industrial "maturity," where manufacturing jobs come to be replaced by service sector jobs. According to Robert Rowthorn and Ramana Ramaswamy, "Deindustrialization is not a negative phenomenon, but is the natural consequence of the industrial dynamism in an already developed economy" (as cited in David Brady and Ryan Denniston, "Economic Globalization, Industrialization, and Deindustrialization in Affluent Democracies," *Social Forces* 85 [2006]: 297–326). In other words, in this naturalized model, deindustrialization is simply a transitional stage of growing pains as a national economy reaches a "higher" level of economic maturity.

30. Although as economists Barry Bluestone and Bennett Harrison noted in 1982, US companies investing abroad were increasingly themselves becoming the "foreign competition." Bluestone and Harrison, *The Deindustrialization of America*.

31. John Hoerr offers a detailed discussion of some of the mistakes and intense antagonism generated by US steel industry executives (although he is also critical of labor). See Hoerr, *And the Wolf Finally Came*. Southeast Chicago residents also sometimes told anecdotal stories of workers trying to abuse the "system" by sleeping on the job or in other ways trying to get out of work (see also Modell, *A Town without Steel*,

58–60). Older workers might also contrast the work ethic of the younger generations with those of their own. However, several points need to be made about such
accounts. First, as Hoerr notes, such alienation has to be placed in the context of
historical antagonism between steelworkers and steel industry management. In the
post–World War II years, labor-management confrontations were "solved" by ex-
changing high wages and benefits for the ability of management to organize work
production without worker input regarding production decisions that might have
decreased job alienation. (Unions were also nervous about helping increase "efficiency" for fear that it would result in the loss of jobs.) Second, as the classic auto
worker memoir *Rivethead*, by Ben Hamper (New York: Warner Books, 1992), demonstrates, the substance abuse that was part of drug experimentation among middle-
class youth in the 1970s was also found among working-class youth. Although the
intense strain of factory and mill work also resulted in heavy alcohol use by earlier
generations, abuse issues appeared to be particularly common among younger workers who didn't yet have the pressing responsibilities of mortgages and families.

Most persuasively, however, Kathryn Dudley in *The End of the Line* offers a perceptive anthropological analysis of shop floor culture in the automobile industry, in
which workers demonstrated skill by finding shortcuts to assembly line tasks and
boasted of "leisure" time that they were able to accumulate by outwitting both the
tasks and management. Rather than being an example of not caring about their work,
such actions could be virtuoso demonstrations of "skill" as defined within shop floor
culture. This analysis explains Hamper's simultaneous self-depiction as taking a great
pride in his consummate skill at riveting (hence, being known as the "rivethead") as
well as pride in finding ways to outwit the task and the clock and create leisure time
on the job. See also sociologist David Halle's discussion of chemical factory workers
and the importance of workplace sociality and the creation of "leisure." David Halle,
*America's Working Man* (Chicago: University of Chicago, 1987). It should also be
noted that it was common for companies to shut down factories and relocate to low-
wage areas even when the factories in question demonstrated high levels of quality
work and efficiency (for two examples, see Dudley, *The End of the Line*; and Steve May
and Laura Morrison, "Making Sense of Restructuring: Narrative of Accommodation
among Downsized Workers," in Cowie and Heathcott, *Beyond the Ruins*, 259–79).

32. Southeast Chicago differed from some other rust belt regions in that almost all residents of the area were working class, in contrast to towns like Kenosha, Wisconsin,
or cities like Youngstown, Ohio, that had their own elites. In the latter instances,
more educated residents might see the loss of industry as positive rather than negative, both because of hopes for a more "classy" postindustrial economy and, as Kate
Dudley persuasively shows, out of resentment of the relatively high wages that industrial workers were paid. The fact that advanced education was not needed for
such jobs was seen as evidence that such work was unworthy and did not deserve
"middle-class" wages. See Dudley, *The End of the Line*. For discussion of local elites in
Youngstown who do not look upon an industrial past with nostalgia, see Linkon and
Russo, *Steeltown, U.S.A.* For Homestead, Pennsylvania, see Modell, *A Town without
Steel*, 58–60.

33. In 1981–82 US Steel spent $91 million dollars to reline the number 8 blast furnace at
South Works (a furnace that was never lit) and had an ultramodern rod mill. Nevertheless, South Works began laying off large numbers of employees in 1981, using
profits not to modernize the steel mills, but to diversify and acquire Marathon Oil
Company for $6 billion. However, the acquisition of Marathon Oil meant that US

Steel also acquired a $3 billion debt load and steep interest payments. In 1984, US Steel told South Works employees that they would build a new rolling mill if South Works employees agreed to wage concessions and if the state provided tax and environmental breaks. Both the state and union agreed. US Steel stalled on construction raising questions about its intentions (particularly since it had continued to disinvest in South Works even in 1981 when profits rose to 13.3 percent). Finally, US Steel proposed another round of concessions which the union refused. US Steel then took out a full page ad in Chicago newspapers blaming the loss of the rail mill on the selfishness of the union. See discussion in Bensman and Lynch, *Rusted Dreams*; and Bluestone and Harrison, *The Deindustrialization of America*, 6.

34. Bensman and Lynch, *Rusted Dreams*, 87.

35. See, for example, the discussion in Jefferson Cowie, *Stayin' Alive: The 1970s and the Last Days of the Working Class* (New York: New Press, 2010).

36. The discussion here builds on such accounts as Bluestone and Harrison, *The Deindustrialization of America*; Harvey, *The Condition of Postmodernity*; Donald Bartlett and James Steele, *America: What Went Wrong?* (Kansas City, Mo.: Andrews and McMeel, 1992); Ho, *Liquidated*.

37. The company would later return to the name US Steel in 2001, when the company's steel holdings were once again spun off as a separate enterprise.

38. An article by Eric Dash in the *New York Times* entitled "Executive Pay: A Special Report" (April 9, 2006) notes that in 1940, half of executives earned more than 56 times the average worker's pay; in 2004, half of executives earned more than 104 times the average worker's pay. See also discussion in Ho, *Liquidated*; and David Owen, "The Pay Problem," *New Yorker*, October 12, 2009, 58–63.

39. David Cay Johnston, "Income Gap Is Widening, Data Shows," *New York Times*, March 29, 2007. The article also notes, "The new [tax] data also shows that the top 300,000 Americans collectively enjoyed almost as much income as the bottom 150 million Americans. Per person, the top group received 440 times as much as the average person in the bottom half earned, nearly doubling the gap from 1980." For other measures of economic inequality that rival those of the nineteenth century, see "Ever Higher Society, Ever Harder to Ascend"; and Freeland, "The Rise of the New Ruling Class," 48. In 2011, the Congressional Budget Office noted that the top 15 percent of income earners had more than doubled their share of the national wealth over the last three decades. Pear, "Top Earners Doubled Share of Nation's Income."

40. Information on the decline of the share of manufacturing jobs in the workforce was compiled from US Bureau of Labor Statistics. Thanks to Marie Burke and Caterina Scaramelli for gathering this information.

41. For discussions of Mittal, see Martin Baker, "He's Got the Whole World in His Hands," *Observer*, February 5, 2006; and "Lakshmi Mittal," BBC International News Profile, BBC, July 3, 2006, accessed online on June 19, 2008, http://news.bbc.co .uk/2/hi/business/5142202.stm. See also Eric Sergio Boria, "Borne in the Industrial Everyday: Reterritorializing Claims-Making in a Global Steel Economy" (PhD diss., Loyola University, Chicago, 2006).

42. Bluestone and Harrison, *The Deindustrialization of America*; Bartlett and Steele, *America: What Went Wrong?*

43. Cowie and Heathcott, *Beyond the Ruins*, 14.

44. Some of deregulatory and other policy choices that led to such economic transformations included the Reagan-era dismantling of antitrust enforcement, changes in capital investment rules allowing companies to merge with little oversight, changes

in the tax code, and changes in bankruptcy rules. For example, changes in the federal tax code helped spur the wave of leveraged buyouts by allowing companies to deduct interest on loans for purchases. In addition companies were allowed to take net operating loss deductions under which they could deduct for past operating losses including shutting down plants and interest on debt for buyouts which could then be used to deduct federal taxes on future income. The revision of bankruptcy laws made it easier for companies to operate while under Chapter 11 bankruptcy (as opposed to liquidation under Chapter 7), making it possible for corporations to write off the past losses of bankrupt subsidiaries against the income generated in the acquisition of new companies. Other tax code policies like that of "transfer pricing" helped subsidize the growth of multinationals and the transfer of jobs and assets to other countries. In addition, other changes in investment rules that allowed pension funds, mutual funds, and savings and loan and insurance companies to engage in riskier investments generated the large capital flows needed to accommodate the economic shift toward financial transactions including takeovers, mergers, and acquisitions in contrast to production. For insight into such changes from both the production end and the Wall Street end, see Bluestone and Harrison, *The Deindustrialization of America*; Bartlett and Steele, *America: What Went Wrong?*; and Ho, *Liquidated*.

45. See Kathleen Thelen, *How Institutions Evolve: The Political Economy of Skills in Germany, Britain, the United States, and Japan* (Cambridge: Cambridge University Press, 2004).

46. However, President Obama has recently called for a "renaissance" in American manufacturing and, in the buildup to the 2012 election, has unveiled a manufacturing initiative. See Kathleen Hennessey, "Obama Hails Job Report, Pitches Manufacturing Initiative," *Los Angeles Times*, March 9, 2012. However, it is unclear how worker friendly such policies will ultimately be or whether low wages and decreased rates of unionization will be used as a selling point for manufacturers to return to the United States. In other words, will low wages be considered part of the United States' new so-called comparative economic advantage? See, for example, the report by Harold L. Sirkin, Michael Zinser, and Douglas Hohner, *Made in America, Again: Manufacturing Will Return to the U.S.* (Boston: Boston Consulting Group, 2011). For a critique, see Mike Alberti, "On Manufacturing Policy, White House Remains in the Grip of 'Ratchet-Down' Consultants," *Remapping Debate*, January 18, 2012, http://www.remappingdebate.org/article/manufacturing-policy-white-house-remains -grip-%E2%80%9Cratchet-down%E2%80%9D-consultants. My home institution of MIT has been heavily involved in the Obama administration's Advanced Manufacturing Partnership (AMP), intended to promote the rebuilding of manufacturing in the United States; see Peter Dizikes, "Rebuilding American Manufacturing," MIT News Office, November 30, 2011, http://web.mit.edu/newsoffice/2011.

47. See High, *Industrial Sunset*, 122–30.

48. Over the last few years, however, there has been a more recent loss of industrial jobs in central Canada, which some have linked to an overly strong Canadian dollar. The value of the Canadian dollar climbed from sixty-two cents on the dollar in 2002 to above par with the US dollar in 2012. The shift was attributed in part to the influence of Canadian commodity exports like oil. The result has been that Canadian manufactured goods intended for export have become prohibitively expensive (much like the situation in the United States during the 1980s), leading to a recent massive shedding of industrial jobs around Ontario and a 22 percent contraction in manufacturing. See, for example, "As Dollar Climbed over Past Decade, 500,000 Factory Jobs Vanished," *Guardian*, March 1, 2012.

CHAPTER THREE

1. For example, see the special report "Meritocracy in America," in the *Economist*, January 1–7, 2005; and Wessel, "As Rich-Poor Gap Widens in U.S., Class Mobility Stalls."

2. Alfred Lubrano, *Limbo: Blue-Collar Roots, White Collar Dreams* (Hoboken, N.J.: John Wiley and Sons, 2004).

3. The scholarly literature on this is now very extensive. For example, see Sennett and Cobb, *The Hidden Injuries of Class*. For poststructuralist revisionings of Marxist theory, see Laclau and Mouffe, "Recasting Marxism"; and Gibson-Graham, *The End of Capitalism*. For a useful new paradigm for thinking about class, labor, and the use of personal narratives, see Russo and Linkon, "What's New about New Working-Class Studies?" For the way class becomes part of our everyday dispositions or "habitus," see works by Pierre Bourdieu, including perhaps most influentially *Distinction* and *Outline of a Theory of Practice*. See also Bourdieu's *Sketch for a Self-Analysis*, which offers a fraught personal account of upward mobility through education that offers many common concerns with this one. For anthropological takes on intersections of race, gender, and class, see Ortner, "Reading America"; and Bettie, *Women without Class*. For anthropological discussions of these intersections and urban places, see Gregory, *Black Corona*; and Jackson, *Harlemworld*. For discussions of deindustrialization, see J. Nash, *From Tank Town to High Tech*; Dudley, *The End of the Line*; Pappas, *The Magic City*; Modell, *A Town without Steel*; Katherine Newman, "Introduction: Urban Anthropology and the Deindustrialization Paradigm," *Urban Anthropology* 14 (1985): 5–20; and Micaela di Leonardo, "Deindustrialization as a Folk Model," *Urban Anthropology* 14 (1985): 237–57.

4. This sense of being ill at ease in cross-class encounters is widely discussed in the class literature. For example, see Bourdieu, *Distinction*; and Lubrano, *Limbo*.

5. This is not to say that we were even a "we"; our presence, I suspect, merely provoked mild puzzlement about our personal tackiness or not being "cool." I should also note how different this situation is from contemporary elite prep schools, which have become increasingly diverse in recent years. Yet, as Shamus Khan notes in *Privilege*, his study of the St. Paul's prep school, such diversity works to create the deceptive idea that issues of inequality have been addressed in American society, while ignoring underlying realities of socioeconomic inequality that have become ever more extreme. In other words, token upward mobility for a few becomes a substitute for addressing broader structural inequalities at a societal level. Shamus Khan, *Privilege: The Making of an Adolescent Elite at St Paul's School* (Princeton: Princeton University Press, 2011).

6. D. H. Lawrence, *Sons and Lovers* (New York: Modern Library, 1999); Steedman, *Landscape for a Good Woman*; Richard Rodriguez, *Hunger of Memory: The Education of Richard Rodriguez: An Autobiography* (New York: Bantam Dell, 1982); C. L. Barney Dews and Carolyn Leste Law, eds. *This Fine Place So Far from Home: Voices of Academics from the Working Class* (Philadelphia: Temple University Press, 1995); Jake Ryan and Charles Sackrey, eds., *Strangers in Paradise: Academics from the Working Class* (Lanham, Md.: University Press of America, 1996); and Michelle M. Tokarczyk and Elizabeth A. Fay, eds. *Working-Class Women in the Academy: Laborers in the Knowledge Factory* (Amherst: University of Massachusetts Press, 1993).

7. Rodriguez, *Hunger of Memory*.

8. See Bourdieu, *Distinction*.

9. See the PBS film *People like Us: Social Class in America*, directed by Louis Alvarez and Andy Kolker (2001).

10. Friends have asked me whether such reactions were linked to my being a girl. My sense is that it was not. In the fraction of the white working class in which I grew up (like that of many working-class African-Americans), it was at that time considerably more acceptable in gendered terms for girls to be academically successful or "smart" than it was for boys. For boys, spending time reading and studying rather than in sports and more physical activities would have led them to be viewed as "unmasculine" and subjected to homophobic taunts. This is the opposite of the situation in elite educational contexts, even for a fairly gender-conscious discipline like anthropology. In anthropology, there is still a tendency for men to dominate "high theory" discussions while women often do the more labor intensive "gruntwork" of detailed ethnographic fieldwork and analysis.

11. Shamus Khan implies that students from disadvantaged backgrounds at elite prep schools do extremely well on college admissions because they have already shown colleges that they can navigate elite educational institutions and are less risky choices for such colleges to admit than students who continue to live in disadvantaged settings (Khan, *Privilege*, 189). Although Khan is primarily talking about African-American students here, I imagine a similar logic was at work in my own admission process.

12. Lila Abu-Lughod has described the importance of this phenomenon for "halfie" anthropologists from mixed ethnic and cultural backgrounds. I would argue that class "halfies," like myself, have similar stories to tell. Abu-Lughod, "Writing against Culture."

13. See Christine J. Walley, *Rough Waters: Nature and Development in an East African Marine Park* (Princeton: Princeton University Press, 2004).

14. Along the East African coast, many residents came from mixed backgrounds—backgrounds that included Arab forebears as well as Africans from a wide variety of mainland and coastal ethnic groups. Historically, the logic of kinship was traced in different ways for different ethnic groups—bilaterally through both mother and father's side among KiSwahili-speaking coastal populations, matrilineally, or through the mother's side, for those of Central African ethnicities who were historically brought to the coast as slaves, and patrilineally, or through the father's side, for many Muslim Arabs. What "ethnicity" or "tribe" one belonged to was linked more to such kinship understandings than physical phenotype. Later, British colonialism brought in other understandings of ethnicity and race that were linked to biological criteria in a very different way, and administered through colonial legal structures based on "tribal" distinctions that encouraged essentialized understandings of ethnicity. The complexity of race, ethnicity, and belonging in such a historical context made it very difficult to take for granted the essentialized understandings of race historically common in a US context.

15. Lubrano, *Limbo*, 65.

16. See also the description offered in Hoerr, *And the Wolf Finally Came*.

17. My father's account parallels that of Southeast Chicago union leader Ed Sadlowski as conveyed in a portrait of him by Alex Kotlowicz in *Never a City So Real: A Walk in Chicago* (New York: Crown Publishers, 2004), 26–48.

18. C. Wright Mills, *White Collar: The American Middle Classes* (Oxford: Oxford University Press, 1951).

19. This tendency, however, coexisted with a kind of homegrown relativism in which, no matter how heated the conversation, there was often a recognition that "people think differently" on issues, rather than any attempt to force a common view of the

"truth." Jack Metzgar makes the same point about his steelworker father. Metzgar, *Striking Steel*.

20. This tendency, I believe, is linked to the historical tensions that emerged between the American liberal/left intelligentsia and the white working class in the context of the Vietnam War era of the 1960s and 1970s. White working-class men were dispropor- tionately sent to Vietnam as troops, and, even the large number of working-class individuals who did not support the war were often angry at middle-class college students for what was perceived as the use of class privilege to avoid military service. For example, see discussion in Christian Appy's *Working-Class War: American Combat Soldiers and Vietnam* (Chapel Hill: University of North Carolina Press, 1993); and Cowie, *Stayin' Alive*. In turn, many in the liberal/left intelligentsia came to view white working-class men as reactionary conservatives because of their perceived greater support for the war. After this period, there was a greater tendency for scholarly social scientific accounts to emphasize race and gender but to pay only lip service to class in contrast to earlier sociological accounts. In these post-1960s accounts, the white working class is increasingly seen as suspect, a position that carries over into some of the deindustrialization literature. One example of this is anthropologist Micaela di Leonardo's article "Deindustrialization as a Folk Model," which argues that the emerging deindustrialization literature of the 1980s has an inherently conservative bent to it because of its focus on manufacturing jobs predominantly held by white working-class men in contrast to service industry and other jobs held by women or African-Americans. This account ignores the negative impact that deindustrialization would have on low-end wage workers of all genders and races through generalized wage depression and the shift to temporary labor. Furthermore, it implies that merely focusing attention on white working-class men is a politically conservative position and reduces white working-class men to simply being patriarchal representatives of the status quo. For a similar analysis to this one regarding the fallout of the Vietnam War on relations between the white working classes and the intelligentsia in the United States and its impact on political reactions to deindustrialization, see High, *Industrial Sunset*.

21. As mentioned previously, J. K. Gibson-Graham is the pen name of two women, Julie Graham and Katherine Gibson, who write as if they were one person. See Gibson- Graham, *The End of Capitalism*.

22. It is also important to recognize, however, that there *are* important discussions to have about how class dynamics and tensions play out in different ways *within* both middle-class and elite groups. For example, C. Wright Mills explored the tensions around class positioning for the 1940s middle class that he saw as revolving around issues of status competition and competitive consumption and the soul-deadening effects of bureaucratic jobs that bring a modicum of status but little intellectual stim- ulation. See Mills, *White Collar*. Others describe the particular social dynamics and tensions found among elites. For example, Nelson Aldrich, Jr., describes the psycho- logical dynamics of East Coast hereditary elites that includes fears that others value one only because of one's wealth or background (encouraging elites to stick with other elites to discourage "gold diggers"), a sense that one's accomplishments will always be dismissed as resulting from one's wealth and position rather than one's skill, hard work, or personal worth, and a certain sense of ennui, aimlessness, and lack of discipline linked to having so many options that it becomes difficult to find meaning in one's life. See Nelson W. Aldrich, Jr., *Old Money: The Mythology of Wealth in America* (New York: Allworth Press, 1997). For an intriguing discussion of different

outlooks found among different fractions of middle-class African-Americans, see Karyn R. Lacy, *Blue-Chip Black: Race, Class, and Status in the New Black Middle Class* (Berkeley: University of California Press, 2007).

CHAPTER FOUR

1. As this book goes to press, there has been increased activity at some of these sites, as will be described later in this chapter. However, it is still unclear whether these plans will materialize.

2. Much of the environmental justice literature focuses on environmental health exposures found in specific locations and makes the point that differential exposure to toxic pollutants is often bound up with inequalities of race and income. Although the analysis offered here builds upon this approach, it also underscores that our individual bodies have exposure histories that move with us as we geographically change locations.

3. Numerous historical accounts make references to smoke signifying "food on the table," for example, Brosch et al., *The Historical Development of Three Chicago Millgates*, 11. This theme is also referenced in lectures by local historian Rod Sellers and by interviewees in a video about the Calumet entitled *The Changing Calumet*, directed by Chris Boebel (Calumet Ecological Park Association, 2006). For similar views in neighboring Gary, see Hurley, *Environmental Inequalities*, 44. For comparable views in Youngstown, Ohio, see Linkon and Russo, *Steeltown, U.S.A*, 76.

4. Civic organizations in Southeast Chicago protested landfills and expressed concern about air pollution during the 1960s; see, for example, "S.E.C.O to Fight Proposed Dump," *Chicago Tribune*, March 31, 1963; and "Community Units Join Forces for Combined Pollution Control," *Chicago Tribune*, June 19, 1969. (Such organizations included the South East Community Organization, Avalon Trails Improvement Association [Hegewisch], the Bush Association, Fair Elms Civic League [East Side], Washington PTA, Addams PTA, Gallistel PTA, Concerned Parents of Sheridan, East Side Community Organization, and South East Air Pollution Committee.) Concerns about toxic waste in particular would escalate, as they did elsewhere, in the post–Love Canal period of the late 1970s.

5. Steel industry representatives regularly claimed that environmental regulation and expensive antipollution measures could force them to cut workers or force them to relocate. For example, in a *Chicago Tribune* article ("US Steel Agrees to Curb Pollution," August 11, 1977), Edward Smith, a US Steel vice president, described the court-induced decision to recycle its wastewater at Gary Works as a "step backward as far as financial impact on a financially troubled industry," adding that it might have to lay off workers because of the steel industry slump and because the clean water projects would mean it had fewer funds to stay competitive. See also Hurley, *Environmental Inequalities*, 74. Such arguments have a long history. Colten notes, for example, how preliminary efforts in the early twentieth century to regulate industrial wastes led to similar responses by business supporters who also argued that such efforts could force industries out of business (see Colten, *Industrial Wastes in the Calumet Area*, 22–23). It should also be noted that ensuring environmental compliance could be extremely expensive; for example, see discussion of Wisconsin Steel in Bensman and Lynch, *Rusted Dreams*, 45.

6. Even prior to this period, there was some activism in the 1950s in relation to the first sizable garbage dump in the area. See Brosch et al., *The Historical Development of Three Chicago Millgates*, 52–55. This activism centered around what some argued

was the illegal dumping of waste by the city of Chicago itself in the northern third of Lake Calumet, constituting what critics argued was the largest dump site in Cook County. Civic groups and residents opposed the dumping and pressured their local alderman to protest to the city. For a discussion of dumping and antidumping activism in Southeast Chicago during the 1980s and 1990s, see Bensman and Lynch, *Rusted Dreams*, 105–7 and 187–92, and James Schwab, *Deeper Shades of Green: The Rise of Blue Collar and Minority Environmentalism in America* (San Francisco: Sierra Club Books, 1994), 160–206. For a related discussion of environmental activism in neighboring Gary, Indiana, see Hurley, *Environmental Inequalities*.

7.   The class was taught by Faye Ginsburg, professor of anthropology at New York University, to whom I am eternally grateful.

8.   Martha Balshem notes similar explanations for disease in a working-class community in Philadelphia. Martha Balshem, *Cancer in the Community: Class and Medical Authority* (Washington, D.C.: Smithsonian Institution Press, 1993).

9.   See comment on site history in Illinois Environmental Protection Agency, *Focused Feasibility Study Report: Lake Calumet Cluster Site*, IEPA ID: 0316555084 Cook County (Springfield: Illinois EPA, 2006), 1–2.

10.   For discussion of the early Lake Calumet and Southeast Chicago region as a hunting and fishing paradise, see Brosch et al., *The Historical Development of Three Chicago Millgates*, 6–12; and City of Chicago, Department of Planning and Development, "Calumet Area Land Use Plan," December 2001, 8.

11.   See discussion of history of area in City of Chicago, Department of Planning and Development, "Calumet Area Land Use Plan," 8.

12.   For discussion of filling in wetlands, small lakes, and the fringes of Lake Michigan with slag and/or dredged sludge from the Calumet, see Colten, *Industrial Wastes in the Calumet Area*; Craig Colten, "Chicago's Waste Lands: Refuse Disposal and Urban Growth, 1840–1990," *Journal of Historical Geography* 20 (1994):124–42; Brosch et al, *The Historical Development of Three Chicago Millgates*; and virtually all Illinois EPA reports cited for this region.

13.   A 1907 article painted the following graphically metaphoric images of the smoke generated by Southeast Chicago's US Steel–South Works:

> This plant, as you see it from the deck of a yacht out in the lake, is just an opaque mass of smoke, thirty million dollars' worth of smoke. You may descry, it is true, certain dim outlines of multitudinous buildings, like the faint surmises of a dream. You may be diverted by the long rows of slender smoke-stacks, rearing their heads through the smoke and standing shoulder to shoulder at rigid attention as if about to salute. You may be thrilled by the three thin, wavering tongues of flame that spurt up from the throats of the Bessemer converters and fight their way through the thick layers of their imprisonment, like fleeting spirits, to the clear air above. But these things are mere modifications of the central theme, which is smoke, a mountain of smoke, or, rather, a cave of smoke. For the mountain is hollow, and in its interior ten thousand men are at work.

> See Hard, "Making Steel and Killing Men," 579–91. For mention of early twentieth-century "antismoke" drives protesting air pollution from Southeast Side steel mills, see Colten, *Industrial Wastes in the Calumet Area*, 28. For more recent discussions of air pollution, see Environmental Protection Agency (US EPA), *Environmental Loadings Profile for Cook County, IL and Lake County, IN, EPA 747-R-01-002* (US Environmental Protection Agency, Office of Pollution Prevention and Toxics, Washington, D.C., April 2001).

14. For discussion of chemicals generated in the process of steelmaking including naphthalene, phenols, and cyanides, as well as sulfuric acid pickling liquors used to remove rust from steel, see Colten, *Industrial Wastes in the Calumet Area*, 6, 25; Hurley, *Environmental Inequalities*, chap. 2; and Devra Davis, *When Smoke Ran like Water: Tales of Environmental Deception and the Battle against Pollution* (New York: Basic Books, 2002).

15. In 1954, the US Army Corp of Engineers sued Southeast Chicago's Republic, Interlake, and Wisconsin Steel Companies for dumping so much waste into the Calumet River that it became difficult for them to keep the river navigable. Court records documented that Republic Steel put ten thousand tons of solid waste per year into the Calumet River; Wisconsin Steel twenty-seven thousand tons, and Interlake twenty thousand tons in addition to a total daily discharge of 4.9 million gallons of untreated wastewater. See Joel Greenberg, *A Natural History of the Chicago Region* (Chicago: University of Chicago Press, 2002), 237; and Colten, *Industrial Wastes in the Calumet Area*.

16. See Arcadis G&M, "Steel Production Area Remedial Action Plan: Former Wisconsin Steel Works, Chicago Illinois" (report prepared for International Truck and Engine Corporation, 2006, regarding the matter of *People of the State of Illinois v. Navistar International Transportation Corp.*, case 96CH0014146, Illinois EPA); Wisconsin Steel is listed as a CERCLA site under superfund law. Commonly, only those CERCLA sites listed on the National Priority List (NPL), however, are referred to as "superfund" sites. As Schwab explains, sites enter the NPL based on perceived threats to public health rather than degrees of toxicity per se. Despite the widespread toxic pollution in the Calumet region and the fact that many sites have contaminated groundwater, the region has fewer NPL superfund sites than might be expected, due to the fact that residents do not drink groundwater but instead get their drinking supply from Lake Michigan; see Schwab, *Deeper Shades of Green*, 170–71.

17. For an account of pollutants released by nearby nonsteel industry, including chemical and paint companies that have produced DDT, arsenic, varnishes, and so on, see Colten, *Industrial Wastes in the Calumet Area*, 5–6, 28.

18. These fifty-one landfills and waste disposal areas located in the Calumet region include thirteen hazardous waste sites, fifteen solid and industrial waste landfills, and twenty-three unauthorized and random dumps. There are 423 hazardous waste sites in the vicinity of the Calumet River as regulated under the Resource Conservation and Recovery Act (RCRA), and more than 460 underground storage tanks. The Illinois EPA once ranked the Calumet region as possessing the largest concentration of hazardous waste disposal sites on the North American continent, and the region continues to remain one of the largest. See Colten, *Industrial Wastes in the Calumet Area*, 79; and Greenberg, *A Natural History of the Chicago Region*, 238.

19. There are concerns that toxic substances deposited into Lake Calumet are being transported into Lake Michigan, the source of Chicago's drinking supply, via the Calumet River, after heavy rains lead to a reversal of river flow into the lake. See William P. Fitzpatrick and Nani G. Bhowmik, *Pollutant Transport to Lake Calumet and Adjacent Wetlands and an Overview of Regional Hydrology*, Illinois State and Water Survey, Waste Management and Research Center Report RR-E50, September 1990; and Colten, *Industrial Wastes in the Calumet Area*. For further discussion of groundwater contamination, see Colten, "Chicago's Waste Lands," 124–42

20. The Alburn incinerator illegally burned PCBs during the 1970s. For discussion of

community opposition to the Chemical Waste Management incinerator, which was one of three in the country licensed to burn PCBs and which operated illegally at times, see James Schwab, *Deeper Shades of Green*, 178–85.

21. Paxton II was reportedly originally acquired in the 1960s by brothers involved in the Mafia. Local legend held that it was used to dispose of dead bodies but that the owners later discovered the lucrative nature of the garbage business. The site was later acquired by Steve Martell, a notorious polluter in the Chicago area (personal interview with Marian Byrnes, July 3, 2002). The landfill, which began operation in 1971, was improperly constructed and 170 feet high (100 feet higher than legally permitted), making it the highest nonstructural point in Cook County at its top. It was also repeatedly cited for environmental violations and closed in 1992. In 1999, an engineering study warned of a potential catastrophic collapse of the Paxton II landfill. There were fears of a "garbalanche" that could release up to three hundred thousand cubic yards of garbage and millions of gallons of contaminated leachate onto Stony Island Avenue and adjacent properties. There were also fears of potential fires and explosions if flammable gases were suddenly exposed to oxygen. Five years' worth of work by the Illinois EPA and approximately 20 million dollars were then spent on regrading and capping the landfill. Prairie grasses were planted on the landfill to help prevent future site erosion. A herd of goats (with guard dogs to protect them from wild dogs and coyotes) was added in 2005 to eat invasive weeds that were crowding out the prairie grasses that provided the best erosion protection. See Illinois Environmental Protection Agency, "Hawks, Deer Are Calling Remediated Urban Landfill Home," *Environmental Progress* (Winter 2003); and Illinois Environmental Protection Agency, "Work Moves Forward on Lake Calumet Cluster Sites/Paxton II Landfill Repair Maintenance," *Environmental Progress*, vol. 23 (2007).

22. US Department of the Interior, *Calumet Ecological Park Feasibility Study*, August 1998, 36.

23. Environmental Protection Agency, *Environmental Loadings Profile for Cook County*, 2–6.

24. For discussions of the presumed mechanisms by which endocrine disruption works, see Theo Colborn, Diane Dumanoski, and J. P. Myers, *Our Stolen Future* (New York: Dutton, 1996); see also T. Colborn, F. S. vom Saal, and A. M. Soto, "Developmental Effects of Endocrine Disrupting Chemicals in Wildlife and Humans," *Environmental Health Perspectives* 101 (1993): 378–83; and Linda S. Birnbaum and Suzanne E. Fenton, "Cancer and Developmental Exposure to Endocrine Disruptors," *Environmental Health Perspectives* 111 (2003): 389–94. For discussion of the social, environmental, and policy implications of endocrine disruption, Sheldon Krimsky, *Hormonal Chaos: The Scientific and Social Origins of the Environmental Endocrine Hypothesis* (Baltimore: Johns Hopkins University Press, 2000); Nancy Langston "The Retreat From Precaution: Regulating Diethylstilbestrol (DES), Endocrine Disruptors, and Environmental Health," *Environmental History* 13 (2008): 41–65; and Sarah Vogel, "From 'the Dose Makes the Poison' to 'the Timing Makes the Poison': Conceptualizing Risk in the Synthetic Age," *Environmental History* 13 (2008): 667–73. The EPA now lists not only whether chemicals are carcinogenic but whether they are potential endocrine disruptors.

25. This discussion is based on information found on the US EPA website as well as in discussions found in Nancy Langston, *Toxic Bodies: Hormone Disruptors and the Legacy of DES* (New Haven: Yale University Press, 2011); Davis, *When Smoke Ran like Water*; Colborn et al., *Our Stolen Future*; Sandra Steingraber, *Living Downstream: An Ecolo-*

*gist's Personal Investigation of Cancer and the Environment* (Cambridge, Mass.: Da Capo Press, 2010); Hurley, *Environmental Inequalities*; and Colten, *Industrial Wastes in the Calumet Area.*

26. For the ongoing impact of now banned substances like PCBs in the Calumet region, see, for example, Seung-Muk Yi et al., "Emissions of Polychlorinated Biphenyls (PCBs) from Sludge Drying Beds to the Atmosphere in Chicago," *Chemosphere* 71 (2008): 1028–34.

27. Health studies of the region are hindered by a range of factors, including the fact that much available information is aggregated for Cook County or the city of Chicago as a whole and not for subregions such as Southeast Chicago. In general, the limitations of epidemiological and toxicological studies are widely discussed in the environmental health literature. For example, see discussion in Jason Corburn, *Street Science: Community Knowledge and Environmental Health Justice* (Cambridge, Mass.: MIT Press, 2005); and Linda Nash, *Inescapable Ecologies: A History of Environment, Disease, and Knowledge* (Berkeley: University of California Press, 2007). Nevertheless, in 1986, an Illinois EPA study of cancer mortality in the Lake Calumet Area did conclude that there was excessive mortality for some cancers in the area compared to national averages and found excessive instances of lung and prostate cancer in white males and excessive bladder cancer in females. Speculation regarding probable causes centered upon possible occupational and health exposures. See Illinois Environmental Protection Agency, *The Southeast Chicago Study: An Assessment of Environmental Pollution and Public Health Impacts* (Springfield: Illinois Environmental Protection Agency, 1986). See also discussion of the aforementioned study in Fitzpatrick and Bhowmik, *Pollutant Transport to Lake Calumet*, 9. In addition, as a result of community environmental activism, the US EPA in later years agreed to compile an enormous cumulative toxic loadings profile of the region that has looked at a variety of pollutants in all media and has gathered together the disparate scientific literature on the Calumet region. While a valuable undertaking, the voluminous report does not offer interpretations of the reams of information that would make it useful at the community level. In addition, the EPA used 1996 as its base year. Given the fact that most area steel mills, which were the largest polluters in the region, shut down in the early 1980s and due to the long latency period for cancer and many other health effects, this ahistorical perspective is extremely problematic. See Environmental Protection Agency, *Environmental Loadings Profile for Cook County.*

28. The vast brownfields of Southeast Chicago suffer from different levels of toxicity that limit what can be done with these sites. Those steel mill sites, for example, that had coking operations are considerably more toxic than others. The US Steel–South Works site, for example, was deemed less polluted since it did not have a coke plant (personal communication, Rod Sellers, August, 2004). (Although it should also be noted that brownfield remediation programs, such as the one operative for the US Steel–South Works site, generally entail reduced environmental standards for cleanup; see Jessica Higgins, "Evaluating the Chicago Brownfields Initiative: The Effects of City-Initiated Brownfield Redevelopment on Surrounding Communities," *Northwestern Journal of Law and Social Policy* 3 [2008]: 240–62). As discussed later in this chapter, there are proposals to locate housing on the South Works site in the future. Wisconsin Steel, in addition to having coking operations, underwent a major PCB cleanup as well as a cleanup for other contaminants. (The US government had to challenge the sale of the mill to hold International Harvester and its successor company, Navistar, responsible for the cleanup.) According to the remediation report for the Wisconsin Steel site, it

is recommended that the site be used only for industrial purposes or restricted-access commercial use in the future. Arcadis G&M, "Steel Production Area Remedial Action Plan: Former Wisconsin Steel Works."

29. This discussion of the airport proposal draws upon a range of newspaper articles and both pro- and antiairport newsletters. See Dan Rezek, "Airport Opposition Rallies at Opening," *East Side Times*, February 6, 1992; Gary Washburn, "Lake Calumet Airport Talks Press Deadline," *Chicago Tribune*, February 9, 1992; Michael Gillis and Fran Spielman, "A Bumpy Flight Path: Lake Calumet Airport Far from a Safe Landing," *Chicago Sun-Times*, February 21, 1992; Scott Fornek and Philip Franchine, "Lake Calumet Airport: Devastated Neighbors Find Little Optimism," *Chicago Sun-Times*, February 21, 1992; Fran Spielman, "Lake Calumet Airport: Daley: Man in Control Tower," *Chicago Sun-Times*, February 21, 1992; City of Chicago, Department of Aviation, "Lake Calumet Airport Update," vol. 1, no. 1 (Fall 1990); and Tenth Ward Committee to Stop the Lake Calumet Airport, "10th Ward Airport News," September 1991. For numbers of people and homes affected, see Michael Gillis and Don Hayner, "Airport Deal Set," *Chicago Sun-Times*, February 20, 1992.

30. For example, see the discussion in chap. 5, "From Industrial Prosperity to Crash Landing," in Schwab, *Deeper Shades of Green*; and David Naguib Pellow, "Environmental Inequality Formation: Towards a Theory of Environmental Injustice," *American Behavioral Scientist* 43 (2000): 581–601.

31. For example, see Tenth Ward Committee to Stop the Lake Calumet Airport, "10th Ward Airport News," September 1991.

32. The question of whether Altgeld Gardens is a part of "Southeast Chicago" is a complex one and depends on whether regions are defined through social links, through spatial interactions, or around environmental or geological features. Historians that focus on the steel industry and "old-timer" Southeast Chicago residents tend to define Southeast Chicago in terms of those neighborhoods that historically arose in conjunction with the steel industry and other heavy manufacturing. For them, Southeast Chicago includes South Chicago, South Deering, the East Side, and Hegewisch. (Although racial and ethnic divisions may be profound within these neighborhoods, there is a recognition that these communities have been linked through their historical relationship to the steel industries. For example, many older white residents who voiced antipathy to African-Americans and Latinos living in "their" neighborhoods, nevertheless, recognized historical ties to largely minority communities like South Chicago and South Deering because they were often raised in these neighborhoods and then moved to the East Side and Hegewisch in a pattern that sociologists have referred to as ethnic "succession.") Environmentalists, however, conceive of Chicago's "Calumet region" and Southeast Chicago in terms of environmental topography. Consequently, for them, the entire region surrounding Lake Calumet and its related rivers and wetlands, including Altgeld Gardens and Pullman, is considered to be part of Southeast Chicago, even though social linkages among these areas were historically more tenuous. In addition to these historical and geographic questions, however, the issue of racial and class divisions, as discussed in the text, have been equally central in terms of defining what gets counted as "community." Presumably, the fact that Altgeld Gardens has been largely socially oriented toward predominantly African-American communities in Roseland and Riverdale to the west of Lake Calumet (and in neighborhood population censuses is included as part of those communities), rather than toward Southeast Chicago, stems from a combination of these historical, geographic, and racial factors.

33. Luke W. Cole and Sheila R. Foster, *From the Ground Up: Environmental Racism and the Rise of the Environmental Justice Movement* (New York: New York University Press, 2001); David Schlosberg, *Defining Environmental Justice: Theories, Movements, and Nature* (Oxford: Oxford University Press, 2007).

34. Some have estimated that 70–80 percent of local environmental justice group leaders and their membership have been women. See Citizen's Clearinghouse on Hazardous Waste as cited in Barbara Epstein, "The Environmental Justice/Toxics Movement: Politics of Race and Gender," *Capitalism, Nature, Socialism* 8 (1997): 69. Some attribute the predominance of women to their central role in caring for their children's health and their tendency to depict their activism as an extension of their role as mothers. Others note that, since men have historically been more likely to work in polluting industrial jobs, women's own identities and job security might be in less direct conflict with anti-toxics protesting than men's. See Epstein "The Environmental Justice/Toxics Movement"; and Shannon Bell and Yvonne Braun, "Coal, Identity, and the Gendering of Environmental Justice Activism in Central Appalachia," *Gender and Society* 24 (2010): 794–813.

35. The information on PCR has been compiled largely from the PCR website www .peopleforcommunityrecovery.org, as well as commentary by Cheryl Johnson at the "Disruptive Environments: Activists, Academics and Journalists in Conversation" conference at the MIT Museum, April 10–11, 2008, and an interview conducted with Cheryl Johnson on July 23, 2009.

36. See *Chicago's Southeast Side: An Environmental History: Industry vs. Nature*, a booklet compiled by students at Washington High School as part of an Annennberg Challenge Grant project under the supervision of Rod Sellers (n.d.).

37. I have been unable to uncover the root causes of these tensions, as many community leaders from this time period are now elderly and no longer give interviews. It has been noted elsewhere, however, that tensions arose between the largely Hispanic organization United Neighborhood Organization (UNO) and both white and African-American groups from Hegewisch and Altgeld Gardens regarding the question of incinerators. While the Hegewisch and Altgeld Garden groups opposed incinerators, the UNO did not. See David Naguib Pellow, *Garbage Wars: The Struggle for Environmental Justice in Chicago* (Cambridge, Mass.: MIT Press, 2002). Also the UNO (based largely in less affected South Chicago and South Deering) did not oppose the Lake Calumet airport proposal, frustrating Hegewisch residents; see Schwab, *Deeper Shades of Green*, 202–3.

38. See Schwab, *Deeper Shades of Green*, 181.

39. For another discussion of the different strategies taken by environmental groups in these two regions, see Kathleen A. Gillogly and Eve C. Pinsker, "Networks and Fragmentation among Community Environmental Groups of Southeast Chicago" (SfAA Environmental Anthropology Fellows, EPA Region 5 Socioeconomic Profiling Project, June 5, 2000); and Kathleen A. Gillogly and Eve C. Pinsker, "Not Good at Partnering? Community Fragmentation and Environmental Activism in Southeast Chicago" (paper presented at the annual meetings of the Society of Applied Anthropology, San Francisco, March 2000).

40. For example, see discussion in Hurley, *Environmental Inequalities*.

41. Most environmental justice literature includes references to class but came out of concerns that centered primarily on issues of race, such as Benjamin Chavis, Jr., and Charles Lee, "Toxic Waste and Race in the United States" (United Church of Christ Commission on Racism, 1987); and Robert Bullard, *Unequal Protection: Environmen-*

*tal Justice and Communities of Color* (San Francisco: Sierra Club, 1994). Academic work on Southeast Chicago from an environmental justice perspective similarly tends to depict the region as composed almost entirely of minority populations, erasing white working-class residents from the picture. For example, Joni Seager refers to "the predominantly African American and Hispanic southeast side of Chicago[, which] has the greatest concentration of hazardous-waste sites in the nation," during a period when this was considerably less than the case now. Joni Seager, *Earth Follies* (New York: Routledge, 1993), 184. David Pellow has a chapter on Southeast Chicago that similarly ignores its white residents and appears to take numbers for minority populations from Altgeld Gardens and extrapolate them to all of Southeast Chicago. The author mentions in passing in a single footnote that the South Side has "not always been heavily populated with African-Americans" but offers no discussion of the history of Southeast Chicago or area mills, how waste came to be located in the region, or the complex racial and ethnic diversity of the region which continues into the present. Pellow, *Garbage Wars*. In addition, in a 1987 Greenpeace activist video, *Rush to Burn*, against garbage incinerators, environmental activists from Altgeld Gardens and Hegewisch are presented in different sections of the film, with Altgeld Gardens featured in a special section on environmental racism. There is no acknowledgment that these activists were fighting the same incinerator as part of a coalition. For an insightful, in-depth anthropological perspective on environmental racism, see Melissa Checker's work, which offers a compelling account of environmental issues and race but again downplays the experience of working-class whites in adjoining areas. Melissa Checker, *Polluted Promises: Environmental Racism and the Search for Social Justice in a Southern Town* (New York: New York University Press, 2005).

In general, industrial patterns and immigration histories in Chicago and potentially many other northern and midwestern cities has meant that waste sites were historically first located in working-class areas that were often populated by European immigrants beginning in the late nineteenth and early twentieth centuries, a situation which often lasted up until at least the 1960s. Acknowledging this history, however, does not necessitate the dismissal of race as a crucial factor in toxic exposures. Many of these formerly industrial areas now have large minority populations, as whites have moved away. Race powerfully affects the ability of minority residents to leave heavily polluted areas due to employment and residential barriers. In addition, it is often harder for minority communities to gain access to political leaders and other routes for having their environmental concerns addressed. Nevertheless, in analyzing the way social inequalities intersect with, and are reproduced in relation to, environmental hazards, we also have to leave space for unanticipated outcomes. For example, a 1997 study of waste sites in Chicago found waste sites in some instances to be correlated with *high*-income groups due to the real estate boom of the time period and the tendency to convert old industrial spaces to high-end lofts. See Brett Baden and Don Coursey, "The Locality of Waste Sites within the City of Chicago: A Demographic, Social, and Economic Analysis" (Chicago: Irving B. Harris School of Public Policy Studies, University of Chicago, 1997), 31.

42. See Michael Hawthorne, "Environmental Justice Groups Fight Pollution Problems on Southeast Side," *Chicago Tribune*, September 15, 2011; Gregory Tejeda, "Chicago's Other Latino Neighborhoods Reach Out to Southeast Side," *Northwest Indiana Times*, September 21, 2011.

43. For example, see discussion in n. 27. See also Michael Hawthorne and Darnell Little, "Our Toxic Air: Chicago Area Residents Face Some of the Risks of Getting Sick from

Pollution, but the EPA Isn't Making It Widely Known," *Chicago Tribune*, September 29, 2008.

44. In addition to the erasure of working-class whites in some of the environmental justice literature, there has also been a tendency to ignore middle-class and upper-middle-class African-Americans in the academic literature, as scholars working on this topic have noted; see Mary Patillo-McCoy, *Black Picket Fences: Privilege and Peril among the Black Middle Class* (Chicago: University of Chicago Press, 1999); and Lacy, *Blue-Chip Black*.

45. Earlier academics who focused on class, often from a more Marxist orientation, tended to see it as the primary determinant of social experience and downplayed other factors such as race and gender. For post-1960s scholars, in contrast, there has been a tendency to downplay issues of class or to subordinate such interests to a focus on race and ethnicity or gender, despite frequent calls to consider all three. As some scholars have noted, actually achieving the goal of considering the intersection of race, gender, and class simultaneously can be challenging. See David Roediger, "More Than Two Things: The State of the Art of Labor History," in Russo and Linkon, *New Working-Class Studies*. In general, there is a strong need to theorize how such forms of difference and inequality come to be "coconstituted" in relation to the other, without assuming one to be dominant, and leaving room for unexpected intersections and independent trajectories, rather than simply layering three levels of oppression onto each other. As already mentioned, Julie Bettie's *Women without Class* offers an excellent ethnographic example of how class, race/ethnicity, and gender are formed in relation to the other. Other scholars have argued that the use of personal narratives can achieve similar ends, since the personal experiences of class, race, and gender are often seamlessly integrated in such accounts, see Russo and Linkon, "What's New about New Working-Class Studies?," 1–15. Politically, the difficulty of adequately addressing issues of class in relation to race and ethnicity stems, in part, from the tendency of conservatives in the United States to use references to "class" to downplay racial inequities (consider, for example, debates over affirmative action or the social fallout of 2005's Hurricane Katrina in New Orleans).

46. "Olympics Stadium? Casino? Possible at Wisconsin Steel," *Southeast Chicago Observer*, October 11, 2006.

47. For example, Lisa Chamberlain, "Mayor Daley's Green Crusade," *Metropolis Magazine*, July 2004; Evan Osnos, "Letter from Chicago: The Daley Show," *New Yorker*, March 8, 2010.

48. This discussion builds on the analysis in Jessica Higgins, "Evaluating the Chicago Brownfields Initiative: The Effects of City-Initiated Brownfield Redevelopment on Surrounding Communities," *Northwestern Journal of Law and Social Policy* 3 (2008): 240–62. See also Matt Schulz, "Chicago Program Cuts Risk of Liability Suits for Banks Developing Contaminated Sites," *American Banker* 161 (1996): 8.

49. For a discussion of hunting and fishing traditions among midwestern industrial working-class residents, see Lisa Fine, "Rights of Men, Rights of Passage: Hunting and Masculinity at Reo Motors of Lansing Michigan, 1945–1975," *Journal of Society History* 33 (2000): 805–23. The Hegewisch Rod and Gun Club on Wolf Lake has long been a central institution in the region (now the Southeast Sportsmen's Club).

50. City of Chicago, Department of Planning and Development, "Calumet Area Land Use Plan," December 2001.

51. See discussion of the Chicago Lakeside Project in Jonathan Black, "Nasutsa Mabwa Makes No Small Plans," *UIC Alumni Magazine*, Fall 2011, 21–25.

52. See Dave Hoekstra, "Dave Matthews Band Caravan Using U.S. Steel Site for 3 Day Concert," *Chicago Sun Times*, February 12, 2011; and Steve Jackson, "Smooth Music, Rocky Environs at Caravan," *Chicago Tribune*, July 10, 2011.

53. Such concerns were also discussed by Higgins, noting, for example, the gentrification around the brownfield rehabilitation site for University of Illinois–Circle Campus, closer to downtown. See Higgins, "Evaluating the Chicago Brownfields Initiative." Regarding the increasing tendency for those with high incomes to be located near toxic waste sites through loft conversion, see the comment in Baden and Coursey, "The Locality of Waste Sites," 31.

54. Conversion of capped landfills to golf courses has become a popular environmental remediation technique in the United States; see "Re-using Cleaned Up Superfund Sites: Golf Facilities Where Waste Is Left on Site, EPA-540-R-03-003," US Environmental Protection Agency, Office of Superfund Remediation and Technology Innovation, Washington, D.C., October 2003; and Kent Curtis, "Greening Anaconda: EPA, ARCO, and the Politics of Space in Post-industrial Montana," in Cowie and Heathcott, *Beyond the Ruins*, 91–111. Babcock notes that some area residents contended they did not use the course both because it was extremely expensive and "because they found the idea of golfing on top of a landfill unappealing and possibly dangerous to their health." See Elizabeth Babcock, "Environmentalism and Perceptions of Nature in the Lake Calumet Region" (Chicago: Field Museum of Chicago, Office of Environmental and Conservation Programs, 1998), 10.

55. See also the conclusion in Dudley, *The End of the Line*.

CONCLUSION

1. Linkon, "Navigating Past and Present."

2. See also the discussion in Bensman and Lynch, *Rusted Dreams*; and Putterman and Steelworkers Research Project, *Chicago Steelworkers*.

3. See also Gusterson and Besteman, *Insecure American*.

4. While the movement of whites to working- and lower-middle-class suburbs has been about race, it has also been about class, as many jobs increasingly shift to the suburbs. For a discussion of the "suburbanization" of former working-class jobs, see William Julius Wilson, *When Work Disappears: The World of the New Urban Poor* (New York, Vintage, 1997). African-Americans have also moved out of the city in search of work; see Monica Davey, "Chicago Now Smaller and Less Black, Census Shows," *New York Times*, February 15, 2011.

5. For a discussion of police, firefighters, and other city workers who similarly must stay within Chicago city limits, see the discussion of "Beltway" in William Julius Wilson and Richard R. Taub, *There Goes the Neighborhood: Racial, Ethnic and Class Tensions in Four Chicago Neighborhoods and Their Meaning for America* (New York: Alfred A. Knopf, 2006). Regarding the expansion in "social service" jobs of health care and education for women and health care for low-skilled women, see Wilson, *When Work Disappears*, 27; for African-American women, see Wilson, *When Work Disappears*, 33.

6. According to Richard Lloyd, 58 percent of the Hispanic workforce in Chicago was employed in manufacturing in 1970, in contrast to 39 percent by 1991; Richard Lloyd, *Neo-Bohemia: Art and Commerce in the Postindustrial City* (New York: Routledge, 2006), 39. See also discussion in Wilson and Taub, *There Goes the Neighborhood*.

7. One overview of NAFTA's impact noted that while five hundred thousand manufacturing jobs were created in Mexico between 1994 and 2002, the Mexican agricultural sector had lost 1.3 million jobs since 1994 and migration was one common coping

mechanism. See John J. Audley et al., *NAFTA's Promise and Reality: Lessons from Mexico for the Hemisphere* (Washington, D.C.: Carnegie Endowment for International Peace, 2004), 6. The destabilization of the agricultural sector in Mexico has been linked in part to lowered prices for corn following NAFTA, which displaced many small scale agricultural farmers, while larger commercial operations turned to vegetable production. Amanda King, "Trade and Totomoxtle: Livelihood Strategies in the Totonaca Region of Veracruz," *Agriculture and Human Values* 24 (2007): 29–40.

8.  For the impact of immigration on depression of wages on bottom end of the scale, see Wilson, *When Work Disappears*, 34; and Peter Kwong, "Walling Out Immigrants," in *The Insecure American*, ed. Hugh Gusterson and Catherine Besteman ( Berkeley: University of California Press, 2009).

9.  For influential discussions of the impact of deindustrialization, unemployment, and economic dislocation on African-American residents in Chicago, see Wilson, *When Work Disappears*; and William Julius Wilson, *The Truly Disadvantaged: The Inner City, the Underclass, and Public Policy* (Chicago: University of Chicago Press, 1987).

10.  For a discussion of the historic social stability of Southeast Chicago neighborhoods, see Richard Taub, *Paths of Neighborhood Change* (Chicago: University of Chicago Press, 1987).

11.  For articles on the decline in African-American population in Chicago during the last census, Davey, "Chicago Now Smaller and Less Black, Census Shows."

12.  William Julius Wilson in *When Work Disappears* offered evidence that in the late 1960s, more than half of urban blacks classified in blue-collar occupations were employed in manufacturing. He also noted that the number of black men employed in manufacturing between 1973 and 1987 went from three in eight to one in five (*When Work Disappears*, 31).

13.  Gary, Indiana, offers a telling example. Between the 1920s and 1940s, thirty-five thousand African-American migrants from the South moved to Gary, and three out of every four African-American men who did so worked in the industrial sector. In the 1950s, *Ebony* magazine ranked Gary as the best place to be in the United States for blacks, and, by 1969, Gary's blacks had a higher median income than their counterparts in any other US city. See Hurley, *Environmental Inequalities*, 113.

14.  Marc Doussard, Jamie Peck, and Nik Theodore, "After Deindustrialization: Uneven Growth and Economic Inequality in 'Postindustrial Chicago,'" *Economic Geography* 85 (2009): 183–207.

15.  Coke oven emissions are a known cause of lung cancer. PAHs, chromium, and arsenic, all of which are part of the Wisconsin Steel environmental cleanup, are also carcinogenic and associated with lung cancer.

16.  This argument in many ways parallels that made in Thomas Frank, *What's the Matter with Kansas? How Conservatives Won the Heart of America* (New York: Holt Books, 2004).

17.  Books that have been reevaluating what has been lost in recent decades include Jefferson Cowie, *Stayin' Alive*; and Judith Stein, *The Pivotal Decade: How the United States Traded Factories for Finance in the 1970s* (New Haven: Yale University Press, 2011). In the context of England, see the popular account by Owen Jones, *Chavs: The Demonization of the Working Class* (London: Verso, 2011).

18.  See discussion in chap. 2, n. 46.

# BIBLIOGRAPHY

Abbott, Edith. *Women in Industry: A Study in American Economic History.* New York: D. Appleton and Company, 1910.

Abu-Lughod, Lila. "Can There Be a Feminist Ethnography?" *Women and Performance* 5 (1990): 7–27.

Abu-Lughod, Lila. "Writing against Culture." In *Recapturing Anthropology*, edited by Richard Fox, 137–62. Santa Fe, N.M.: School of American Research Press, 1991.

Alberti, Mike. "On Manufacturing Policy, White House Remains in the Grip of 'Ratchet-Down' Consultants." *Remapping Debate*, January 18, 2012. http://www.remappingdebate.org/article/manufacturing-policy-white-house-remains-grip-%E2%80%9Cratchet-down%E2%80%9D-consultants.

Aldrich, Nelson W., Jr. *Old Money: The Mythology of Wealth in America.* New York: Allworth Press, 1997.

Appy, Christian. *Working-Class War: American Combat Soldiers and Vietnam.* Chapel Hill: University of North Carolina Press, 1993.

Arcadis G&M. "Steel Production Area Remedial Action Plan: Former Wisconsin Steel Works, Chicago Illinois." Report prepared for International Truck and Engine Corporation regarding the matter of People of the State of Illinois v. Navistar International Transportation Corp., case 96CH0014146, Illinois EPA, 2006.

"As Dollar Climbed over Past Decade: 500,000 Factory Jobs Vanished." *Guardian*, March 1, 2012.

Audley, John J., et al. *NAFTA's Promise and Reality: Lessons from Mexico for the Hemisphere.* Washington, D.C.: Carnegie Endowment for International Peace, 2004.

Babcock, Elizabeth. "Environmentalism and Perceptions of Nature in the Lake Calumet Region." Chicago: Field Museum of Chicago, Office of Environmental and Conservation Programs, 1998.

Baden, Brett, and Don Coursey. "The Locality of Waste Sites within the City of Chicago: A Demographic, Social, and Economic Analysis." Chicago: Irving B. Harris School of Public Policy Studies, University of Chicago, 1997.

Baker, Martin. "He's Got the Whole World in His Hands." *Observer*, February 5, 2006.

Balshem, Martha. *Cancer in the Community: Class and Medical Authority.* Washington, D.C.: Smithsonian Institution Press, 1993.

Bartlett, Donald, and James Steele. *America: What Went Wrong?* Kansas City, Mo.: Andrews and McMeel, 1992.

Bell, Shannon, and Yvonne Braun. "Coal, Identity, and the Gendering of Environmental Justice Activism in Central Appalachia." *Gender and Society* 24 (2010): 794–813.

Bensman, David, and Roberta Lynch. *Rusted Dreams: Hard Times in a Steel Community*. Berkeley: University of California Press, 1987.

Bergsvik, Robert. "Rally Marks 9th Anniversary of Wisconsin Steel's Closing." *Daily Calumet*, March 29, 1989.

Bettie, Julie. *Women without Class*. Berkeley: University of California Press, 2003.

Birnbaum, Linda S., and Suzanne E. Fenton. "Cancer and Developmental Exposure to Endocrine Disruptors." *Environmental Health Perspectives* 111 (2003): 389–94.

Black, Jonathan. "Nasutsa Mabwa Makes No Small Plans." *UIC Alumni Magazine*, Fall 2011, 21–25.

Bluestone, Barry, and Bennett Harrison. *The Deindustrialization of America*. New York: Basic Books, 1982.

Boebel, Chris, dir. *The Changing Calumet*. A video made for the Calumet Ecological Park Association, 2006.

Boria, Eric Sergio. "Borne in the Industrial Everyday: Reterritorializing Claims-Making in a Global Steel Economy." PhD diss., Loyola University, Chicago, 2006.

Bourdieu, Pierre. *Outline of a Theory of Practice*. Cambridge: Cambridge University Press, 1977.

Bourdieu, Pierre. *Distinction: A Social Critique of the Judgement of Taste*. Cambridge, Mass.: Harvard University Press, 1984.

Bourdieu, Pierre. *Sketch for a Self-Analysis*. Chicago: University of Chicago Press, 2008.

Brady, David, and Ryan Denniston. "Economic Globalization, Industrialization, and Deindustrialization in Affluent Democracies." *Social Forces* 85 (2006): 297–326.

Brosch, David, Marcia Kijewski, and Robert Bulanda. *The Historical Development of Three Chicago Millgates*. Chicago: Illinois Labor History Society, 1972.

Broyard, Anatole. *Intoxicated by My Illness*. New York: Ballantine Books, 1993.

Bruno, Robert. *Steelworker Alley: How Class Works in Youngstown*. Ithaca: Cornell University Press, 1999.

Bullard, Robert. *Unequal Protection: Environmental Justice and Communities of Color*. San Francisco: Sierra Club, 1994.

Byington, Margaret. *Homestead: Households of a Mill Town*. 1910, reprint, New York: Arno Press, 1969.

Chamberlain, Lisa. "Mayor Daley's Green Crusade." *Metropolis Magazine*, July 2004.

Chavis, Benjamin, Jr., and Charles Lee. "Toxic Waste and Race in the United States." United Church of Christ Commission on Racism, 1987.

Checker, Melissa. *Polluted Promises: Environmental Racism and the Search for Justice in a Southern Town*. New York: New York University Press, 2005.

City of Chicago, Department of Aviation. "Lake Calumet Airport Update." Vol. 1, no. 1 (Fall 1990).

City of Chicago, Department of Planning and Development. "Calumet Area Land Use Plan." December, 2001.

Clark, Gordon L. "Piercing the Corporate Veil: The Closure of Wisconsin Steel in South Chicago." *Regional Studies* 24 (1990): 405–20.

Cohen, Lizabeth. *Making a New Deal: Industrial Workers in Chicago, 1919–1939*. Cambridge: Cambridge University Press, 1990.

Colborn, Theo, Diane Dumanoski, and J. P. Myers. *Our Stolen Future*. New York: Dutton, 1996.

Colborn, T., F. S. vom Saal, and A. M. Soto. "Developmental Effects of Endocrine Disrupting Chemicals in Wildlife and Humans." *Environmental Health Perspectives* 101 (1993): 378–83.

Cole, Luke W., and Sheila R. Foster. *From the Ground Up: Environmental Racism and the Rise of the Environmental Justice Movement.* New York: New York University Press, 2001.

Colten, Craig. 1985. *Industrial Wastes in the Calumet Area, 1869–1970: A Historical Geography.* Hazardous Waste Research and Information Center: Champaign: Illinois Department of Energy and Natural Resources, 1985.

Colten, Craig. "Chicago's Waste Lands: Refuse Disposal and Urban Growth, 1840–1990." *Journal of Historical Geography* 20 (1994): 124–42.

"Community Units Join Forces for Combined Pollution Control." *Chicago Tribune,* June 19, 1969.

Corburn, Jason. *Street Science: Community Knowledge and Environmental Health Justice.* Cambridge, Mass.: MIT Press, 2005.

Cowie, Jefferson. *Stayin' Alive: The 1970s and the Last Days of the Working Class.* New York: New Press, 2010.

Cowie, Jefferson, and Joseph Heathcott, eds. *Beyond the Ruins: The Meanings of Deindustrialization.* Ithaca: Cornell University Press, 2003.

Cronon, William. *Nature's Metropolis: Chicago and the Great West.* New York: W. W. Norton and Company, 1991.

Curtis, Kent. "Greening Anaconda: EPA, ARCO, and the Politics of Space in Post-industrial Montana." In *Beyond the Ruins: The Meanings of Deindustrialization,* edited by Jefferson Cowie and Joseph Heathcott, 91–111. Ithaca: Cornell University Press, 2003.

Dash, Eric. "Executive Pay: A Special Report." *New York Times,* April 9, 2006.

Davey, Monica. "Chicago Now Smaller and Less Black, Census Shows." *New York Times,* February 15, 2011.

Davis, Devra. *When Smoke Ran like Water: Tales of Environmental Deception and the Battle against Pollution.* New York: Basic Books, 2002.

Dennis, Michael. *The Memorial Day Massacre and the Movement for Industrial Democracy.* New York: Palgrave Macmillan, 2010.

Dews, C. L. Barney, and Carolyn Leste Law, eds. *This Fine Place So Far from Home: Voices of Academics from the Working Class.* Philadelphia: Temple University Press, 1995.

di Leonardo Micaela. *The Varieties of Ethnic Experience: Kinship, Class and Gender among California's Italian-Americans.* Ithaca: Cornell University Press, 1984.

di Leonardo, Micaela. "Deindustrialization as a Folk Model." *Urban Anthropology* 14 (1985): 237–57.

Dizikes, Peter. "Rebuilding American Manufacturing." MIT News Office. Accessed November 30, 2011. http://web.mit.edu/newsoffice/2011.

Doussard, Marc, Jamie Peck, and Nik Theodore. "After Deindustrialization: Uneven Growth and Economic Inequality in 'Postindustrial Chicago.'" *Economic Geography* 85 (2009): 183–207.

Dudley, Kathryn. *The End of the Line: Lost Jobs, New Lives in Post-industrial America.* Chicago: University of Chicago Press, 1994.

Environmental Protection Agency (US EPA). *Environmental Loadings Profile for Cook County, IL and Lake County, IN, EPA 747-R-01-002.* US Environmental Protection Agency, Office of Pollution Prevention and Toxics, Washington, D.C., April 2001.

Environmental Protection Agency (US EPA). *Re-using Cleaned Up Superfund Sites: Golf Facilities Where Waste Is Left on Site, EPA-540-R-03-003.* US Environmental Protection Agency, Office of Superfund Remediation and Technology Innovation, Washington, D.C., October 2003.

Epstein, Barbara. "The Environmental Justice/Toxics Movement: Politics of Race and Gender." *Capitalism, Nature, Socialism* 8 (1997): 63–87.

"Ever Higher Society, Ever Harder to Ascend." Special Report. *Economist*, January 1, 2005.

Ewick, Patricia, and Susan Silbey. "Subversive Stories and Hegemonic Tales: Towards a Sociology of Narrative." *Law and Society Review* 29 (1995): 197–226.

Fine, Lisa. *The Souls of the Skyscrapers: Female Clerical Workers in Chicago, 1870–1930*. Philadelphia: Temple University Press, 1990.

Fine, Lisa. "Rights of Men, Rights of Passage: Hunting and Masculinity at Reo Motors of Lansing Michigan, 1945–1975." *Journal of Social History* 33 (2000): 805–23.

Fitzpatrick, William P., and Nani G. Bhowmik. *Pollutant Transport to Lake Calumet and Adjacent Wetlands and an Overview of Regional Hydrology*. Illinois State and Water Survey, Waste Management and Research Center Report RR-E50, September 1990.

Fornek, Scott, and Philip Franchine. "Lake Calumet Airport: Devastated Neighbors Find Little Optimism." *Chicago Sun-Times*, February 21, 1992.

Frank, Thomas. *What's the Matter with Kansas? How Conservatives Won the Heart of America*. New York: Holt Books, 2004.

Freeland, Chrystia. "The Rise of the New Ruling Class: How the Global Elite Is Leaving You Behind." *Atlantic*, February 2011, 44–55.

Fuechtmann, Thomas G. *Steeples and Stacks: Religion and Steel Crisis in Youngstown*. Cambridge: Cambridge University Press, 1989.

Geoghegan, Thomas. *Which Side Are You On? Trying to Be for Labor When It's Flat On Its Back*. New York: Farrar, Straus and Giroux, 1991.

Gibson-Graham, J. K. *The End of Capitalism (as We Knew It): A Feminist Critique of Political Economy*. Oxford: Blackwell, 1996.

Gillis, Michael, and Don Hayner. "Airport Deal Set." *Chicago Sun-Times*, February 20, 1992.

Gillis, Michael, and Fran Spielman. "A Bumpy Flight Path: Lake Calumet Airport Far from a Safe Landing." *Chicago Sun-Times*, February 21, 1992.

Gillogly, Kathleen A., and Eve C. Pinsker. "Not Good at Partnering? Community Fragmentation and Environmental Activism in Southeast Chicago." Paper presented at the annual meetings of the Society for Applied Anthropology, San Francisco. March, 2000.

Gillogly, Kathleen A., and Eve C. Pinsker. "Networks and Fragmentation among Community Environmental Groups of Southeast Chicago." SfAA Environmental Anthropology Fellows, EPA Region 5 Socioeconomic Profiling Project, June 5, 2000.

Greenburg, Joel. *A Natural History of the Chicago Region*. Chicago: University of Chicago Press, 2002.

Gregory, Steven. *Black Corona: Race and the Politics of Place in an Urban Community*. Princeton: Princeton University Press, 1998.

Gordon, Linda. "Social Insurance and Public Assistance: The Influence of Gender in Welfare Thought in the United States, 1890–1935." *American Historical Review* 97, no. 1 (1992): 19–54.

Gruber, William. "Fearless Buying: Tiny Firm Tackles Ailing Steel Outfit." *Chicago Tribune*, August 7, 1977.

Gusterson, Hugh, and Catherine Besteman. *The Insecure American*. Berkeley: University of California Press, 2009.

Halle, David. *America's Working Man*. Chicago: University of Chicago Press, 1987.

Hamilton, Martha M. "Jobless Benefits." *Washington Post*, February 19, 1981.

Hamper, Ben. *Rivethead*. New York: Warner Books, 1992.

Haraway, Donna. "Situated Knowledges: The Science Question in Feminism and the Privilege of Partial Perspective." *Feminist Studies* 14 (1988): 575–99.

Hard, William. "Making Steel and Killing Men." *Everybody's Magazine* 17 (1907): 579–91.

Hartigan, John, Jr. *Racial Situations: Class Predicaments of Whiteness in Detroit.* Princeton: Princeton University Press, 1999.

Harvey, David. *The Condition of Postmodernity.* London: Basil Blackwell, 1989.

Hawthorne, Michael. "Environmental Justice Groups Fight Pollution Problems on Southeast Side." *Chicago Tribune*, September 15, 2011.

Hawthorne, Michael, and Darnell Little. "Our Toxic Air: Chicago Area Residents Face Some of the Highest Risks of Getting Sick from Pollution, but the EPA Isn't Making It Widely Known." *Chicago Tribune*, September 29, 2008.

Higgins, Jessica. "Evaluating the Chicago Brownfields Initiative: The Effects of City-Initiated Brownfield Redevelopment on Surrounding Communities." *Northwestern Journal of Law and Social Policy* 3 (2008): 240–62.

High, Steven. *Industrial Sunset: The Making of the North America's Rustbelt, 1969–1984.* Toronto: University of Toronto Press, 2003.

Hirsch, Arnold R. "Massive Resistance in the Urban North: Trumbull Park, Chicago, 1953–1966. *Journal of American History* 82 (1995): 522–50.

Ho, Karen. *Liquidated: An Ethnography of Wall Street.* Durham: Duke University Press, 2008.

Hoekstra, Dave. "Dave Matthews Band Caravan Using U.S. Steel Site for 3 Day Concert." *Chicago Sun Times*, February 12, 2011.

Hoerr, John P. *And the Wolf Finally Came: The Decline of the American Steel Industry.* Pittsburgh: University of Pittsburgh Press, 1988.

Hurley, Andrew. *Environmental Inequalities: Class, Race and Industrial Pollution in Gary, Indiana, 1945–1980.* Chapel Hill: University of North Carolina Press, 1995.

Illinois Environmental Protection Agency. *The Southeast Chicago Study: An Assessment of Environmental Pollution and Public Health Impacts.* Springfield: Illinois EPA, 1986.

Illinois Environmental Protection Agency. "Hawks, Deer Are Calling Remediated Urban Landfill Home." *Environmental Progress*, Winter 2003.

Illinois Environmental Protection Agency. *Focused Feasibility Study Report: Lake Calumet Cluster Site.* IEPA ID: 0316555084, Cook County. Springfield: Illinois EPA, 2006.

Illinois Environmental Protection Agency. "Work Moves Forward on Lake Calumet Cluster Sites/Paxton II Landfill Repair Maintenance." *Environmental Progress* 23 (Winter–Spring 2007), 5–8.

Jackson, John L. *Harlemworld: Doing Race and Class in Contemporary Black America.* Chicago: University of Chicago Press, 2003.

Jackson, Steve. "Smooth Music, Rocky Environs at Caravan." *Chicago Tribune*, July 10, 2011.

Johnson, Erika. "Scandinavians Preferred: Nordic Ethnic Identity, Gender and Work in Chicago, 1879–1993." PhD diss., Michigan State University, 2010.

Johnston, David Cay. "Income Gap Is Widening, Data Shows." *New York Times*, March 29, 2007.

Jones, Owen. *Chavs: The Demonization of the Working Class.* London: Verso, 2011.

Kefalas, Maria. *Working-Class Heroes: Protecting Home, Community and Nation in a Chicago Neighborhood.* Berkeley: University of California Press, 2003.

Khan, Shamus Rahman. *Privilege: The Making of an Adolescent Elite at St. Paul's School.* Princeton: Princeton University Press, 2011.

King, Amanda. "Trade and Totomoxtle: Livelihood Strategies in the Totonaca Region of Veracruz, Mexico." *Agriculture and Human Values* 24 (2007): 29–40.

Kornblum, William. *Blue Collar Community.* Chicago: University of Chicago Press, 1974.

Kotlowicz, Alex. *Never a City So Real: A Walk in Chicago.* New York: Crown Publishers, 2004.

Krimsky, Sheldon. *Hormonal Chaos: The Scientific and Social Origins of the Environmental Endocrine Hypothesis.* Baltimore: Johns Hopkins University Press, 2000.

Kwong, Peter. "Walling Out Immigrants." In *The Insecure American,* edited by Hugh Gusterson and Catherine Besteman. Berkeley: University of California Press, 2009.

Laclau, Ernesto, and Chantal Moffee. "Recasting Marxism: Hegemony and New Social Movements." *Socialist Review* 12 (1982): 91–113.

Lacy, Karyn R. *Blue-Chip Black: Race, Class, and Status in the New Black Middle Class.* Berkeley: University of California Press, 2007.

"Lakshmi Mittal." BBC International News Profile. BBC, July 3, 2006. Accessed June, 19, 2008. http://news.bbc.co.uk/2/hi/business/5142202.stm.

Langston, Nancy. "The Retreat from Precaution: Regulating Diethylstilbestrol (DES), Endocrine Disruptors, and Environmental Health." *Environmental History* 13 (2008): 41–65.

Langston, Nancy. *Toxic Bodies: Hormone Disruptors and the Legacy of DES.* New Haven: Yale University Press, 2011.

Lawrence, D. H. *Sons and Lovers.* New York: Modern Library, 1999.

Leonhardt, David. "What's Really Squeezing the Middle Class?," *New York Times,* April 25, 2007.

Liechty, Mark. *Suitably Modern: Making Middle-Class Culture in a New Consumer Society.* Princeton: Princeton University Press, 2003.

Linkon, Sherry Lee. "Navigating Past and Present in the Deindustrial Landscape." Paper presented at the Working Class Studies Conference, University of Illinois at Chicago, June 23, 2011.

Linkon, Sherry Lee, and John Russo. *Steeltown, U.S.A.: Work and Memory in Youngstown.* Lawrence: University Press of Kansas, 2003.

Lubrano, Alfred. *Limbo: Blue-Collar Roots, White Collar Dreams.* Hoboken, N.J.: John Wiley and Sons, 2004.

Lloyd, Richard. *Neo-Bohemia: Art and Commerce in the Postindustrial City.* New York: Routledge, 2006.

Marx, Karl. *Capital.* Edited by David McLellan. Oxford: Oxford University Press, 1995.

Marx, Karl. *The Marx-Engels Reader.* Edited by Robert C. Tucker. New York: W. W. Norton and Company, 1972.

May, Steve, and Laura Morrison. "Making Sense of Restructuring: Narratives of Accommodation among Downsized Workers." In *Beyond the Ruins: The Meanings of Deindustrialization,* edited by Jefferson Cowie and Joseph Heathcott, 259–79. Ithaca: Cornell University Press, 2003.

Maynes, Mary Jo, Jennifer L. Pierce, and Barbara Laslett. *Telling Stories: The Use of Personal Narratives in the Social Sciences and History.* Ithaca: Cornell University Press, 2008.

McIntyre, James R. *The History of Wisconsin Steel Works of the International Harvester Company.* Wisconsin Steel Works: International Harvester, 1951.

"Meritocracy in America." *Economist,* January 1–7, 2005.

Metzgar, Jack. *Striking Steel: Solidarity Remembered.* Philadelphia: Temple University Press, 2000.

Meyerowitz, Joanne. *Women Adrift: Independent Wage Earners in Chicago, 1880–1930.* Chicago: University of Chicago Press, 1988.

Mills, C. Wright. *White Collar: The American Middle Classes.* Oxford: Oxford University Press, 1951.

Mintz, Steven, and Susan Kellogg. *Domestic Revolutions: A Social History of American Life.* New York: Free Press, 1988.

Modell, Judith. *A Town without Steel: Envisioning Homestead.* Pittsburgh: University of Pittsburgh Press, 1998.

Myerhoff, Barbara. *Number Our Days.* New York: Simon and Schuster, 1972.

Narayan, Kirin. *My Family and Other Saints.* Chicago: University of Chicago Press, 2007.

Nash, June. *From Tank Town to High Tech.* Albany: SUNY Press, 1989.

Nash, Linda. *Inescapable Ecologies: A History of Environment, Disease and Knowledge.* Berkeley: University of California Press, 2007.

Neckerman, Kathryn, and Forencia Torche. "Inequality: Causes and Consequences." *Annual Review of Sociology* 33 (2007): 335–57.

Newman, Katherine. "Introduction: Urban Anthropology and the Deindustrialization Paradigm." *Urban Anthropology* 14 (1985): 5–20.

Newman, Katherine. *Falling from Grace: Downward Mobility in the Age of Affluence.* Berkeley: University of California Press, 1999.

Ochs, Elinor, and Lisa Capps. *Living Narrative: Creating Lives in Everyday Storytelling.* Cambridge, Mass.: Harvard University Press, 2001.

O'Hara, S. Paul. "Envisioning the Steel City: The Legend and Legacy of Gary, Indiana." In *Beyond the Ruins: The Meanings of Deindustrialization,* edited by Jefferson Cowie and Joseph Heathcott, 219–36. Ithaca: Cornell University Press, 2003.

"Olympics Stadium? Casino? Possible at Wisconsin Steel." *Southeast Chicago Observer,* October 11, 2006.

Ortner, Sherry B. "Reading America: Preliminary Notes on Class and Culture." In *Recapturing Anthropology: Working in the Present,* edited by Richard G. Fox, 163–90. Santa Fe, N.M.: School of American Research Press, 1991.

Ortner, Sherry B. *New Jersey Dreaming: Capital, Culture and the Class of 1958.* Durham: Duke University Press, 2003.

Osnos, Evan. "Letter from Chicago: The Daley Show." *New Yorker,* March 8, 2010.

Owen, David. "The Pay Problem." *New Yorker,* October 12, 2009.

Pacyga, Dominic A. *Polish Immigrants and Industrial Chicago.* Chicago: University of Chicago Press, 1991.

Pacyga, Dominic A. *Chicago: A Biography.* Chicago: University of Chicago Press, 2011.

Panourgia, Neni. *Fragments of Death, Fables of Identity: An Athenian Anthropography.* Madison: University of Wisconsin Press, 1995.

Pappas, Gregory. *The Magic City: Unemployment in a Working-Class Community.* Ithaca: Cornell University Press, 1989.

Patillo-McCoy, Mary. *Black Picket Fences: Privilege and Peril among the Black Middle Class.* Chicago: University of Chicago Press, 1999.

Pear, Robert. "Top Earners Doubled Share of Nation's Income, Study Finds." *New York Times,* October 25, 2011.

Pellow, David Naguib. "Environmental Inequality Formation: Towards a Theory of Environmental Injustice." *American Behavioral Scientist* 43 (2000): 581–601.

Pellow, David Naguib. *Garbage Wars: The Struggle for Environmental Justice in Chicago.* Cambridge, Mass.: MIT Press, 2002.

Personal Narratives Group, eds. *Interpreting Women's Lives: Feminist Theory and Personal Narratives.* Bloomington: Indiana University Press, 1989.

Piketty, Thomas, and Emmanuel Saez. "Income Inequality in the United States, 1913–1998." *Quarterly Journal of Economics* 118 (2003): 1–39.

Portelli, Alessandro. *The Death of Luigi Trastulli and Other Stories: Form and Meaning in Oral History.* Albany: State University of New York Press, 1991.

Putterman, Julie, and the Steelworkers Research Project. *Chicago Steelworkers: The Cost of*

*Unemployment.* Chicago: Hull House Association and Local 65 United Steelworkers of America, 1985.

Reed-Danahay, Deborah. "Introduction." In *Auto/Ethnography: Rewriting the Self and the Social,* edited by Deborah Reed-Danahay. New York: Berg Press, 1997.

Renny, Christopher. "Shame and the Search for Home," *Feminist Studies* 30, no. 1 (2004): 178–92.

Rezek, Dan. 1992. "Airport Opposition Rallies at Opening." *East Side Times,* February 6, 1992.

Rieder, Jonathan. *Canarsie: The Jews and Italians of Brooklyn against Liberalism.* Cambridge, Mass.: Harvard University Press, 1985.

Rodriguez, Richard. *Hunger of Memory: The Education of Richard Rodriguez: An Autobiography.* New York: Bantam Dell, 1982.

Roediger, David. "More Than Two Things: The State of the Art of Labor History." In *New Working-Class Studies,* edited by John Russo and Sherry Lee Linkon, 32–41. Ithaca: Cornell University Press, 2005.

Russo, John, and Sherry Lee Linkon, eds. *New Working-Class Studies.* Ithaca: Cornell University Press, 2005.

Russo, John, and Sherry Lee Linkon. "What's New about New Working-Class Studies?" In *New Working-Class Studies,* edited by John Russo and Sherry Lee Linkon, 1–15. Ithaca: Cornell University Press, 2005.

Ryan, Jake, and Charles Sackrey, eds. *Strangers in Paradise: Academics from the Working Class.* Lanham, Md.: University Press of America, 1996.

Saez, Emmanuel. "Striking It Richer: The Evolution of Top Incomes in the United States." June 17, 2010. http://www.econ.berkeley.edu/~saez/saez-UStopincomes-2008.pdf.

Schlosberg, David. *Defining Environmental Justice: Theories, Movements, and Nature.* Oxford: Oxford University Press, 2007.

Schwab, James. *Deeper Shades of Green: The Rise of Blue Collar and Minority Environmentalism in America.* San Francisco: Sierra Club Books, 1994.

Seager, Joni. *Earth Follies.* New York: Routledge, 1993.

"S.E.C.O. to Fight Proposed Dump." *Chicago Tribune,* March 31, 1963.

Sellers, Rod, and Dominic A. Pacyga. *Chicago's Southeast Side.* Charleston, S.C.: Arcadia, 1998.

Sellers, Rod. 2001. *Chicago's Southeast Side Revisited.* Chicago: Arcadia.

Sennett, Richard, and Jonathan Cobb. *The Hidden Injuries of Class.* New York: Knopf, 1972.

Sinclair, Upton. 2002. *The Jungle.* New York: Modern Library.

Sirkin, Harold L., Michael Zinser, and Douglas Hohner. *Made in America, Again: Manufacturing Will Return to the U.S.* Boston: Boston Consulting Group, 2011.

Sklar, Kathryn Kish. "Hull House in the 1890s: A Community of Women Reformers." In *American Vistas: 1877 to the Present,* edited by Leonard Dinnerstein and Kenneth T. Jackson, 108–27. New York: Oxford University Press, 1995.

Small, M. L., D. J. Harding, and M. Lamont. "Reconsidering Culture and Poverty." *Annals of the American Academy of Political and Social Sciences* 629 (2010): 6–27.

Solzman, David M. *The Chicago River: An Illustrated History and Guide to the River and Its Waterways.* Chicago: University of Chicago Press, 2006.

Spielman, Fran. "Lake Calumet Airport: Daley: Man in Control Tower." *Chicago Sun-Times,* February 21, 1992.

Spinney, Robert G. *City of Big Shoulders: A History of Chicago.* DeKalb: Northern Illinois University Press, 2000.

Stacey, Judith. "Can There Be a Feminist Ethnography?" *Women's Studies* 11 (1988): 21–27.

Steedly, Mary. *Hanging without a Rope: Narrative Experience in Colonial and Post-colonial Karoland.* Princeton: Princeton University Press, 1993.

Steedman, Carolyn. *Landscape for a Good Woman: A Story of Two Lives.* New Brunswick: Rutgers University Press, 1986.

Steingraber, Sandra. *Living Downstream: An Ecologist's Personal Investigation of Cancer and the Environment.* Cambridge, Mass.: Da Capo Press, 2010.

Susser, Ida. *Norman Street: Poverty and Politics in an Urban Neighborhood.* Oxford: Oxford University Press, 1982.

Taub, Richard. *Paths of Neighborhood Change: Race and Crime in Urban America.* Chicago: University of Chicago Press, 1987.

Tejeda, Gregory. "Chicago's Other Latino Neighborhoods Reach Out to Southeast Side." *Northwest Indiana Times,* September 21, 2011.

Tenth Ward Committee to Stop the Lake Calumet Airport. "10th Ward Airport News." September 1991.

Terkel, Studs. *Working.* New York: New Press, 2004. First published 1972.

Thelen, Kathleen. *How Institutions Evolve: The Political Economy of Skills in Germany, Britain, the United States, and Japan.* Cambridge: Cambridge University Press, 2004.

Tokarczyk, Michelle M., and Elizabeth A. Fay, eds. *Working-Class Women in the Academy: Laborers in the Knowledge Factory.* Amherst: University of Massachusetts Press, 1993.

Torgovnick, Marianna De Marco. *Crossing Ocean Parkway.* Chicago: University of Chicago Press, 1997.

US Steel. "Steel Serves the Nation." Golden Anniversary Publication, 1951.

"US Steel Agrees to Curb Pollution." *Chicago Tribune,* August 11, 1977.

Vogel, Sarah. "From 'the Dose Makes the Poison' to 'the Timing Makes the Poison': Conceptualizing Risk in the Synthetic Age." *Environmental History* 13 (2008): 667–73.

Walley, Christine J. "Steeltown Stories: Deindustrialization on Chicago's Southeast Side." MA thesis, New York University, 1993.

Walley, Christine J. *Rough Waters: Nature and Development in an East African Marine Park.* Princeton: Princeton University Press, 2004.

Walley, Christine J. "Deindustrializing Chicago: A Daughter's Story." In *The Insecure American,* edited by Hugh Gusterson and Catherine Besteman. Berkeley: University of California Press, 2009.

Waterson, Alisse and Barbara Rylko-Bauer. "Out of the Shadows of History and Memory: Personal Family Narratives in Ethnographies of Rediscovery," *American Ethnologist,* 330 (2006): 397–412.

Weber, Max. *From Max Weber: Essays in Sociology.* H. H. Gerth and C. Wright Mills, eds. New York: Oxford University Press, 1946.

Weber, Max. *The Protestant Ethic and the Spirit of Capitalism.* New York: Charles Scribner's Sons, 1958.

Washburn, Gary. "Lake Calumet Airport Talks Press Deadline." *Chicago Tribune,* February 9, 1992.

Wasik, John F. "End of the Line at Wisconsin Steel." *Progressive* 52 (1988): 15.

Wessel, David. "As Rich-Poor Gap Widens in U.S., Class Mobility Stalls." *Wall Street Journal,* May 13, 2005.

Weston, Kath. *Traveling Light: On the Road with America's Poor.* Boston: Beacon Press, 2009.

Willis, Paul. *Learning to Labor.* Aldershot, UK: Gower, 1977.

Wilson, William Julius. *The Truly Disadvantaged: The Inner City, the Underclass, and Public Policy.* Chicago: University of Chicago Press, 1987.

Wilson, William Julius. *When Work Disappears: The World of the New Urban Poor.* New York: Vintage Books, 1996.

Wilson, William Julius, and Richard R. Taub. *There Goes the Neighborhood: Racial, Ethnic and Class Tensions in Four Chicago Neighborhoods and Their Meaning for America.* New York: Alfred A. Knopf, 2006.

Yi, Seung-Muk, et al. "Emissions of Polychlorinated Biphenyls (PCBs) from Sludge Drying Beds to the Atmosphere in Chicago." *Chemosphere* 71 (2008): 1028–34.